Biblical Genealogy and History – From Creation to Restoration

° – indicates order of birth where person on central line should come
(Levi) – indicates general relation to family, specifics unknown
... – additional siblings not given
Boaz–Ruth – marriage relationship
Pharez Zerah – sibling relationship
The list includes only those names of greater significance
   The central line shows those persons counted as part of the line
of David and his predecessors
Other persons of singular importance in Bible history are indicated by boxes
Continuing and Intervening generations are indicated by lines with no names attached

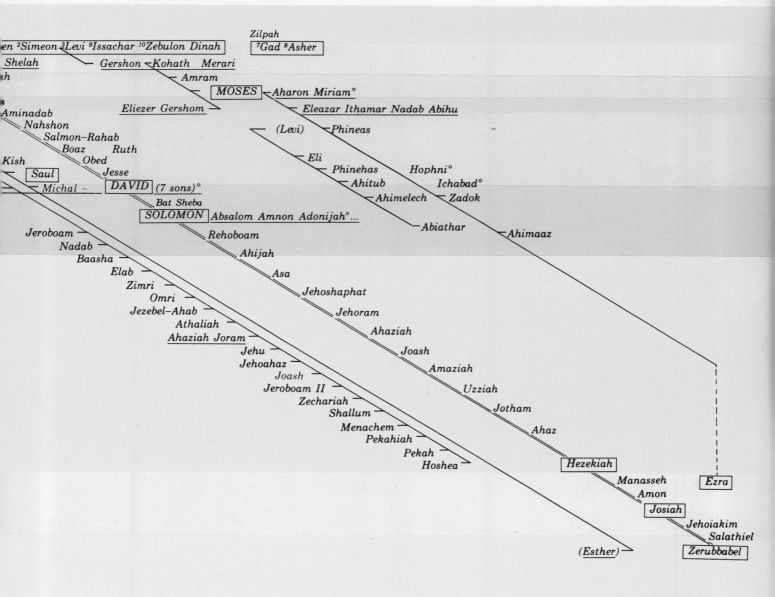

THE GLORY OF THE OLD TESTAMENT

VILLARD BOOKS / NEW YORK / 1984

THE GLORY OF THE
OLD TESTAMENT

Concept and design: SHLOMO S. (YOSH) GAFNI

Editor: GEORGETTE CORCOS

Assistant editor: GALEN MARQUIS

Managing editor: RACHEL GILON

Language editor: YAEL LOTAN

Main Photographers: DAVID HARRIS
A. VAN DER HEYDEN
ZEV RADOVAN
ERICH LESSING

The Publishers wish to express their sincere gratitude to the following persons for their help:
Mrs Irène Lewitt; Mr Mietek Orbach; Mr Uri Palit; Mr Constantin Presman; Mrs Margalit
Bassan; Mr Yoel Zimmerman; Mrs Judith Meissner-Joseph; Miss Susan Fogg; Miss Hilary Cemel;
Mr Yehuda Reshef; Miss Hanna Dahan.

Title page:
The Shore near Solomon's Bay, in the
Gulf of Elath with the mountain
range of Central Sinai in the
background.

Library of Congress Cataloging in Publication Data
Main entry under title:

The Glory of the Old Testament

Includes index.
1. Palestine – Description and travel – Views
2. Bible O.T. – Illustrations
DS108.5.G56   1984   221.9'1'0222   83-848323
ISBN 0-394-53658-4

The scripture quotations in this publication are from the Authorized Version of the King James' Bible.

Phototypesetting: S.T.I. Scientific Translations International Ltd., Jerusalem

Manufactured in Hong Kong by Mandarin Offset (International) Ltd.

9   8   7   6   5   4   3   2
First Edition

CONTENTS

INTRODUCTION

The Old Testament is the story of a people and also the story of mankind. The events it depicts take place at a specific time yet they are timeless. They occur in a certain space yet are universal. Countless generations have studied the Old Testament, loved it and revered it, finding in its pages a record of a unique civilization of the ancient past, which has brought comfort for the present and inspiration for the future.

Its framework is the development of a small nation in a small area of the then-known world. Greater nations — the Egyptians, the Assyrians, the Babylonians — were making the history of mankind; the Israelites were making the history of the human spirit.

The Old Testament contains stories of many individuals, portraying their faults and foibles, as well as their greatness. But the total concept is universal and all-powerful. It tells of the birth of monotheism, the belief in the One God, in an environment of paganism and polytheism, and of how this belief became the burning mission of one people. It tells how this people took the idea of the One God to its logical conclusion — the brotherhood of man, with its implications of a wide-ranging social ethic. Its pages combine history, theology and ethics to present a way of life, a civilization.

At the same time, it is one of the great works of world literature. Written in Hebrew, the language of the Israelites, it is more than a book — it is a library. Historical chronicles stand side by side with the most sublime poetry and the wisest observations.

The Old Testament is the masterpiece of the Jewish people, which regarded itself bound in a unique covenant with its God, to live according to its dictates and to bring its message to other peoples. It has become known to the world largely through the medium of the two faiths which owe much of their origin to the Old Testament — Christianity and Islam. For Christianity, the Old Testament is a basic book of faith. Constantly cited in the Gospels, it was read, studied and recited by Christians, and the Book of Psalms, in particular, formed a pillar of Christian liturgical devotions. Through Mohammed's retelling of the Old Testament in the Koran, its message became fundamental also to Islam. Abraham, Moses and David are the heroes of the adherents of the three great religions who have in common their belief in the One God. The Bible reached many peoples, bringing hope to those distressed with its optimistic belief in freedom, human dignity and God's love for mankind. Its vision of life has molded states and societies, peoples and individuals who have found an inexhaustible treasure in its pages. In the words of Walt Whitman: "How many ages and generations have brooded and wept and agonized over this book! What untellable joys and ecstasies, what support to martyrs at the stake, from it! To what myriads has it been the shore and rock of safety — the refuge from driving tempest and wreck! Translated in all languages, how it has united this diverse world! Of its thousands, there is not a verse, not a word, but is thick-studded with human emotion."

Though the Old Testament is universal, it is contained in a very particular setting, and only rarely does it move outside the boundaries of the Land of Israel — which indeed was seen as God's covenant-land. Its message is deeply and vividly comprehended in its original setting, which is illustrated in the pages of this volume. Although later generations were to envisage a Heavenly Jerusalem, the Jerusalem of the Old Testament was a very real city, with all the characteristics of an ancient city. Artists in past ages were moved to depict scenes from the Bible, but lacking first-hand knowledge they made them resemble the environment they knew. Italian paintings of Old Testament scenes actually showed Italians in Italy, a Dutch painting showed Dutchmen in Holland, and so on. Only in the 19th century did a new realism set in, as the real Middle East became known to the rest of the world, especially with the advent of photography.

This book presents the authentic look of the Old Testament. Its pictures show the Hills of Judea and the Wilderness of Zin, the Red Sea and the Dead Sea, the River Jordan and Mount Hermon, as they have looked since time immemorial. It also introduces new discoveries that shed a new light on the Bible. Archaeologists have uncovered the walls of Jericho and the City of David, the palace of Ahab and Hezekiah's Siloam tunnel, Canaanite "high places" and the Chronicles of the Babylonian monarchs. Moreover, we can now see not only sites and specific historical relics but, through modern discoveries, we can relive the everyday life of the people of Bible times: we can reconstruct their homes, their weapons and tools, their agriculture and food, their clothing and pottery. All these add new dimensions to our reading of the Bible. No longer are the biblical figures faceless images. From the finds in Israel and elsewhere in the Middle East, we know how they lived, what they wore, where they made their homes. In this way, the Bible receives a new life. These visualizations permit a more realistic and profound understanding of and identification with the vast panorama of the Old Testament. The judicious selection and fine reproduction of the pictures in this volume enhance the eternal significance of the Book of Books, in which each generation finds a message for its own time.

Geoffrey Wigoder

1. The Tree of Life depicted in the pavement mosaic of the 8th-century palace of the Umayyad Caliph Hisham.
The mosaic, in green, gold and brown, depicts the tale of three deer that came to eat from the leaves of a tree and were attacked by a lion.

2. The serpent is almost the first creature to be mentioned in the Bible. This is not surprising as the serpent held a special significance throughout the Orient, from the earliest times: it was worshipped, feared and hated.

In the beginning God created the heaven and the earth.

And the earth was without form, and void; and darkness was upon the face of the deep. And the Spirit of God moved upon the face of the waters.

(1:1–2)

And the evening and the morning were the fifth day.

And God said, Let the earth bring forth the living creature after his kind, cattle, and creeping thing, and beast of the earth after his kind: and it was so.

(1:23–24)

And the LORD God formed man of the dust of the ground, and breathed into his nostrils the breath of life; and man became a living soul.

And the LORD God planted a garden eastward in Eden; and there he put the man whom he had formed.

And out of the ground made the LORD God to grow every tree that is pleasant to the sight, and good for food; the tree of life also in the midst of the garden, and the tree of knowledge of good and evil.

(2:7–9)

Now the serpent was more subtil than any beast of the field which the LORD God had made. And he said unto the woman, Yea, hath God said, Ye shall not eat of every tree of the garden?

And the woman said unto the serpent, We may eat of the fruit of the trees of the garden:

But of the fruit of the tree which is in the midst of the garden, God hath said, Ye shall not eat of it, neither shall ye touch it, lest ye die.

And the serpent said unto the woman, Ye shall not surely die:

For God doth know that in the day ye eat thereof, then your eyes shall be opened, and ye shall be as gods, knowing good and evil.

(3:1–5)

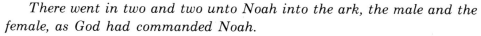

There went in two and two unto Noah into the ark, the male and the female, as God had commanded Noah.

And it came to pass after seven days, that the waters of the flood were upon the earth.

In the six hundredth year of Noah's life, in the second month, the seventeenth day of the month, the same day were all the fountains of the great deep broken up, and the windows of heaven were opened.

And the rain was upon the earth forty days and forty nights.

In the selfsame day entered Noah, and Shem, and Ham, and Japheth, the sons of Noah, and Noah's wife, and the three wives of his sons with them, into the ark;

They, and every beast after his kind, and all the cattle after their kind, and every creeping thing that creepeth upon the earth after his kind, and every fowl after his kind, every bird of every sort.

And they went in unto Noah into the ark, two and two of all flesh, wherein is the breath of life.

And they that went in, went in male and female of all flesh, as God had commanded him: and the LORD shut him in.

And the flood was forty days upon the earth; and the waters increased, and bare up the ark, and it was lift up above the earth.

And the waters prevailed, and were increased greatly upon the earth; and the ark went upon the face of the waters.

And the waters prevailed exceedingly upon the earth; and all the high hills, that were under the whole heaven, were covered.

Fifteen cubits upward did the waters prevail; and the mountains were covered.

And all flesh died that moved upon the earth, both of fowl, and of cattle, and of beast, and of every creeping thing that creepeth upon the earth, and every man:

And in whose nostrils was the breath of life, of all that was in the dry land, died.

And every living substance was destroyed which was upon the face of the ground, both man, and cattle, and the creeping things, and the fowl of the heaven; and they were destroyed from the earth: and Noah only remained alive, and they that were with him in the ark.

And the waters prevailed upon the earth an hundred and fifty days.

(7:9–24)

6. The "Lion Hunt Stele," found at the site of biblical Erech (Mesopotamia), shows a lion hunter using a spear and a heavy bow.

6

7. "The Standard of Ur," a mosaic made of lapis lazuli, shell, colored stones and mother-of-pearl, depicting the Sumerian army in a battle scene and victory parade.

The Sumerians were the earliest of the peoples inhabiting southern Mesopotamia since the 5th millennium B.C. They are not mentioned in the Bible but Sumerian cultural contributions to later Mesopotamian civilization had a great influence on the cultures of the Near East.

The panel of the inlaid standard shown here shows the triumph of a king over his enemies. In the upper register: to the left is an empty four-wheeled chariot, driven by a helmeted soldier armed with an axe, and drawn by four onagers (wild asses). The chariot consists of a frame-work of low, panelled sides, and a higher front-shield mounted on axles, to which are attached four wheels. In front of the animals are a groom and three soldiers carrying axes and spears. In the center of the register is a large figure, probably a king. Before him are prisoners escorted by soldiers. In the middle register: to the left is a line of helmeted soldiers, wearing fringed skirts and capes and armed with short spears. In the right half of the register are depicted soldiers engaged with the enemies. In the lower register: four chariots, each with a driver and a warrior. The first three chariots charge, their onagers at a gallop, over a battlefield covered with corpses, while the fourth follows at a walk.

7

Now these are the generations of the sons of Noah, Shem, Ham, and Japheth: and unto them were sons born after the flood.

The sons of Japheth; Gomer, and Magog, and Madai, and Javan, and Tubal, and Meshech, and Tiras.

And the sons of Gomer; Ashkenaz, and Riphath, and Togarmah.

And the sons of Javan; Elishah, and Tarshish, Kittim, and Dodanim.

By these were the isles of the Gentiles divided in their lands; every one after his tongue, after their families, in their nations.

And the sons of Ham; Cush, and Mizraim, and Phut, and Canaan.

And the sons of Cush; Seba, and Havilah, and Sabtah, and Raamah, and Sabtecha: and the sons of Raamah; Sheba, and Dedan.

And Cush begat Nimrod: he began to be a mighty one in the earth.

He was a mighty hunter before the LORD: wherefore it is said, Even as Nimrod the mighty hunter before the LORD.

And the beginning of his kingdom was Babel, and Erech, and Accad, and Calneh, in the land of Shinar.

Out of that land went forth Asshur, and builded Nineveh, and the city Rehoboth, and Calah,

And Resen between Nineveh and Calah: the same is a great city.

8. Head of a warrior depicted on glazed tile from Mesopotamia, 2nd millennium B.C. (Louvre, Paris).

The genealogical data included in Genesis 10, "The Table of Nations", is a mine of geographical and ethnographical information. All the generations of the world are traced back to the three sons of Noah, Shem, Ham and Japheth. The organization of the genealogy is basically geographic, the Japhethites conceived of as inhabiting the lands north and west of Israel, the Semites those to the east and southeast, and the Hamites those to the southwest. This geographic order, however, is not strictly observed, nor can any overall grouping according to language or race be ascertained. The classificaton of the various peoples is apparently dictated mainly by historical and political considerations.

Shinar, in Mesopotamia, is the biblical name for Babylonia. The kingdom of Nimrod, portrayed as the first of the world's great conquerors, included Babel, Erech (Sumer) and Accad, in the land of Shinar, and later formed the kingdom of Babylonia. These cities, including those founded by Nimrod himself, Nineveh and Calah, were the largest in Mesopotamia.

9. Terracotta head of a Nubian, from the temple of Ramses III, 12th century B.C.

"Cush," in the Old Testament, designates Ethiopia. The name Cush came to apply to all the natives of Africa who dwelt in the southern regions of the biblical world. The sons of Cush, insofar as they can be identified, are found alongside the African and Asiatic peoples of the Red Sea.

10. Terracotta head of a Philistine (Private Collection).

The Philistines are said to have come to Palestine from Caphtor (Amos 9:7, Jeremiah 47:4), though they were not natives of Crete which, together with the other Sea Peoples, they conquered c.1400 B.C., before settling on the mainland in the early 12th century. The name "Palestine" is derived from that of the Philistines, though they inhabited only a narrow strip along the southern coast of present-day Israel and Gaza. The Sea Peoples were a troublesome, piratical group of invaders of Mycenaean origin.

11. Egyptian scribe. Detail from an Egyptian wall painting, 19th century B.C., from a tomb at Beni Hassan, Egypt.

Mizraim is the biblical name for Egypt. The ethnic type of the Egyptians cannot be defined precisely, though the ancient Egyptians were basically a Hamitic people, incorporating mixed elements as well.

8

10

9

11

12

14

12. Elamite soldier from the "Frieze of Archers" of Susa, 5th century B.C.
Madai was the third son of Japheth. The Medes were an Indo-European people who dwelt east of Mesopotamia. They reached their prime in the 7th century B.C. and were one of the factors bringing about the downfall of the neo-Assyrian empire, and later, in the 6th century, the weakening of the neo-Babylonian empire. The country of the Medes was conquered by the Persians under Cyrus in 550 B.C. The Persians were the southern branch of the same people.

13. "The Prince," from a fresco at Knossos, Crete, 1700/1400 B.C. (Heraklion Museum, Crete).
Caphtor is generally accepted as signifying Crete, and this is confirmed by the mention of *kptr* in the cuneiform tablets from Ras Shamara, ancient Ugarit, as a place overseas considered as the home of the arts.

14. Detail of "The Charioteer of Polyzales," from the temple of Apollo at Delphi (Delphi Museum, Greece).
Javan is the Hebrew rendering of the Greek *Iaon*, "Ionian," and designates the Greeks. Javan is the fourth son of Japheth. The Greeks settled in the regions surrounding the Aegean Sea. Javan is mentioned in Akkadian documents already in the 9–8th centuries and he, Tubal and Meshech are mentioned as slave traders and brass merchants in the book of Ezekiel (27:13).

15. Head of a Libyan depicted on glazed tile from the temple of Ramses III, 12th century B.C.
Ludim, as one of the sons of Mizraim, that is, Egypt, should probably be identified with the Libyans of African descent. The Libyans were a very ancient people who dwelt west of Egypt. They were subdued by the Egyptians and served as mercenaries in their army. In the 10th century B.C. they themselves conquered Egypt and founded a strong dynasty, established by the biblical Shishak.

13

15

And Mizraim begat Ludim, and Anamim, and Lehabim, and Naphtuhim,

And Pathrusim, and Casluhim, (out of whom came Philistim,) and Caphtorim.

And Canaan begat Sidon his firstborn, and Heth, (10:1–15)

And the whole earth was of one language, and of one speech.

And it came to pass, as they journeyed from the east, that they found a plain in the land of Shinar; and they dwelt there.

And they said one to another, Go to, let us make brick, and burn them throughly. And they had brick for stone, and slime had they for morter.

And they said, Go to, let us build us a city and a tower, whose top may reach unto heaven; and let us make us a name, lest we be scattered abroad upon the face of the whole earth.

16. Stele of Naram-Sin, king of Accad (c. 2250 B.C.).
The name of Accad referred to the northern part of the kingdom of Babylon in Mesopotamia in the days of the third Dynasty of Ur (c. 2200–2100 B.C.). The southern region of Mesopotamia was known as Sumer. Babylonia grew out of these two territories, and in Babylonian texts her rulers were still called "kings of Accad" (Akkad).

17. In the royal tombs at Ur, an important Sumerian city, gold and ivory statues were found, as well as helmets, weapons and works of art, such as this gold bull's head.

And the LORD came down to see the city and the tower, which the children of men builded.

And the LORD said, Behold, the people is one, and they have all one language; and this they begin to do: and now nothing will be restrained from them, which they have imagined to do.

Go to; let us go down, and there confound their language, that they may not understand one another's speech.

So the LORD scattered them abroad from thence upon the face of all the earth: and they left off to build the city.

Therefore is the name of it called Babel: because the LORD did there confound the language of all the earth: and from thence did the LORD scatter them abroad upon the face of all the earth.

(11:1–9)

18. Reconstruction of the Gate of Ishtar at Babylon.
Extensive remains of two palaces were discovered during excavations. Along the eastern side of the two palaces ran a ceremonial street connected with the interior by the Gate of Ishtar, which it was possible to reconstruct, as shown here. It is decorated with glazed bricks on which wild oxen and legendary animals were depicted.

19. A great achievement of Oriental archaeology was the discovery of the Sumerian culture of southern Mesopotamia, one of the oldest of all human civilizations. The Sumerians developed many of the basic skills of civilized life, and attained a highly developed urban culture as early as 4000 B.C. The cities were built around a huge temple, crowned with a stepped tower called "ziggurat." The description of the Tower of Babel fits that of the (reconstructed) ziggurat of Ur shown here.

19

20

And Abram passed through the land unto the place of Sichem, unto the plain of Moreh. And the Canaanite was then in the land.

And the LORD appeared unto Abram, and said, Unto thy seed will I give this land: and there builded he an altar unto the LORD, who appeared unto him.

And he removed from thence unto a mountain on the east of Beth-el, and pitched his tent, having Beth-el on the west, and Hai on the east: and there he builded an altar unto the LORD, and called upon the name of the LORD.

(12:6–8)

20.& 21. Shechem, one of the most important Canaanite cities on the main road from Jerusalem to the north, appears from early times in Egyptian sources. It occupies a prominent place in the history of the Patriarchs and is often mentioned in the Bible. Biblical Shechem (Sichem) is identified with Tell Balatah, to the east of modern Nablus. Archaeological investigation has shown that the town already existed in the early 4th millennium B.C. Remains from that period include a defensive wall and an Egyptian seal ring of the 12th Dynasty. Shechem flourished under the Hyksos in the 18th to the 16th century B.C.
Here Abraham built an altar to the Lord on his arrival in Canaan (Genesis 12:6–7).
When Jacob came from Padan-Aram he pitched his tent outside the city and bought a parcel of land there (Genesis 33:18–19). Here, according to tradition, Jacob dug a well, which is shown to this day. The incident concerning his daughter Dinah took place at Shechem (Genesis 34). It was at Shechem that Joshua assembled the tribes before his death (Joshua 24).
A double defensive wall was built around it with a triple city gate and, inside, a great temple with massive walls and entrance pillars. The excavators also found remains of shrines, fortifications, and various objects. The archaeological evidence shows that the town was not devastated by war when the Israelites conquered the country. The excavators assume that the Shechemites were on friendly terms with the Israelites. Nowadays, Nablus is a thriving city of some 70,000 inhabitants – including the adjoining villages – and is the largest urban center in Samaria.

21

And the LORD appeared unto him in the plains of Mamre: and he sat in the tent door in the heat of the day;

And he lift up his eyes and looked, and, lo, three men stood by him: and when he saw them, he ran to meet them from the tent door, and bowed himself toward the ground,

And said, My Lord, if now I have found favour in thy sight, pass not away, I pray thee, from thy servant: (18:1–3)

And he said, I will certainly return unto thee according to the time of life; and, lo, Sarah thy wife shall have a son. And Sarah heard it in the tent door, which was behind him.

Now Abraham and Sarah were old and well stricken in age; and it ceased to be with Sarah after the manner of women.

Therefore Sarah laughed within herself, saying, After I am waxed old shall I have pleasure, my lord being old also?

And the LORD said unto Abraham, Wherefore did Sarah laugh, saying, Shall I of a surety bear a child, which am old?

Is any thing too hard for the LORD? At the time appointed I will return unto thee, according to the time of life, and Sarah shall have a son. (18:10–14)

And the LORD said, Shall I hide from Abraham that thing which I do;

Seeing that Abraham shall surely become a great and mighty nation, and all the nations of the earth shall be blessed in him?

For I know him, that he will command his children and his household after him, and they shall keep the way of the LORD, to do justice and judgment; that the LORD may bring upon Abraham that which he hath spoken of him. (18:17–19)

22. The Plain of Mamre. From a point near Mamre it was possible for Abraham to see all the way down to Sodom and watch the smoke billowing as a result of the fiery destruction of that area.

The Hebrew Bible uses the words *alonei mamre*, which mean "oaks of Mamre," to refer to a grove of oaks named after Mamre the Amorite, who dwelt in Hebron. Abraham built an altar to the Lord there (Genesis 13:18), and it was there that he learnt of the capture of his brother's son, Lot (Genesis 14:13).

23. A landmark on the way to Sodom: this cliff with the outline of a human figure known today as "Lot's Wife." The Arabs call the Dead Sea "the Sea of Lot."

24. Salt mounds float on the surface of the Dead Sea where the salinity of the water is four times that of the ocean.

25. A stark view of the Salt Sea or Dead Sea as it has come to be known.
The Dead Sea is a large lake in the lower part of the Jordan Valley between the hills of Moab and the Judean Hills. It is the lowest place on dry land, lying about 1200 feet below sea level. Its name derives from the high proportions of minerals present in the water. The bitumen it contains was exploited in ancient times and used in Egypt for embalming.
The area of the Dead Sea is not all desert. One discovers a lush oasis hidden among the stony crags, with cascades of water, vineyards, and banana plantations.

26. Tell Beer-sheba in the Negev.
The Negev was already inhabited in prehistoric times, but the nature of this settlement is still obscure. The first permanent settlements are of the Chalcolithic period, when in the second half of the 4th millennium B.C. a highly developed culture, the so-called Beer-sheba Culture, flourished in the northern Negev. Remains of this culture have been discovered at Bir-es-Safadi and other sites in the vicinity. At the time of the Patriarchs, the area was probably inhabited by semi-nomads.

27. Abraham's Well is located within the modern city of Beersheba. Here the Patriarch made his covenant with Abimelech, the Philistine king of Gerar. In honor of the agreement, the site was named Beersheba, meaning "Well of the Oath" in Hebrew.

28. An ivory statuette (the archaeologists called it "Pinocchio") of the Chalcolithic period, found at Bir-es-Safadi, about a mile south of Beersheba in the Negev.

24

And it came to pass in the days of Amraphel king of Shinar, Arioch king of Ellasar, Chedorlaomer king of Elam, and Tidal king of nations;

That these made war with Bera king of Sodom, and with Birsha king of Gomorrah, Shinab king of Admah, and Shemeber king of Zeboiim, and the king of Bela, which is Zoar.

All these were joined together in the vale of Siddim, which is the salt sea.
(14:1–3)

And Abraham drew near, and said, Wilt thou also destroy the righteous with the wicked? (18:23)

And he said, Oh let not the Lord be angry, and I will speak yet but this once: Peradventure ten shall be found there. And he said, I will not destroy it for ten's sake. (18:32)

Then the LORD rained upon Sodom and upon Gomorrah brimstone and fire from the LORD out of heaven;

And he overthrew those cities, and all the plain, and all the inhabitants of the cities, and that which grew upon the ground.

But his wife looked back from behind him, and she became a pillar of salt. (19:24–26)

23

25

26

And Abimelech said unto Abraham, What mean these seven ewe lambs which thou hast set by themselves?

And he said, For these seven ewe lambs shalt thou take of my hand, that they may be a witness unto me, that I have digged this well.

Wherefore he called that place Beer-sheba; because there they sware both of them.

Thus they made a covenant at Beer-sheba: then Abimelech rose up, and Phichol the chief captain of his host, and they returned into the land of the Philistines.

And Abraham planted a grove in Beer-sheba, and called there on the name of the LORD, the everlasting God.

And Abraham sojourned in the Philistines' land many days.

(21:29–34)

And it came to pass the same day, that Isaac's servants came, and told him concerning the well which they had digged, and said unto him, We have found water.

And he called it Shebah: therefore the name of the city is Beer-sheba unto this day.

(26:32–33)

And it came to pass after these things, that God did tempt Abraham, and said unto him, Abraham: and he said, Behold, here I am.

And he said, Take now thy son, thine only son Isaac, whom thou lovest, and get thee into the land of Moriah; and offer him there for a burnt offering upon one of the mountains which I will tell thee of.

And Abraham rose up early in the morning, and saddled his ass, and took two of his young men with him, and Isaac his son, and clave the wood for the burnt offering, and rose up, and went unto the place of which God had told him.

Then on the third day Abraham lifted up his eyes, and saw the place afar off.

And Abraham said unto his young men, Abide ye here with the ass; and I and the lad will go yonder and worship, and come again to you.

And Abraham took the wood of the burnt offering, and laid it upon Isaac his son; and he took the fire in his hand, and a knife; and they went both of them together.

And Isaac spake unto Abraham his father, and said, My father: and he said, Here am I, my son. And he said, Behold the fire and the wood: but where is the lamb for a burnt offering?

And Abraham said, My son, God will provide himself a lamb for a burnt offering: so they went both of them together.

And they came to the place which God had told him of; and Abraham

29. The Dome of the Rock stands on Mount Moriah, traditionally identified with the Temple Mount. At Moriah Abraham was ordered to sacrifice his son Isaac – the supreme example of self-sacrifice in obedience to God's will. In the center of the Dome of the Rock is the *Even Shetyya* (in Hebrew – the foundation rock). In Jewish legend it is the focal point of the world, or "the rock from which the world was woven," on which stood the altar of the Temple which King Solomon built.

built an altar there, and laid the wood in order, and bound Isaac his son, and laid him on the altar upon the wood.

And Abraham stretched forth his hand, and took the knife to slay his son.

And the angel of the LORD called unto him out of heaven, and said, Abraham, Abraham: and he said, Here am I.

And he said, Lay not thine hand upon the lad, neither do thou any thing unto him: for now I know that thou fearest God, seeing thou hast not withheld thy son, thine only son from me.

And Abraham lifted up his eyes, and looked, and behold behind him a ram caught in a thicket by his horns: and Abraham went and took the ram, and offered him up for a burnt offering in the stead of his son.

And Abraham called the name of that place Jehovah-jireh: as it is said to this day, In the mount of the LORD it shall be seen.

And the angel of the LORD called unto Abraham out of heaven the second time,

And said, By myself have I sworn, saith the LORD, for because thou hast done this thing, and hast not withheld thy son, thine only son:

That in blessing I will bless thee, and in multiplying I will multiply thy seed as the stars of the heaven, and as the sand which is upon the sea shore; and thy seed shall possess the gate of his enemies;

And in thy seed shall all the nations of the earth be blessed; because thou hast obeyed my voice.

So Abraham returned unto his young men, and they rose up and went together to Beer-sheba; and Abraham dwelt at Beer-sheba.

And it came to pass after these things, that it was told Abraham, saying, Behold, Milcah, she hath also born children unto thy brother Nahor;

Huz his firstborn, and Buz his brother, and Kemuel the father of Aram,

And Chesed, and Hazo, and Pildash, and Jidlaph, and Bethuel.

And Bethuel begat Rebekah: these eight Milcah did bear to Nahor, Abraham's brother.

And his concubine, whose name was Reumah, she bare also Tebah, and Gaham, and Thahash, and Maachah.

(22:1–24)

30. The sacrifice of Isaac depicted on the mosaic pavement of the ancient synagogue of Beth Alpha, dated to the early 6th century. On the right side, Abraham is shown dressed in a long robe holding the knife with which he is about to kill Isaac. Isaac himself appears to the right of Abraham with his hands tied behind his back. The altar upon which the sacrifice will be offered is near Isaac, and the fire upon which Isaac's body is to be placed is burning brightly. On the left side, two of Abraham's servants lead a donkey. Above Abraham, a hand appears in a cloud with the rays of the sun shining behind it. This hand is the symbol of divine power, as it is usually represented in the religious art of the Jews and early Christians.

And Sarah was an hundred and seven and twenty years old: these were the years of the life of Sarah.

And Sarah died in Kirjath-arba; the same is Hebron in the land of Canaan: and Abraham came to mourn for Sarah, and to weep for her.

And Abraham stood up from before his dead, and spake unto the sons of Heth, saying,

I am a stranger and a sojourner with you: give me a possession of a buryingplace with you, that I may bury my dead out of my sight.

And the children of Heth answered Abraham, saying unto him,

Hear us, my lord: thou art a mighty prince among us: in the choice of our sepulchres bury thy dead; none of us shall withhold from thee his sepulchre, but that thou mayest bury thy dead.

And Abraham stood up, and bowed himself to the people of the land, even to the children of Heth.

And he communed with them, saying, If it be your mind that I should bury my dead out of my sight; hear me, and intreat for me to Ephron the son of Zohar,

That he may give me the cave of Machpelah, which he hath, which is in the end of his field; for as much money as it is worth he shall give it me for a possession of a buryingplace amongst you.

(23:1–9)

31. Interior of the sanctuary built over the Cave of Machpelah in Hebron. The massive building at the heart of Hebron is called "Haram al Khaleel" by the Arabs (The Shrine of the Beloved of God). The base of the present edifice dates back to the reign of Herod the Great, who built it of great square-cut stones. A mosque was added in the 7th century, and was converted by the Crusaders into a church, only to revert to its original function after the Mamelukes conquered the country. It was the Mamelukes who developed Hebron, and built the present structure.

Inside, over the tombs directly below in the cave, are the cenotaphs of the Patriarchs Abraham and Isaac and those of their wives Sarah and Rebecca, respectively. The cenotaphs of Jacob and Leah are in another building, north of the main court. All of the cenotaphs are covered with gold-embroidered silk brocade – green for the Patriarchs, and crimson for their wives. The Jews have worshipped at the shrine since the time of Abraham. Today Jews and Moslems both worship in the place where their joint forefather Abraham is buried.

32. View of Hebron with the Haram al Khaleel in the center.

Hebron, a short distance south of Jerusalem, is 2800 feet above sea level in the Judean Hills. According to the Bible (Numbers 13:22), Hebron was founded seven years before Zoan, the capital of the Hyksos in Egypt, which, it is known, was founded in c. 1720 B.C. Between the time of Abraham and that of Moses it was inhabited by Hittites from northern Syria, who administered the area on behalf of the Hyksos who ruled Egypt at that time. It was one of the important localities visited by the twelve spies sent by Moses "to spy out the land of Canaan" (Numbers 13:18).

After the death of Saul, David chose Hebron as his royal city and was anointed there as king over Judah and eventually as king over all Israel (II Samuel 2:1–4; 5:1–3), before making Jerusalem his capital.

The town was partly destroyed by the Romans when they crushed the great Jewish revolt (A.D. 70). However, it remained inhabited, and during the Byzantine period churches and synagogues were built there. According to Moslem tradition, Noah was also buried there.

33

33. Rachel's tomb on the road between Jerusalem and Bethlehem.
The matriarch Rachel was not buried in the ancestral patriarchal vault at the Cave of Machpelah in Hebron, but at the place where she died.
The site has been venerated since at least the 4th century A.D., and attracts many pilgrims, especially women who pray for good health, or an easy birth, or for children if they are barren.

34. The tomb is housed in a dome-topped structure which was built in the 19th century to replace the dilapidated one which had stood at the site since the 12th century. According to travelers' descriptions, the tomb consisted of eleven stones which were laid by the eleven sons of Jacob on the grave; a large stone was placed over them by Jacob. The tomb was roofed over with a dome which was supported by four pillars. A picture of the tomb of Rachel was commonly used as a decoration in Jewish homes throughout the world. The photograph shown here was taken in 1908. (Collection Dr. N. Gidal, Jerusalem).

35. Joseph forced into a pit by his brothers, depicted in a French 13th-century psalter (now at the Bibliothèque Nationale, Paris).
In the left part of the illustration, Joseph's brothers are shown bargaining the sale of their brother.

And they journeyed from Beth-el; and there was but a little way to come to Ephrath: and Rachel travailed, and she had hard labour.

And it came to pass, when she was in hard labour, that the midwife said unto her, Fear not; thou shalt have this son also.

And it came to pass, as her soul was in departing, (for she died) that she called his name Ben-oni: but his father called him Benjamin.

And Rachel died, and was buried in the way to Ephrath, which is Bethlehem.

And Jacob set a pillar upon her grave: that is the pillar of Rachel's grave unto this day.

(35:16–20)

And when they saw him afar off, even before he came near unto them, they conspired against him to slay him.

And they said one to another, Behold, this dreamer cometh.

Come now therefore, and let us slay him, and cast him into some pit, and we will say, Some evil beast hath devoured him: and we shall see what will become of his dreams.

And Reuben heard it, and he delivered him out of their hands; and said, Let us not kill him.

And Reuben said unto them, Shed no blood, but cast him into this pit that is in the wilderness, and lay no hand upon him; that he might rid him out of their hands, to deliver him to his father again.

And it came to pass, when Joseph was come unto his brethren, that they stript Joseph out of his coat, his coat of many colours that was on him.

And they took him, and cast him into a pit: and the pit was empty, there was no water in it.

And they sat down to eat bread: and they lifted up their eyes and looked, and, behold, a company of Ishmeelites came from Gilead with their camels bearing spicery and balm and myrrh, going to carry it down to Egypt.

And Judah said unto his brethren, What profit is it if we slay our brother and conceal his blood?

Come, and let us sell him to the Ishmeelites, and let not our hand be upon him; for he is our brother and our flesh. And his brethren were content.

Then there passed by Midianites merchantmen; and they drew and lifted up Joseph out of the pit, and sold Joseph to the Ishmeelites for twenty pieces of silver: and they brought Joseph into Egypt.

(37:18–28)

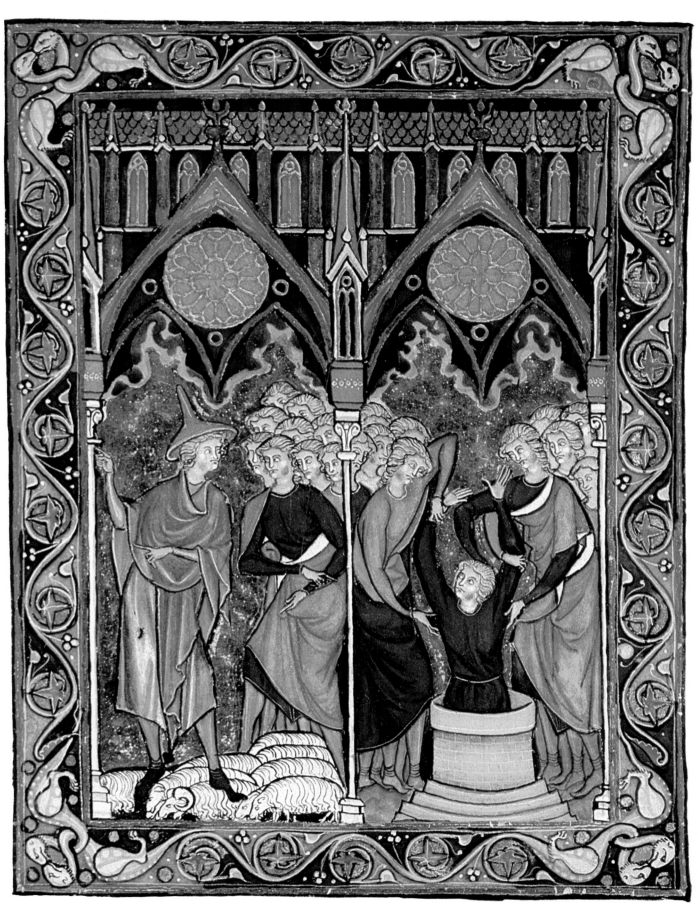

And Jacob rent his clothes, and put sackcloth upon his loins, and mourned for his son many days.

And all his sons and all his daughters rose up to comfort him; but he refused to be comforted; and he said, For I will go down into the grave unto my son mourning. Thus his father wept for him.

And the Midianites sold him into Egypt unto Potiphar, an officer of Pharaoh's, and captain of the guard.

(37:34–36)

And Joseph was brought down to Egypt; and Potiphar, an officer of Pharaoh, captain of the guard, an Egyptian, bought him of the hands of the Ishmeelites, which had brought him down thither.

And the LORD was with Joseph, and he was a prosperous man; and he was in the house of his master the Egyptian.

And his master saw that the LORD was with him, and that the LORD made all that he did to prosper in his hand.

And Joseph found grace in his sight, and he served him: and he made him overseer over his house, and all that he had he put into his hand.

And it came to pass from the time that he had made him overseer in his house, and over all that he had, that the LORD blessed the Egyptian's house for Joseph's sake; and the blessing of the LORD was upon all that he had in the house, and in the field.

And he left all that he had in Joseph's hand; and he knew not ought he had, save the bread which he did eat. And Joseph was a goodly person, and well favoured.

(39:1–6)

36

36. Clay figurine of a mourner, found at Azor (near Jaffa).
Certain prescribed customs, common to the Israelites and other peoples of the Ancient Near East, were observed on the death of a person or when calamity befell an individual or a group of people (see Samuel 3:31, 12:15–6; Numbers 14:1–6).

37. Egyptian hieroglyphic writing from the second millennium B.C.

37

38. Part of the Great Hypostyle at Karnak, Egypt, comprising 134 pillars in 16 rows 69 feet high and 33 feet in circumference. The capitals are so immense that each could accommodate a hundred persons. The building was planned by Ramses I (1320–1318 B.C.), but the greater part was built by his son and grandson, and other Pharaohs also contributed to its completion.

39

40

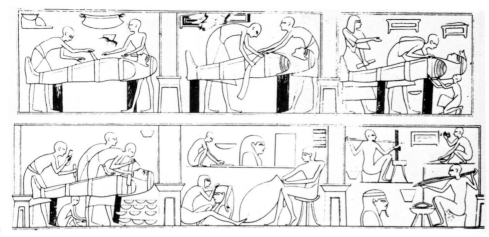

41

39. Statue of a scribe in ancient Egypt.

40. Egyptian wall painting from the latter part of the 19th century B.C., from a tomb at Beni Hassan, Egypt, showing a group of men and women of a West Semitic clan going to Egypt to bring paint and other goods for Pharaoh.
Most of the men and women are wearing many-colored clothes (reminding us of Joseph's "coat of many colors" – Genesis 37:3) and sandals; some carry skin water-bottles, bows, javelins, heavy throw sticks and a lyre. Asses were used for transportation. On the right are two Egyptian scribes who are introducing the clan to an official who is not shown. They wear the white linen skirts so common in Egypt. At the top Egyptian hieroglyphs are cut in stone. At the right the scribe shows a letter, written in ink on papyrus.

41. The Egyptians believed that the soul leaves the body of a dying person but returns to it at a later time. They therefore thought it appropriate to preserve the body – the eternal resting place of the soul – by embalming it. The art of preserving a dead body from decay by means of aromatics, or by desiccation, originated in Egypt and was mainly practiced there. From the Bible it is known that embalming was also practiced by the ancient Hebrews. The process is shown here in a wall painting in an Egyptian tomb.

And he charged them, and said unto them, I am to be gathered unto my people: bury me with my fathers in the cave that is in the field of Ephron the Hittite,

In the cave that is in the field of Machpelah, which is before Mamre, in the land of Canaan, which Abraham bought with the field of Ephron the Hittite for a possession of a buryingplace.

There they buried Abraham and Sarah his wife; there they buried Isaac and Rebekah his wife; and there I buried Leah.

The purchase of the field and of the cave that is therein was from the children of Heth.

And when Jacob had made an end of commanding his sons, he gathered up his feet into the bed, and yielded up the ghost, and was gathered unto his people.   (49:29–33)

And Joseph fell upon his father's face, and wept upon him, and kissed him.

And Joseph commanded his servants the physicians to embalm his father: and the physicians embalmed Israel.

And forty days were fulfilled for him; for so are fulfilled the days of those which are embalmed: and the Egyptians mourned for him threescore and ten days.   (50:1–3)

And Joseph took an oath of the children of Israel, saying, God will surely visit you, and ye shall carry up my bones from hence.

So Joseph died, being an hundred and ten years old: and they embalmed him, and he was put in a coffin in Egypt.   (50:25–26)

Now there arose up a new king over Egypt, which knew not Joseph.

And he said unto his people, Behold, the people of the children of Israel are more and mightier than we:

Come on, let us deal wisely with them; lest they multiply, and it come to pass, that, when there falleth out any war, they join also unto our enemies, and fight against us, and so get them up out of the land.

Therefore they did set over them taskmasters to afflict them with their burdens. And they built for Pharaoh treasure cities, Pithom and Raamses.

But the more they afflicted them, the more they multiplied and grew. And they were grieved because of the children of Israel.

And the Egyptians made the children of Israel to serve with rigour:

And they made their lives bitter with hard bondage, in morter, and in brick, and in all manner of service in the field: all their service, wherein they made them serve, was with rigour.

(1:8–14)

42. Statue of Ramses II in one of the temples at Abu Simbel, on the west bank of the Nile, which Ramses built as a monument to himself and his deeds.

It is assumed that the "the new king over Egypt" referred to is Ramses II who reigned from 1304 B.C. During his long reign, which lasted 67 years, Ramses II built some of the most imposing burial structures and temples erected in Egypt by any of the pharaohs. These structures served to protect their mummified remains and to record their deeds for posterity.

At Abu Simbel Ramses II erected two colossal temples cut out of the rock. One of these is dedicated to the sun-god Ra and to Amon of Thebes, to Ptah of Memphis and to Ramses II himself. Local deities, depending on the success of the ruler in the locality, would become most influential in a larger area and finally achieve national status when their worship became a state cult.

Such was the religious world of the Egyptians at the time Moses led the Children of Israel out of Egypt.

43. Scenes of field work depicted in a wall painting in the tomb of Mennah, scribe of Tuthmose IV.

The bondage of the children of Israel consisted not only of brick making, but also "all manner of service in the field." Such labor was quite rigorous, especially in the hot Egyptian sun.

44. The Nile: in the Bible it is referred to as simply "the river." "The river" symbolized the land of Egypt (Ezekiel 29).
The whole life of Egypt depended, as it still does, on the waters of the Nile. Its floodwaters irrigate and renew the fertility of the valley and delta and make them habitable, in contrast to the surrounding arid desert.

44

And there went a man of the house of Levi, and took to wife a daughter of Levi.

And the woman conceived, and bare a son: and when she saw him that he was a goodly child, she hid him three months.

And when she could not longer hide him, she took for him an ark of bulrushes, and daubed it with slime and with pitch, and put the child therein; and she laid it in the flags by the river's brink.

And his sister stood afar off, to wit what would be done to him.

And the daughter of Pharaoh came down to wash herself at the river; and her maidens walked along by the river's side; and when she saw the ark among the flags, she sent her maid to fetch it.

And when she had opened it, she saw the child: and, behold, the babe wept. And she had compassion on him, and said, This is one of the Hebrew's children.

Then said his sister to Pharaoh's daughter, Shall I go and call to thee a nurse of the Hebrew women, that she may nurse the child for thee?

And Pharaoh's daughter said to her, Go. And the maid went and called the child's mother.

And Pharaoh's daughter said unto her, Take this child away, and nurse it for me, and I will give thee thy wages. And the woman took the child, and nursed it.

And the child grew, and she brought him unto Pharaoh's daughter, and he became her son. And she called his name Moses: and she said, Because I drew him out of the water.

(2:1–10)

45. Moses taken from his floating ark: detail from a series of frescoes depicting biblical scenes, in the synagogue of Dura-Europos, an ancient city on the Euphrates River, which was destroyed in c. A.D. 258.
The remains of the synagogue were discovered in 1932.

45

And it came to pass in process of time, that the king of Egypt died: and the children of Israel sighed by reason of the bondage, and they cried, and their cry came up unto God by reason of the bondage. (2:23)

Now Moses kept the flock of Jethro his father in law, the priest of Midian: and he led the flock to the backside of the desert, and came to the mountain of God, even to Horeb.

And the angel of the LORD appeared unto him in a flame of fire out of the midst of a bush: and he looked, and, behold, the bush burned with fire, and the bush was not consumed.

And Moses said, I will now turn aside, and see this great sight, why the bush is not burnt.

And when the LORD saw that he turned aside to see, God called unto him out of the midst of the bush, and said, Moses, Moses. And he said, Here am I.

And he said, Draw not nigh hither: put off thy shoes from off thy feet, for the place whereon thou standest is holy ground.

Moreover he said, I am the God of thy father, the God of Abraham, the God of Isaac, and the God of Jacob. And Moses hid his face; for he was afraid to look upon God.

And the LORD said, I have surely seen the affliction of my people which are in Egypt, and have heard their cry by reason of their taskmasters; for I know their sorrows;

And i am come down to deliver them out of the hand of the Egyptians, and to bring them up out of that land unto a good land and a large, unto a land flowing with milk and honey; unto the place of the Canaanites, and the Hittites, and the Amorites, and the Perizzites, and the Hivites, and the Jebusites.

Now therefore, behold, the cry of the children of Israel is come unto me: and I have also seen the oppression wherewith the Egyptians oppress them.

Come now therefore, and I will send thee unto Pharaoh, that thou mayest bring forth my people the children of Israel out of Egypt.

And Moses said unto God, Who am I, that I should go unto Pharaoh, and that I should bring forth the children of Israel out of Egypt?

(3:1–11)

46. In the courtyard, against a chapel wall of the Monastery of Santa Caterina in the Sinai, grows a trailing raspberry bush, which is believed to have grown from the original burning bush.

47. On the way to Mount Sinai.
The triangular Sinai Peninsula lies between the two branches of the Red Sea and Mediterranean. The northern part is a sandy plateau with low hills. The southern part has red granite mountains reaching to a height of 8660 feet. Here the Egyptians exploited turquoise mines.
The climate in the peninsula is that of a desert – dry, with an insignificant rainfall. Some brackish water may be found by digging the *wadis*, but there are few springs. Two of the larger ones produced the oasis of Kadesh-barnea.
The Sinai was the habitat of nomads, who found some pasture in the valleys. It is the land bridge connecting Egypt with Palestine, Syria and Mesopotamia, and through it passed major trade routes since early times.

48. Serabit el-Khadem (Pillars of the Slaves, as it is called in Arabic) in southern Sinai. The Bedouin have given this name to the site where a hieroglyphic inscription carved on pillars relates the story of a Semitic slave being beaten by an Egyptian official.
This region of the Sinai desert was a source of turquoise and copper for the ancient Egyptians.

49. Semitic captives making bricks in an Egyptian brickyard, shown in a wall painting in the tomb of Rekhmire, 15th century B.C.
Bricks were produced by a simple method. A hole was dug in the ground and filled with water. The mud thus produced was then mixed with straw, and trodden until it became a thick, pliable substance. At first this was shaped with the hands into brick but later a wooden mold was used. The newly made bricks were then laid out to dry in the sun. This method was used until the Roman period.
In ancient Egypt, the enslaved Israelites labored at brick making. They had to gather the straw themselves and still produce the same number of bricks.

And Pharaoh commanded the same day the taskmasters of the people, and their officers, saying,

Ye shall no more give the people straw to make brick, as heretofore: let them go and gather straw for themselves.

And the tale of the bricks, which they did make heretofore, ye shall lay upon them; ye shall not diminish ought thereof: for they be idle; therefore they cry, saying, Let us go and sacrifice to our God.

Let there more work be laid upon the men, that they may labour therein: and let them not regard vain words.

And the taskmasters of the people went out, and their officers, and they spake to the people, saying, Thus saith Pharaoh, I will not give you straw.

Go ye, get you straw where ye can find it: yet not ought of your work shall be diminished.

So the people were scattered abroad throughout all the land of Egypt to gather stubble instead of straw.

And the taskmasters hasted them, saying, Fulfil your works, your daily tasks, as when there was straw.

And the officers of the children of Israel which Pharaoh's taskmasters had set over them, were beaten, and demanded, Wherefore have ye not fulfilled your task in making brick both yesterday and to day, as heretofore?

(5:6–14)

And they shall eat the flesh in that night, roast with fire, and unleavened bread; and with bitter herbs they shall eat it.

(12:8)

Seven days shall ye eat unleavened bread; even the first day ye shall put away leaven out of your houses: for whosoever eateth leavened bread from the first day until the seventh day, that soul shall be cut off from Israel.

And in the first day there shall be an holy convocation, and in the seventh day there shall be an holy convocation to you; no manner of work shall be done in them, save that which every man must eat, that only may be done of you.

And ye shall observe the feast of unleavened bread; for in this selfsame day have I brought your armies out of the land of Egypt: therefore shall ye observe this day in your generations by an ordinance for ever.

In the first month, on the fourteenth day of the month at even, ye shall eat unleavened bread, until the one and twentieth day of the month at even.

Seven days shall there be no leaven found in your houses: for whosoever eateth that which is leavened, even that soul shall be cut off from the congregation of Israel, whether he be a stranger, or born in the land.

Ye shall eat nothing leavened; in all your habitations shall ye eat unleavened bread.

(12:15–20)

50. Miniature from the *Darmstadt Haggadah*, a manuscript of the 15th century (preserved in the Darmstadt Landesbibliothek). The *Haggadah* is a set form of benedictions, prayers, comments and psalms which accompany the recital of the story of the exodus from Egypt.

Passover, commemorating the exodus of the Children of Israel under the leadership of Moses, is one of the most important Jewish festivals. It is celebrated in the spring, and lasts seven days (eight days outside Israel). The highlight of the festival is the *seder* service on the first night with the recitation of the *Haggadah* before partaking of the evening meal. The *seder* service is celebrated in Jewish homes throughout the world.

During the entire festival it is forbidden to eat or own leaven and only unleavened bread *(mazzah)* is eaten.

And it was told the king of Egypt that the people fled: and the heart of Pharaoh and of his servants was turned against the people, and they said, Why have we done this, that we have let Israel go from serving us?

(14:5)

And the LORD hardened the heart of Pharaoh king of Egypt, and he pursued after the children of Israel: and the children of Israel went out with an high hand.

But the Egyptians pursued after them, all the horses and chariots of Pharaoh, and his horsemen, and his army, and overtook them encamping by the sea, beside Pihahiroth, before Baal-zephon.

(14:8–9)

And Moses stretched out his hand over the sea; and the LORD caused the sea to go back by a strong east wind all that night, and made the sea dry land, and the waters were divided.

(14:21)

51

51. The horses and chariots of Pharaoh, depicted on a chest found in Tutankhamon's tomb (Egyptian pharaoh, 14th century B.C.). The king, of superhuman size, is driving at full gallop, his bow drawn, in front of columns of chariots and infantry.

52. The Red Sea, the sea that the Israelites crossed on their way from Egypt to Canaan. This is the body of water separating northeastern Africa from the Arabian Peninsula and including two arms known, in modern times, as the Gulf of Suez and the Gulf of Aqaba.
The actual site where the Israelites crossed the Red Sea (referred to as the Egyptian sea in Isaiah 11:15, and named *Yam Suf* in Hebrew, meaning "sea of reeds") is much disputed by scholars. Some believe that the reference is to the northwestern branch of the Red Sea, known as the Gulf of Suez; others suggest that it was one of the lakes that lay on the border of Egypt and Sinai, between Suez and the Mediterranean, where reeds still grow. Yet others believe it should be identified with Lake Sirbonis, which was once a continuation of the eastern Nile Delta.

53

54

55

Then said the LORD unto Moses, Behold, I will rain bread from heaven for you; and the people shall go out and gather a certain rate every day, that I may prove them, whether they will walk in my law, or no.

(16:4)

And the LORD spake unto Moses, saying,

I have heard the murmurings of the children of Israel: speak unto them, saying, At even ye shall eat flesh, and in the morning ye shall be filled with bread; and ye shall know that I am the LORD your God.

And it came to pass, that at even the quails came up, and covered the camp: and in the morning the dew lay round about the host.

And when the dew that lay was gone up, behold, upon the face of the wilderness there lay a small round thing, as small as the hoar frost on the ground.

And when the children of Israel saw it, they said one to another, It is manna: for they wist not what it was. And Moses said unto them, This is the bread which the LORD hath given you to eat.

This is the thing which the LORD hath commanded, Gather of it every man according to his eating, an omer for every man, according to the number of your persons; take ye every man for them which are in his tents.

And the children of Israel did so, and gathered, some more, some less.

(16:11–17)

53. A wall painting in an Egyptian tomb at Thebes, depicting the snaring of birds.

54. A tree growing in the Sinai Peninsula, the tamarisk, is believed by some scholars to be the source of manna, or "bread from heaven" referred to in the Bible. It is understood to be the sweet edible drops of fluid secreted by two kinds of tiny insects living on the tamarisk tree. The drops are secreted in the spring, then dry and fall to the ground where they are collected to this day by the Bedouin.

55. Migrating quail still flock to Sinai, and until recently were caught in nets. Trapping was easy, for the birds were tired after their long flight across the Mediterranean.

56. A pool of ice-cold water, fed by a small spring and a narrow waterfall – hidden among the rocks – in the Wilderness of Zin, in the Negev.

56

And all the congregation of the children of Israel journeyed from the wilderness of Sin, after their journeys, according to the commandment of the LORD, and pitched in Rephidim: and there was no water for the people to drink.

Wherefore the people did chide with Moses, and said, Give us water that we may drink. And Moses said unto them, Why chide ye with me? wherefore do ye tempt the LORD?

And the people thirsted there for water; and the people murmured against Moses, and said, Wherefore is this that thou hast brought us up out of Egypt, to kill us and our children and our cattle with thirst?

And Moses cried unto the LORD, saying, What shall I do unto this people? they be almost ready to stone me.

And the LORD said unto Moses, Go on before the people, and take with thee of the elders of Israel; and thy rod, wherewith thou smotest the river, take in thine hand, and go.

Behold, I will stand before thee there upon the rock in Horeb; and thou shalt smite the rock, and there shall come water out of it, that the people may drink. And Moses did so in the sight of the elders of Israel.

And he called the name of the place Massah, and Meribah, because of the chiding of the children of Israel, and because they tempted the LORD, saying, Is the LORD among us, or not?

Then came Amalek, and fought with Israel in Rephidim.

(17:1–8)

And Jethro, Moses' father in law, came with his sons and his wife unto Moses into the wilderness, where he encamped at the mount of God:

And he said unto Moses, I thy father in law Jethro am come unto thee, and thy wife, and her two sons with her.

(18:5–6)

And Moses told his father in law all that the LORD had done unto Pharaoh and to the Egyptians for Israel's sake, and all the travail that had come upon them by the way, and how the LORD delivered them.

And Jethro rejoiced for all the goodness which the LORD had done to Israel, whom he had delivered out of the hand of the Egyptians.

And Jethro said, Blessed be the LORD, who hath delivered you out of the hand of the Egyptians, and out of the hand of Pharaoh, who hath delivered the people from under the hand of the Egyptians.

(18:8–10)

57. This landscape is the kind of scenery one sees most often in the Sinai.

58. The traditional tomb of Nebi Shueib, identified with Jethro, at the foot of the Horns of Hittin in the Galilee, one of the holiest sites of the Druze.
The Druze are a small community numbering about 200,000 souls living in Israel, Syria and southern Lebanon. They have a closed religion of their own based on Ismailism. The Druze permit no conversion either to or from their religion. They have succeeded in maintaining their close-knit identity and religion through almost a thousand years of turbulent history. They hold Jethro, Moses' father-in-law and adviser, in special reverence. Each spring thousands of Druze from all over the country gather at his tomb for a great festival.

And God spake all these words saying

I am
the Lord thy God

Thou
shalt have no other gods before me

Thou
shalt not take the name of the Lord
thy God in vain

Remember
the sabbath day to keep it holy

Honour
thy father and thy mother

Thou
shalt not kill

Thou
shalt not commit adultery

Thou
shalt not steal

Thou
shalt not bear false witness
against thy neighbour

Thou
shalt not covet thy neighbour's wife

59. The Ten Commandments.

60. The tablets of the Law carved in stone.

60

61. Baroque style, carved and gilded doors of the Ark of the Law from an Italian synagogue of the early 18th century (now at the Israel Museum, Jerusalem).
The Ark, or the "Holy Ark" as it is also known, is the receptacle in the synagogue in which the Scrolls of the Law are kept.

61

62

And the LORD said unto Moses, Come up to me into the mount, and be there: and I will give thee tables of stone, and a law, and commandments which I have written; that thou mayest teach them.

And Moses rose up, and his minister Joshua: and Moses went up into the mount of God.

And he said unto the elders, Tarry ye here for us, until we come again unto you: and, behold, Aaron and Hur are with you: if any man have any matters to do, let him come unto them.

And Moses went up into the mount, and a cloud covered the mount.

(24:12–15)

62. & 63. Some three thousand steps lead up to the summit of Jebel Musa, "The Mount of Moses," in the heart of the ragged range in southern Sinai where, according to tradition, Moses received the Commandments.

And thou shalt make a vail of blue, and purple, and scarlet, and fine twined linen of cunning work: with cherubims shall it be made:

And thou shalt hang it upon four pillars of shittim wood overlaid with gold: their hooks shall be of gold, upon the four sockets of silver.

And thou shalt hang up the vail under the taches, that thou mayest bring in thither within the vail the ark of the testimony: and the vail shall divide unto you between the holy place and the most holy. (26:31–33)

64. Embroidered ark curtain from a synagogue in Germany, 18th century (now at the Hechal Shlomo Synagogue Museum, Jerusalem).
Such curtains conceal the doors of the ark in which the Scrolls of the Law are kept in the synagogue ("that you mayest bring in thither within the vail of the ark of testimony").

And these are the garments which they shall make; a breastplate, and an ephod, and a robe, and a broidered coat, a mitre, and a girdle: and they shall make holy garments for Aaron thy brother, and his sons, that he may minister unto me in the priest's office.

And they shall take gold, and blue, and purple, and scarlet, and fine linen.

And they shall make the ephod of gold, of blue, and of purple, of scarlet, and fine twined linen, with cunning work.

It shall have the two shoulderpieces thereof joined at the two edges thereof: and so it shall be joined together.

And the curious girdle of the ephod, which is upon it, shall be of the same, according to the work thereof; even of gold, of blue, and purple, and scarlet, and fine twined linen.

(28:4–8)

And for Aaron's sons thou shalt make coats, and thou shalt make for them girdles, and bonnets shalt thou make for them, for glory and for beauty.

(28:40)

65. Ritual objects used in the Temple, depicted in painted lead on the wood panels of the Holy Ark from a synagogue in Cracow, Poland; early 17th century (Israel Museum, Jerusalem).

66. High-priest vestments, depicted in 16th century Italian illuminated manuscript (Israel Museum, Jerusalem).

65 66

67. The "breastplate," or shield, hanging from the staves of a Scroll of the Law, recalls the breastplate worn by the High Priest. The one shown here is from Munich, 1826 (Israel Museum, Jerusalem).

And thou shalt make the breastplate of judgment with cunning work; after the work of the ephod thou shalt make it; of gold, of blue, and of purple, and of scarlet, and of fine twined linen, shalt thou make it.

Foursquare it shall be being doubled; a span shall be the length thereof, and a span shall be the breadth thereof.

And thou shalt set in it settings of stones, even four rows of stones: the first row shall be a sardius, a topaz, and a carbuncle: this shall be the first row.

And the second row shall be an emerald, a sapphire, and a diamond.

And the third row a ligure, an agate, and an amethyst.

And the fourth row a beryl, and an onyx, and a jasper: they shall be set in gold in their inclosings.

And the stones shall be with the names of the children of Israel, twelve, according to their names, like the engravings of a signet; every one with his name shall they be according to the twelve tribes.

(28:15–21)

68. Moses standing on top of the flaming Mount Sinai holding the tablets of the Law. To his left stands Joshua, and the Israelites encircle the mountain. From the 14th-century illuminated *Sarajevo Haggadah,* executed in Spain (now at the Sarajevo National Museum, Yugoslavia).

And the LORD spake unto Moses, saying,

Speak thou also unto the children of Israel, saying, Verily my sabbaths ye shall keep: for it is a sign between me and you throughout your generations: that ye may know that I am the LORD that doth sanctify you.

Ye shall keep the sabbath therefore; for it is holy unto you: every one that defileth it shall surely be put to death: for whosoever doeth any work therein, that soul shall be cut off from among his people.

Six days may work be done; but in the seventh is the sabbath of rest, holy to the LORD: whosoever doeth any work in the sabbath day, he shall surely be put to death.

Wherefore the children of Israel shall keep the sabbath, to observe the sabbath throughout their generations, for a perpetual covenant.

It is a sign between me and the children of Israel for ever: for in six days the LORD made heaven and earth, and on the seventh day he rested, and was refreshed.

(31:12–17)

And Moses gathered all the congregation of the children of Israel together, and said unto them, These are the words which the LORD hath commanded, that ye should do them.

Six days shall work be done, but on the seventh day there shall be to you an holy day, a sabbath of rest to the LORD: whosoever doeth work therein shall be put to death.

Ye shall kindle no fire throughout your habitations upon the sabbath day.

(35:1–3)

And he made the candlestick of pure gold: of beaten work made he the candlestick; his shaft, and his branch, his bowls, his knops, and his flowers, were of the same:

And six branches going out of the sides thereof; three branches of the candlestick out of the one side thereof, and three branches of the candlestick out of the other side thereof:

Three bowls made after the fashion of almonds in one branch, a knop and a flower; and three bowls made like almonds in another branch, a knop and a flower: so throughout the six branches going out of the candlestick.

And in the candlestick were four bowls made like almonds, his knops, and his flowers:

And a knop under two branches of the same, and a knop under two branches of the same, and a knop under two branches of the same, according to the six branches going out of it.

Their knops and their branches were of the same: all of it was one beaten work of pure gold.

And he made his seven lamps, and his snuffers, and his snuffdishes, of pure gold.

Of a talent of pure gold made he it, and all the vessels thereof.

And he made the incense altar of shittim wood: the length of it was a cubit, and the breadth of it a cubit; it was foursquare; and two cubits was the height of it; the horns thereof were of the same.

(37:17–25)

69. "This is Aaron who pours oil into the lamps": a miniature from a manuscript of Benjamin the Scribe, c. 1280, possibly written in Troyes, France (now at the British Museum).

זה המעירה ואהרן העתת שמן בנירות "

And the priest shall dip his finger in the blood, and sprinkle of the blood seven times before the LORD, before the vail of the sanctuary.

And the priest shall put some of the blood upon the horns of the altar of sweet incense before the LORD, which is in the tabernacle of the congregation; and shall pour all the blood of the bullock at the bottom of the altar of the burnt offering, which is at the door of the tabernacle of the congregation.

(4:6–7)

And the LORD spake unto Moses, saying,

Take Aaron and his sons with him, and the garments, and the anointing oil, and a bullock for the sin offering, and two rams, and a basket of unleavened bread;

And gather thou all the congregation together unto the door of the tabernacle of the congregation.

And Moses did as the LORD commanded him; and the assembly was gathered together unto the door of the tabernacle of the congregation.

And Moses said unto the congregation, This is the thing which the LORD commanded to be done.

(8:1–5)

And Aaron lifted up his hand toward the people, and blessed them, and came down from offering of the sin offering, and the burnt offering, and peace offerings.

And Moses and Aaron went into the tabernacle of the congregation, and came out, and blessed the people: and the glory of the LORD appeared unto all the people.

(9:22–23)

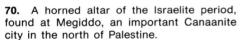

70. A horned altar of the Israelite period, found at Megiddo, an important Canaanite city in the north of Palestine.

Altars were constructed of stone, earth or metal. Altars of earth were explicitly commanded (Exodus 20:20), but none has been found, presumably as they did not resist the ravages of time. Stone altars, however, have been unearthed, especially from the pre-Israelite period. The altar originally was the place where sacrificial slaughter was performed.

In biblical times animals were no longer slaughtered upon the altar but nearby. The altar was not restricted to animal sacrifices; it also received grain, wine, and incense offerings. It also fulfilled other functions, such as testimony (Joshua 22:28 . . . "Behold the pattern of the altar of the Lord, which our fathers made, not for burnt offerings nor for sacrifice, but it is a witness between us and you").

The horns of the altar also provided refuge for those seeking asylum; the fugitive could seize them and claim sanctuary. This sanctuary, however, was not extended to murderers (Exodus 21:14; I Kings 2:28–34).

71

When a man shall have in the skin of his flesh a rising, a scab, or bright spot, and it be in the skin of his flesh like the plague of leprosy; then he shall be brought unto Aaron the priest, or unto one of his sons the priests:

And the priest shall look on the plague in the skin of the flesh: and when the hair in the plague is turned white, and the plague in sight be deeper than the skin of his flesh, it is a plague of leprosy: and the priest shall look on him, and pronounce him unclean. (13:2–3)

And the leper in whom the plague is, his clothes shall be rent, and his head bare, and he shall put a covering upon his upper lip, and shall cry, Unclean, unclean.

All the days wherein the plague shall be in him he shall be defiled; he is unclean: he shall dwell alone; without the camp shall his habitation be. (13:45–46)

71. The consecration of the tabernacle, from one of the wall paintings from Dura-Europos.

72. A priest inspecting possible cases of leprosy for ritual uncleanness, shown in an illustration from the title page of the Hebrew-Latin edition of the *Mishnah* (codification of Jewish Law), published in Amsterdam, 1700–04.

The term "leprosy" used in the Old and the New Testament is not limited to true leprosy, i.e., what is known today as Hansen's disease, but embraces a variety of skin ailments, including non-contagious types.

"The principles of hygiene contained in the medical sections of Leviticus are unique in antiquity as rational assessments of pathology," writes R.K. Harrison in the *Interpreter's Dictionary of the Bible*. In the Ancient Near East disease was generally attributed to evil magic or the punishment of sins. Counter-magic was used to exorcise the disease. In contrast to the pagan priest, the Israelite priest – who was concerned only with the contagious skin diseases – was not a healer, but a sort of "quarantine officer, an ecclesiastical health officer." He prescribed rituals, but only after healing had taken place.

72

And the LORD spake unto Moses, saying,

This shall be the law of the leper in the day of his cleansing: He shall be brought unto the priest:

And the priest shall go forth out of the camp; and the priest shall look, and, behold, if the plague of leprosy be healed in the leper;

Then shall the priest command to take for him that is to be cleansed two birds alive and clean, and cedar wood, and scarlet, and hyssop:

And the priest shall command that one of the birds be killed in an earthen vessel over running water:

As for the living bird, he shall take it, and the cedar wood, and the scarlet, and the hyssop, and shall dip them and the living bird in the blood of the bird that was killed over the running water:

And he shall sprinkle upon him that is to be cleansed from the leprosy seven times, and shall pronounce him clean, and shall let the living bird loose into the open field.

And he that is to be cleansed shall wash his clothes, and shave off all his hair, and wash himself in water, that he may be clean: and after that he shall come into the camp, and shall tarry abroad out of his tent seven days.

But it shall be on the seventh day, that he shall shave all his hair off his head and his beard and his eyebrows, even all his hair he shall shave off: and he shall wash his clothes, also he shall wash his flesh in water, and he shall be clean.

(14:1–9)

73. According to some modern scholars the hyssop is marjoram *(Marjoram syriaca; Origanum maru)*, a small aromatic plant that grows in rocks and stone walls. In the Bible it is contrasted with the lofty cedar of the Lebanon (I Kings 5:13). The two were used together for purposes of purification, as well as in the water for the purification of lepers, and of the house smitten by leprosy. The stems and the leaves of the hyssop contain a volatile oil used in perfume-making. Nowadays marjoram is used as a cooking herb in Mediterranean countries.

74. A Phoenician clay figurine of a woman bathing, dating from the 8th century B.C. It was found at Achzib, in the north of Israel. Washing, bathing and immersion were common religious practices in ancient times. The primitive conditions of life in biblical times would hardly have permitted bathing in the sense understood today, or as it was practiced already in the Roman period. People generally bathed in a natural source of water, such as a river or spring. Ordinary dwellings rarely had bathing facilities, and only in the wealthier houses could one expect to find a special chamber, with a tub used as a bath. The practice seems to have originated in Egypt.

75

75. Ivory wine goblet, 17th century, from southern Germany, showing Moses before Pharaoh. Part of the Hebrew inscription around the rim – "Let my people go" – is visible.

And the LORD spake unto Moses, saying,

Speak unto the children of Israel, and say unto them, Concerning the feasts of the LORD, which ye shall proclaim to be holy convocations, even these are my feasts.

Six days shall work be done: but the seventh day is the sabbath of rest, an holy convocation; ye shall do no work therein: it is the sabbath of the LORD in all your dwellings.

There are the feasts of the LORD, even holy convocations, which ye shall proclaim in their seasons.

In the fourteenth day of the first month at even is the LORD'S passover.

And on the fifteenth day of the same month is the feast of unleavened bread unto the LORD: seven days ye must eat unleavened bread.

In the first day ye shall have an holy convocation: ye shall do no servile work therein.

But ye shall offer an offering made by fire unto the LORD seven days: in the seventh day is an holy convocation: ye shall do no servile work therein.

And the LORD spake unto Moses, saying,

Speak unto the children of Israel, and say unto them, When ye be come into the land which I give unto you, and shall reap the harvest thereof, then ye shall bring a sheaf of the firstfruits of your harvest unto the priest:

And he shall wave the sheaf before the LORD, to be accepted for you: on the morrow after the sabbath the priest shall wave it.

And ye shall offer that day when ye wave the sheaf an he lamb without blemish of the first year for a burnt offering unto the LORD.

And the meat offering thereof shall be two tenth deals of fine flour mingled with oil, an offering made by fire unto the LORD for a sweet savour: and the drink offering thereof shall be of wine, the fourth part of an hin.

And ye shall eat neither bread, nor parched corn, nor green ears, until the selfsame day that ye have brought an offering unto your God: it shall be a statute for ever throughout your generations in all your dwellings.

And ye shall count unto you from the morrow after the sabbath, from the day that ye brought the sheaf of the wave offering; seven sabbaths shall be complete:

Even unto the morrow after the seventh sabbath shall ye number fifty days; and ye shall offer a new meat offering unto the LORD.

Ye shall bring out of your habitations two wave loaves of two tenth deals: they shall be of fine flour; they shall be baken with leaven; they are the firstfruits unto the LORD.

And ye shall offer with the bread seven lambs without blemish of the first year, and one young bullock, and two rams: they shall be for a burnt offering unto the LORD, with their meat offering, and their drink offerings, even an offering made by fire, of sweet savour unto the LORD.

Then ye shall sacrifice one kid of the goats for a sin offering, and two lambs of the first year for a sacrifice of peace offerings.

And the priest shall wave them with the bread of the firstfruits for a wave offering before the LORD, with the two lambs: they shall be holy to the LORD for the priest.

And ye shall proclaim on the selfsame day, that it may be an holy convocation unto you: ye shall do no servile work therein: it shall be a statute for ever in all your dwellings throughout your generations.

And when ye reap the harvest of your land, thou shalt not make clean riddance of the corners of thy field when thou reapest, neither shalt thou gather any gleaning of thy harvest: thou shalt leave them unto the poor, and to the stranger: I am the LORD your God.

76. A page from the *Darmstadt Haggadah*. *Haggadah* in Hebrew means, literally, "recital." The Bible enjoins that the story of the exodus from Egypt must be told (*hagged*, i.e., tell) throughout the generations. The Passover Haggadah is recited at the *seder* ritual on the first evening of Passover. The text of the page shown here reads as follows: "This is the bread of affliction that our fathers ate in the land of Egypt. All who are hungered – let them come and eat: all who are needy – let them come and celebrate the Passover. Now we are here, but next year may we be free." This passage of the Haggadah is not written in Hebrew but in Aramaic, the language spoken among the Jewish people in Palestine after the return from the Babylonian exile.
The invitation to all who are hungry is not a vain formula. The Jew who refuses hospitality to a needy coreligionist on this night is false to the whole spirit of the observance of the Passover.

77. Gathering and winnowing of the harvest shown in a wall painting of an Egyptian tomb, c. 1420 B.C.

78

78. Jerusalem children celebrating Pentecost ("the 50th day" or *Shavuot* in Hebrew, i.e., "weeks"), the 50th day after the first day of Passover, hence its name. In biblical times it marked the beginning of the harvest. It is also known as the "Feast of Weeks" (Exodus 34:22; Deuteronomy 16:10); the "Day of first fruits" (Numbers 28:26) or "The Feast of Harvest" (Exodus 23:16).
After the destruction of the Temple, the festival became the anniversary of the giving of the Law at Sinai. In modern times attempts have been made to revive some of the harvest ceremonies. It is customary to read the Ten Commandments and the Book of Ruth in the synagogue decorated with greenery. Among the reasons given for reading the story of Ruth is that the events took place at harvest time, and that Ruth was the ancestor of David who, traditionally, is said to have died at Pentecost.

And the LORD spake unto Moses, saying,

Speak unto the children of Israel, saying, In the seventh month, in the first day of the month, shall ye have a sabbath, a memorial of blowing of trumpets, an holy convocation.

Ye shall do no servile work therein: but ye shall offer an offering made by fire unto the LORD.

And the LORD spake unto Moses, saying

Also on the tenth day of this seventh month there shall be a day of atonement: it shall be an holy convocation unto you; and ye shall afflict your souls, and offer an offering made by fire unto the LORD.

And ye shall do no work in that same day: for it is a day of atonement, to make an atonement for you before the LORD your God.

For whatsoever soul it be that shall not be afflicted in that same day, he shall be cut off from among his people.

And whatsoever soul it be that doeth any work in that same day, the same soul will I destroy from among his people.

Ye shall do no manner of work: it shall be a statute for ever throughout your generations in all your dwellings.

It shall be unto you a sabbath of rest, and ye shall afflict your souls: in the ninth day of the month at even, from even unto even, shall ye celebrate your sabbath.

And the LORD spake unto Moses, saying,

Speak unto the children of Israel, saying, The fifteenth day of this seventh month shall be the feast of tabernacles for seven days unto the LORD.

On the first day shall be an holy convocation: ye shall do no servile work therein.

Seven days ye shall offer an offering made by fire unto the LORD: on the eighth day shall be an holy convocation unto you; and ye shall offer an offering made by fire unto the LORD: it is a solemn assembly; and ye shall do no servile work therein.

These are the feasts of the LORD, which ye shall proclaim to be holy convocations, to offer an offering made by fire unto the LORD, a burnt offering, and a meat offering, a sacrifice, and drink offerings, every thing upon his day:

79. Farmers bearing produce from their farms as tribute to the local king, depicted on a carved ivory plaque found at Megiddo.

Beside the sabbaths of the LORD, and beside your gifts, and beside all your vows, and beside all your freewill offerings, which ye give unto the LORD.

Also in the fifteenth day of the seventh month, when ye have gathered in the fruit of the land, ye shall keep a feast unto the LORD seven days: on the first day shall be a sabbath, and on the eighth day shall be a sabbath.

And ye shall take you on the first day the boughs of goodly trees, branches of palm trees, and the boughs of thick trees, and willows of the brook; and ye shall rejoice before the LORD your God seven days.

And ye shall keep it a feast unto the LORD seven days in the year. It shall be a statute for ever in your generations: ye shall celebrate it in the seventh month.

Ye shall dwell in booths seven days; all that are Israelites born shall dwell in booths:

That your generations may know that I made the children of Israel to dwell in booths, when I brought them out of the the land of Egypt: I am the LORD your God.

And Moses declared unto the children of Israel the feasts of the LORD.

(23:1–44)

80. The festival of Succot (or the Feast of Tabernacles, or the Feast of the Booths), celebrated at the Western Wall, Jerusalem. The worshippers are wearing the traditional prayer shawl (Numbers 15:38–41) and each holds a citron ("the fruit of goodly trees"), myrtle twigs ("the boughs of thick trees"), a date palm and a willow branch.

81. Prisoners of war depicted on the so-called Cosmetic Palette of the Does from Abydos, Upper Egypt.

And if thy brother that dwelleth by thee be waxen poor, and be sold to unto thee; thou shalt not compel him to serve as a bondservant:

But as an hired servant, and as a sojourner, he shall be with thee, and shall serve thee unto the year of jubile:

And then shall he depart from thee, both he and his children with him, and shall return unto his own family, and unto the possession of his fathers shall he return.

For they are my servants, which I brought forth out of the land of Egypt: they shall not be sold as bondmen.

Thou shalt not rule over him with rigour; but shalt fear thy God.

Both thy bondmen, and thy bondmaids, which thou shalt have, shall be of the heathen that are round about you; of them shall ye buy bondmen and bondmaids.

Moreover of the children of the strangers that do sojourn among you, of them shall ye buy, and of their families that are with you, which they begat in your land: and they shall be your possession.

And ye shall take them as an inheritance for your children after you, to inherit them for a possession; they shall be your bondmen for ever: but over your brethren the children of Israel, ye shall not rule one over another with rigour.

And if a sojourner or stranger wax rich by thee, and thy brother that dwelleth by him wax poor, and sell himself unto the stranger or sojourner by thee, or to the stock of the stranger's family:

After that he is sold he may be redeemed again; one of his brethren may redeem him:

Either his uncle, or his uncle's son, may redeem him, or any that is nigh of kin unto him of his family may redeem him; or if he be able, he may redeem himself.

And he shall reckon with him that bought him from the year that he was sold to him unto the year of jubile: and the price of his sale shall be according unto the number of years, according to the time of an hired servant shall it be with him.

If there be yet many years behind, according unto them he shall give again the price of his redemption out of the money that he was bought for.

And if there remain but few years unto the year of jubile, then he shall count with him, and according unto his years shall he give him again the price of his redemption.

And as a yearly hired servant shall he be with him: and the other shall not rule with rigour over him in thy sight.

And if he be not redeemed in these years, then he shall go out in the year of jubile, both he, and his children with him.

For unto me the children of Israel are servants; they are my servants whom I brought forth out of the land of Egypt: I am the LORD your God.

(25:39–55)

82. Male and female slaves shown in an Egyptian wall painting.

Slavery was an accepted social institution in the ancient world, and the Israelites were no exception. Joseph was sold by Midianite merchants to the Ishmaelites who in turn sold him to the Egyptians (Genesis 37). Slavery did not necessarily mean servitude for life. The Hebrew slave was freed after six years.

There were a number of ways in which a Hebrew could fall into bondage, the most frequent being his inability to pay a debt. If a Hebrew was sold to a stranger his brethren had to redeem him, and the same applied to prisoners of war (see Nehemiah 5:8).

Some slaves reached positions of great eminence; for example Eliezer, the slave of Abraham (Genesis 15:2–4; 24:2), and Joseph (Genesis 39:4). In some cases the master's daughter could be married to a slave (I Chronicles 2:34–5). A master was allowed to strike a slave, but cruelty was punished (Exodus 21:20). According to Deuteronomy 23:15 a fugitive slave was not to be handed back to his owner. The provision for freeing slaves was different for non-Hebrew slaves, who were mainly prisoners of war or women taken as concubines by their masters or masters' sons (Genesis 39:49; Numbers 31:9; Deuteronomy 21:10–14).

After the conquest of Canaan by the Israelites a different form of servitude appeared. Some Israelite tribes paid tribute, in most cases in the form of forced labor.

And the LORD spake unto Moses and unto Aaron, saying,

Every man of the children of Israel shall pitch by his own standard, with the ensign of their father's house: far off about the tabernacle of the congregation shall they pitch.

(2:1–2)

These are those which were numbered of the children of Israel by the house of their fathers: all those that were numbered of the camps throughout their hosts were six hundred thousand and three thousand and five hundred and fifty.

But the Levites were not numbered among the children of Israel; as the LORD commanded Moses.

And the children of Israel did according to all that the LORD commanded Moses: so they pitched by their standards, and so they set forward, every one after their families, according to the house of their fathers.

(2:32–34)

Bring the tribe of Levi near, and present them before Aaron the priest, that they may minister unto him.

And they shall keep his charge, and the charge of the whole congregation before the tabernacle of the congregation, to do the service of the tabernacle.

And they shall keep all the instruments of the tabernacle of the congregation, and the charge of the children of Israel, to do the service of the tabernacle.

And thou shalt give the Levites unto Aaron and to his sons: they are wholly given unto him out of the children of Israel.

(3:6–9)

83. Pentateuch scroll "crown," with hands raised in priestly blessing, in repoussé and perforated silver-gilt, Germany, 1793.
The *cohanim* (plural of *cohen,* priest in Hebrew), descendants of the priestly families who served in the Temple in ancient times, pronounce the priestly blessing: "The Lord bless thee, and keep thee: The Lord make his face shine upon thee, and be gracious unto thee. The Lord lift up his countenance upon thee, and give thee peace."
The *cohanim* invoke the blessing upon the congregation with their prayer shawls drawn forward to cover their heads, their hands outstretched at shoulder level, thumbs touching and the first two fingers of each hand separated from the other two, forming a sort of fan.
In modern times, the claim to an Aaronide priestly descent is mainly a presumptive one which, in the absence of pedigree registers, cannot be proved. However, the rights and privileges of the *cohen,* as well as the prohibitions, are still enforced by orthodox Jews. These privileges are, mainly, the right to be called up to the reading of the Law and to invoke the priestly blessing in the synagogue.

84. The order of the tribes in their tents, as represented in the frontispiece of the Book of Numbers from the *Duke of Sussex Pentateuch,* c. 1300. It shows knights holding banners with the emblems of the four leading tribes of Israel as they camped around the Tabernacle. The emblems are: a lion for Judah (Genesis 49:9), an eagle for Reuben (according to rabbinical interpretations of Genesis 49:3), a bull for Ephraim (Deuteronomy 33:17), and a serpent for Dan (Genesis 49:17). (The manuscript is now at the British Museum, London.)

85. A group of stone weights and scale pans used for weighing ingots, of the Israelite period.

Among the weights mentioned in the Bible are the *shekel* (especially in Chapter 7 of the Book of Numbers), the *talent,* the *ephah,* the *omer,* the *bekah,* the *gerah.* Weights for the most part were made of stone, and the Hebrew Bible refers to weights as "stones."

The *talent* was the largest unit of weight. The *shekel* was the basic unit, as its name, meaning "weight" in Hebrew, implies. It seems that there were three kinds of *shekel:* a silver one, at the going merchants' rate (Genesis 23:16); a *shekel* by the sanctuary weight (Exodus 30:13) and "*shekels* by the king's weight" (II Samuel 14:26), i.e., *shekels* stamped by the royal treasury as proof that they were perfect.

86. A hoard of silver ingots with the clay pot in which it was found near the shores of the Dead Sea. The ingots have markings on them, but no definite shape. Some of them seem to have been broken up into small chunks. Others look like earrings, and in fact jewelry often served as both ornaments and money in ancient times.

And the LORD said unto Moses, They shall offer their offering, each prince on his day, for the dedicating of the altar.

And he that offered his offering the first day was Nahshon the son of Amminadab, of the tribe of Judah:

And his offering was one silver charger, the weight thereof was an hundred and thirty shekels, one silver bowl of seventy shekels, after the shekel of the sanctuary; both of them were full of fine flour mingled with oil for a meat offering:

One spoon of ten shekels of gold, full of incense:

One young bullock, one ram, one lamb of the first year, for a burnt offering:

One kid of the goats for a sin offering:

And for a sacrifice of peace offerings, two oxen, five rams, five he goats, five lambs of the first year: this was the offering of Nahshon the son of Amminadab.

On the second day Nethaneel the son of Zuar, prince of Issachar, did offer:

He offered for his offering one silver charger, the weight whereof was an hundred and thirty shekels, one silver bowl of seventy shekels, after the shekel of the sanctuary; both of them full of fine flour mingled with oil for a meat offering:

One spoon of gold of ten shekels, full of incense:

One young bullock, one ram, one lamb of the first year, for a burnt offering.   (7:11–21)

87

And the LORD spake unto Moses, saying,

Speak unto the children of Israel, and bid them that they make them fringes in the borders of their garments throughout their generations, and that they put upon the fringe of the borders a ribband of blue:

And it shall be unto you for a fringe, that ye may look upon it, and remember all the commandments of the LORD, and do them; and that ye seek not after your own heart and your own eyes, after which ye use to go a whoring:

That ye may remember, and do all my commandments, and be holy unto your God.

I am the LORD your God, which brought you out of the land of Egypt, to be your God: I am the LORD your God.   (15:37–41)

88

89. The Desert of Zin referred to as the "wilderness", has been identified as the stark area south of Kadesh-barnea.

89

Then came the children of Israel, even the whole congregation, into the desert of Zin in the first month: and the people abode in Kadesh; and Miriam died there, and was buried there.

(20:1)

This is the water of Meribah; because the children of Israel strove with the LORD, and he was sanctified in them.

And Moses sent messengers from Kadesh unto the king of Edom, Thus saith thy brother Israel, Thou knowest all the travail that hath befallen us:

How our fathers went down into Egypt, and we have dwelt in Egypt a long time; and the Egyptians vexed us, and our fathers:

And when we cried unto the LORD, he heard our voice, and sent an angel, and hath brought us forth out of Egypt: and, behold, we are in Kadesh, a city in the uttermost of thy border:

Let us pass, I pray thee, through thy country: we will not pass through the fields, or through the vineyards, neither will we drink of the water of the wells: we will go by the king's high way, we will not turn to the right hand nor to the left, until we have passed thy borders.

And Edom said unto him, Thou shalt not pass by me, lest I come out against thee with the sword.

And the children of Israel said unto him, We will go by the high way: and if I and my cattle drink of thy water, then I will pay for it: I will only, without doing any thing else, go through on my feet.

And he said, Thou shalt not go through. And Edom came out against him with much people, and with a strong hand.

(20:13–20)

90. Kadesh-barnea is identified with Ain el-Qudeirat. Remains of an Israelite fortress from the period of the kingdom of Judah have been uncovered, consisting of a casemate-wall fortified with towers. Remains of Roman and Byzantine settlements were also discovered nearby.

91. Kadesh-barnea: this oasis on the border between the Sinai and the Negev was an important junction on the main routes leading from Edom and the Arava to Egypt – the Way of Shur – and from Elath and the central Negev northwards to Arad and Hebron. Kadesh-barnea became known as the Water of Meribah (strife) (Numbers 20:13), and is referred to by Ezekiel as "the waters of strife of Kadesh" (Ezekiel 47:19).

92. The clay figurine shown here was found at Kadesh-barnea during recent excavations. It is dated to the 8th/7th century B.C.

90

91

93. Arad was settled in slightly different locations during different historical periods. Shown here is one of the early settlements. Arad was an important city in the eastern Negev, on the main road to Edom. Remains of the biblical city lie on a plain about twenty-two and a half miles northwest of Beersheba. It is one of the few sites in the Negev that have retained the same names for the past three thousand years.

The Israelites destroyed the district and called it "Hormah," meaning "ban." They did not settle there. However, it seems that some of the inhabitants escaped destruction. Hence, the king of Arad is included in the list of 31 kings later vanquished during Joshua's campaign (Joshua 12:14). According to Judges 1:16, where it is called the "wilderness of Judah," it was settled by Kenites, a people related to the family of Moses.

And when king Arad the Canaanite, which dwelt in the south, heard tell that Israel came by the way of the spies; then he fought against Israel, and took some of them prisoners.

And Israel vowed a vow unto the LORD, and said, If thou wilt indeed deliver this people into my hand, then I will utterly destroy their cities.

And the LORD hearkened to the voice of Israel, and delivered up the Canaanites; and they utterly destroyed them and their cities: and he called the name of the place Hormah.

(21:1–3)

93

And the LORD sent fiery serpents among the people, and they bit the people; and much people of Israel died.

Therefore the people came to Moses, and said, We have sinned, for we have spoken against the LORD, and against thee; pray unto the LORD, that he take away the serpents from us. And Moses prayed for the people.

And the LORD said unto Moses, Make thee a fiery serpent, and set it upon a pole: and it shall come to pass, that every one that is bitten, when he looketh upon it, shall live.

(21:6–8)

94. One of the numerous serpents that are very common in Palestine and the wilderness to the south. Although many are harmless, they are dreaded by the natives, and several kinds are most deadly. The "fiery serpents" refers in reality to the burning sting of the serpents.

And the children of Israel set forward, and pitched in the plains of Moab on this side Jordan by Jericho.

And Balak the son of Zippor saw all that Israel had done to the Amorites.

And Moab was sore afraid of the people, because they were many: and Moab was distressed because of the children of Israel.

And Moab said unto the elders of Midian, Now shall this company lick up all that are round about us, as the ox licketh up the grass of the field. And Balak the son of Zippor was king of the Moabites at that time.

He sent messengers therefore unto Balaam the son of Beor to Pethor, which is by the river of the land of the children of his people, to call him, saying, Behold, there is a people come out from Egypt: behold, they cover the face of the earth, and they abide over against me:

94

Come now therefore, I pray thee, curse me this people; for they are too mighty for me: peradventure I shall prevail, that we may smite them, and that I may drive them out of the land: for I wot that he whom thou blessest is blessed, and he whom thou cursest is cursed. (22:1–6)

And the ass saw the angel of the LORD standing in the way, and his sword drawn in his hand: and the ass turned aside out of the way, and went into the field: and Balaam smote the ass, to turn her into the way.

But the angel of the LORD stood in a path of the vineyards, a wall being on this side, and a wall on that side.

And when the ass saw the angel of the LORD, she thrust herself unto the wall, and crushed Balaam's foot against the wall: and he smote her again.

And the angel of the LORD went further, and stood in a narrow place, where was no way to turn either to the right hand or to the left.

And when the ass saw the angel of the LORD, she fell down under Balaam: and Balaam's anger was kindled, and he smote the ass with a staff.

And the LORD opened the mouth of the ass, and she said unto Balaam, What have I done unto thee, that thou hast smitten me these three times? (22:23–28)

And he brought him into the field of Zophim, to the top of Pisgah, and built seven altars, and offered a bullock and a ram on every altar.

And he said unto Balak, Stand here by thy burnt offering, while I meet the LORD yonder. (23:14–15)

And Balak's anger was kindled against Balaam, and he smote his hands together: and Balak said unto Balaam, I called thee to curse mine enemies, and, behold, thou hast altogether blessed them these three times. (24:10)

95. A view of Moab, the land east of the Dead Sea, between Edom and Ammon. Pisgah has not been identified exactly but it is thought to be in the highest part of the Mountains of Abarim in Moab.
From the peak of Pisgah, Moses saw a great part of the land of Canaan (Deuteronomy 3:27; 34:1–4).

96

96. One of the mountains in Sinai said to be Mount Horeb.

These be the words which Moses spake unto all Israel on this side Jordan in the wilderness, in the plain over against the Red sea, between Paran, and Tophel, and Laban, and Hazeroth, and Dizahab.

(There are eleven days' journey from Horeb by the way of mount Seir unto Kadesh-barnea.)

And it came to pass in the fortieth year, in the eleventh month, on the first day of the month, that Moses spake unto the children of Israel, according unto all that the LORD had given him in commandment unto them;

After he had slain Sihon the king of the Amorites, which dwelt in Heshbon, and Og the king of Bashan, which dwelt at Astaroth in Edrei:

On this side Jordan, in the land of Moab, began Moses to declare this law, saying,

The LORD our God spake unto us in Horeb, saying, Ye have dwelt long enough in this mount:

Turn you, and take your journey, and go to the mount of the Amorites, and unto all the places nigh thereunto, in the plain, in the hills, and in the vale, and in the south, and by the sea side, to the land of the Canaanites, and unto Lebanon, unto the great river, the river Euphrates.

Behold, I have set the land before you: go in and possess the land which the LORD sware unto your fathers, Abraham, Isaac, and Jacob, to give unto them and to their seed after them.

97

And I spake unto you at that time, saying, I am not able to bear you myself alone:

The LORD your God hath multiplied you, and, behold, ye are this day as the stars of heaven for multitude.

(The LORD God of your fathers make you a thousand times so many more as ye are, and bless you, as he hath promised you!)

How can I myself alone bear your cumbrance, and your burden, and your strife?

Take you wise men, and understanding, and known among your tribes, and I will make them rulers over you.

And ye answered me, and said, The thing which thou hast spoken is good for us to do.

So I took the chief of your tribes, wise men, and known, and made them heads over you, captains over thousands, and captains over hundreds, and captains over fifties, and captains over tens, and officers among your tribes.

And I charged your judges at that time, saying, Hear the causes between your brethren, and judge righteously between every man and his brother, and the stranger that is with him.

Ye shall not respect persons in judgment; but ye shall hear the small as well as the great; ye shall not be afraid of the face of man; for the judgment is God's: and the cause that is too hard for you, bring it unto me, and I will hear it.

(1:1–17)

97. A Court of Law depicted on the opening page of the *Arba'a Turim* ("Four Columns" of the Law), by Jacob ben Asher, Mantua, 1436. (Now at the Vatican Library.)

Moses was a judge of his people (Exodus 18:13). Later he delegated his judicial powers. Judges had to be "able men, such as fear God, men of truth, hating covetousness" (Exodus 18:21), and "wise men, and understanding, and known among your tribes..." The judges are told: "Ye shall not respect persons in judgment; but ye shall hear the small as well as the great; ye shall not be afraid of the face of man."

In modern Israel there are secular and rabbinical courts, the latter dealing with religious matters, such as marriage and divorce, and the supervision of dietary laws.

Now these are the commandments, the statutes, and the judgments, which the LORD your God commanded to teach you, that ye might do them in the land whither ye go to possess it:

Hear, O Israel: The LORD our God is one LORD:

And thou shalt love the LORD thy God with all thine heart, and with all thy soul, and with all thy might.

And these words, which I command thee this day, shall be in thine heart:

And thou shalt teach them diligently unto thy children, and shalt talk of them when thou sittest in thine house, and when thou walkest by the way, and when thou liest down, and when thou risest up.

And thou shalt bind them for a sign upon thine hand, and they shall be as frontlets between thine eyes.

And thou shalt write them upon the posts of thy house, and on thy gates.

And it shall be, when the LORD thy God shall have brought thee into the land which he sware unto thy fathers, to Abraham, to Isaac, and to Jacob, to give thee great and goodly cities, which thou buildedst not.

(6:1–10)

98. A silver *mezuzah* from Russia, 1873. The original word *mezuzah* is "door-post" in Hebrew; by association, the word came to mean not the doorpost, but the parchment scroll with selected verses from the Pentateuch (Deuteronomy 6:4;11:13–21) inserted in a small case and affixed to the doorpost of Jewish homes.
The *mezuzah* is one of the most widely observed ritual commandments of Judaism.
In modern times the practice developed of wearing a *mezuzah* around the neck as a charm.

99. The so-called Nash Papyrus, dating from the 2nd century B.C., contains the Ten Commandments. It is the oldest part of the Bible known to exist before the discovery of the Dead Sea Scrolls.

100-106. Wheat; barley; grapes; fig tree; pomegranate; olive tree; dates. Jewish folklore calls these the "seven species," and they are regarded as symbols of the country's fertility.
It is thought that the honey often mentioned in the Old Testament was a thick syrup made from either grapes or dates. Bees' honey, found wild, was sufficiently rare to have been considered among the finest of foods ("honey out of the rock" in Deuteronomy 32:13; Psalms 81:16). It figures in the wedding of Samson (Judges 14:8–9).

For the LORD thy God bringeth thee into a good land, a land of brooks of water, of fountains and depths that spring out of valleys and hills;

A land of wheat, and barley, and vines, and fig trees, and pomegranates; a land of oil olive, and honey;

A land wherein thou shalt eat bread without scarceness, thou shalt not lack any thing in it; a land whose stones are iron, and out of whose hills thou mayest dig brass.

(8:7–9)

These are the statutes and judgments, which ye shall observe to do in the land, which the LORD God of thy fathers giveth thee to possess it, all the days that ye live upon the earth.

Ye shall utterly destroy all the places, wherein the nations which ye shall possess served their gods, upon the high mountains, and upon the hills, and under every green tree:

And ye shall overthrow their altars, and break their pillars, and burn their groves with fire; and ye shall hew down the graven images of their gods, and destroy the names of them out of that place.

Ye shall not do so unto the LORD your God.

But unto the place which the LORD your God shall choose out of all your tribes to put his name there, even unto his habitation shall ye seek, and thither thou shalt come.

(12:1–5)

107. Stele from Ugarit showing the "Baal of the Lightning": the Canaanite god holds a lance in the form of lightning in his left hand.

Seven weeks shalt thou number unto thee: begin to number the seven weeks from such time as thou beginnest to put the sickle to the corn.

And thou shalt keep the feast of weeks unto the LORD thy God with a tribute of a freewill offering of thine hand, which thou shalt give unto the LORD thy God, according as the LORD thy God hath blessed thee:

And thou shalt rejoice before the LORD thy God, thou, and thy son, and thy daughter, and thy manservant, and thy maidservant, and the Levite that is within thy gates, and the stranger, and the fatherless, and the widow, that are among you, in the place which the LORD thy God hath chosen to place his name there.

And thou shalt remember that thou wast a bondman in Egypt: and thou shalt observe and do these statutes.

Thou shalt observe the feast of tabernacles seven days, after that thou hast gathered in thy corn and thy wine:

And thou shalt rejoice in thy feast, thou, and thy son, and thy daughter, and thy manservant, and thy maidservant, and the Levite, the stranger, and the fatherless, and the widow, that are within thy gates.

Seven days shalt thou keep a solemn feast unto the LORD thy God in the place which the LORD shall choose: because the LORD thy God shall bless thee in all thine increase, and in all the works of thine hands, therefore thou shalt surely rejoice.

(16:9–15)

108. The "Gezer Calendar," c. 950 B.C. Engraved on a stone, in old biblical script: Two months of ingathering. Two months of late sowing. A month of pulling flax. A month of barley harvest. A month when everything has been harvested. Two months of pruning [vines]. A month of summer fruit.
This agricultural calendar was discovered in 1908 at Gezer, not far from Tel Aviv.

109

109. A chick emerges in a nest.

If a bird's nest chance to be before thee in the way in any tree, or on the ground, whether they be young ones, or eggs, and the dam sitting upon the young, or upon the eggs, thou shalt not take the dam with the young.

But thou shalt in any wise let the dam go, and take the young to thee; that it may be well with thee, and that thou mayest prolong thy days.

(22:6–7)

If brethren dwell together, and one of them die, and have no child, the wife of the dead shall not marry without unto a stranger: her husband's brother shall go in unto her, and take her to him to wife, and perform the duty of an husband's brother unto her.

And it shall be, that the firstborn which she beareth shall succeed in the name of his brother which is dead, that his name be not put out of Israel.

And if the man like not to take his brother's wife, then let his brother's wife go up to the gate unto the elders, and say, My husband's brother refuseth to raise up unto his brother a name in Israel, he will not perform the duty of my husband's brother.

Then the elders of his city shall call him, and speak unto him: and if he stand to it, and say, I like not to take her;

Then shall his brother's wife come unto him in the presence of the elders, and loose his shoe from off his foot, and spit in his face, and shall answer and say, So shall it be done unto that man that will not build up his brother's house.

And his name shall be called in Israel, The house of him that hath his shoe loosed.

(25:5–10)

110. A *halitza* shoe, made of leather, from Germany, 19th century. Marriage of a widow, whose husband has died without offspring, and the brother of the deceased (levirate marriage) is prescribed in the Bible "that his name be not blotted out of Israel." However, a release from such an obligation is possible by the ceremony of *halitza*: the brother-in-law (*levir* in Latin), wearing on his right foot a special shoe, and the widow, appear before a rabbinical court. The widow declares that the 'levir' refuses to perform his duty of marrying her; she then unties the straps and removes the shoe. The widow thereby releases her brother-in-law from his obligation and, symbolically, from his family's connection with her.

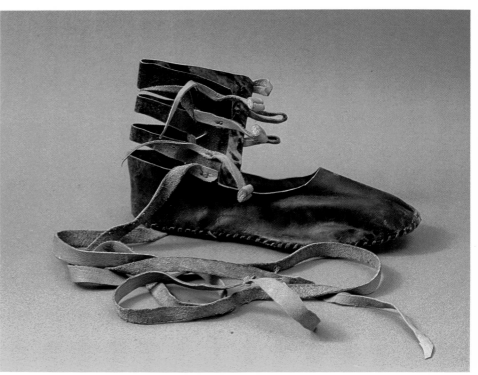

110

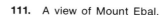

And thou shalt write upon them all the words of this law, when thou art passed over, that thou mayest go in unto the land which the LORD thy God giveth thee, a land that floweth with milk and honey; as the LORD God of thy fathers hath promised thee.

Therefore it shall be when ye be gone over Jordan, that ye shall set up these stones, which I command you this day, in mount Ebal, and thou shalt plaister them with plaister.

And there shalt thou build an altar unto the LORD thy God, an altar of stones: thou shalt not lift up any iron tool upon them.

Thou shalt build the altar of the LORD thy God of whole stones: and thou shalt offer burnt offerings thereon unto the LORD thy God:

And thou shalt offer peace offerings, and shalt eat there, and rejoice before the LORD thy God.

And thou shalt write upon the stones all the words of this law very plainly.

And Moses and the priests the Levites spake unto all Israel, saying, Take heed, and hearken, O Israel; this day thou art become the people of the LORD thy God.

Thou shalt therefore obey the voice of the LORD thy God, and do his commandments and his statutes, which I command thee this day.

And Moses charged the people the same day, saying,

These shall stand upon mount Gerizim to bless the people, when ye are come over Jordan; Simeon, and Levi, and Judah, and Issachar, and Joseph, and Benjamin:

And these shall stand upon mount Ebal to curse; Reuben, Gad, and Asher, and Zebulun, Dan, and Naphtali.

And the Levites shall speak, and say unto all the men of Israel with a loud voice,

Cursed be the man that maketh any graven or molten image, an abomination unto the LORD, the work of the hands of the craftsman, and putteth it in a secret place. And all the people shall answer and say, Amen.

(27:3–15)

111. A view of Mount Ebal.

112. The Mountains of Moab.
The land of Moab extended east of the Jordan and the Dead Sea. The highland of Moab extends southward to the Zered River, eastward to the desert, and westward to the Dead Sea. Its northern boundary was much disputed; sometimes it was limited by the river Arnon and sometimes it extended north of the Dead Sea. The area of Moab is mountainous in the south with ridges rising to about 4000 feet leveling off to a plateau in the north. Its economy was mainly pastoral.

So Moses the servant of the LORD died there in the land of Moab, according to the word of the LORD.

And he buried him in a valley in the land of Moab, over against Beth-peor: but no man knoweth of his sepulchre unto this day.

And Moses was an hundred and twenty years old when he died: his eye was not dim, nor his natural force abated.

And the children of Israel wept for Moses in the plains of Moab thirty days: so the days of weeping and mourning for Moses were ended.

(34:5–8)

113. Pentateuch scroll case, decorated with silver-gilt designs on wood, from Baghdad, Iraq, 1852. The twin glass plates on the inside of the cupola are inscribed with biblical passages.

The scroll of the Law, written with pious care on parchment, is kept in a case or covered with a mantle through which protrude the two staves (called "trees of life" in Hebrew) on which the scroll is rolled. Mounted on each of these staves are two finials called in Hebrew "pomegranates". The name probably developed from the knobs on the top of the staves which were made in the shape of a pomegranate.

114

114. A signpost on the way to Jericho, possibly the oldest city of the world. It was the first Canaanite city west of the Jordan to be conquered by the Israelites.

And Joshua the son of Nun sent out of Shittim two men to spy secretly, saying, Go view the land, even Jericho. And they went, and came into an harlot's house, named Rahab, and lodged there.

And it was told the king of Jericho, saying, Behold, there came men in hither to night of the children of Israel to search out the country.

And the king of Jericho sent unto Rahab, saying, Bring forth the men that are come to thee, which are entered into thine house: for they be come to search out all the country.

And the woman took the two men, and hid them, and said thus, There came men unto me, but I wist not whence they were:

And it came to pass about the time of shutting of the gate, when it was dark, that the men went out: whither the men went I wot not: pursue after them quickly; for ye shall overtake them.

But she had brought them up to the roof of the house, and hid them with the stalks of flax, which she had laid in order upon the roof.

And the men pursued after them the way to Jordan unto the fords: and as soon as they which pursued after them were gone out, they shut the gate.

(2:1–7)

And Joshua rose early in the morning; and they removed from Shittim, and came to Jordan, he and all the children of Israel, and lodged there before they passed over.

And it came to pass after three days, that the officers went through the host;

And they commanded the people, saying, When ye see the ark of the covenant of the LORD your God, and the priests the Levites bearing it, then ye shall remove from your place, and go after it.

Yet there shall be a space between you and it, about two thousand cubits by measure: come not near unto it, that ye may know the way by which ye must go: for ye have not passed this way heretofore.

(3:1–4)

115

115. The Jordan River: it flows from north of the Sea of Galilee to the Dead Sea.
In biblical times it was a barrier between the lands on either side of it. There were a few natural crossing places (there were no bridges then), mostly north of the Sea of Galilee. Close to the Dead Sea there were hardly any passable fords, and these were the sites of many battles.

And thou shalt command the priests that bear the ark of the covenant, saying, When ye are come to the brink of the water of Jordan, ye shall stand still in Jordan.

And Joshua said unto the children of Israel, Come hither, and hear the words of the LORD your God.

And Joshua said, Hereby ye shall know that the living God is among you, and that he will without fail drive out from before you the Canaanites, and the Hittites, and the Hivites, and the Perizzites, and the Girgashites, and the Amorites, and the Jebusites.

Behold, the ark of the covenant of the Lord of all the earth passeth over before you into Jordan.

Now therefore take you twelve men out of the tribes of Israel, out of every tribe a man.

And it shall come to pass, as soon as the soles of the feet of the priests that bear the ark of the LORD, the Lord of all the earth, shall rest in the waters of Jordan, that the waters of Jordan shall be cut off from the waters that come down from above; and they shall stand upon an heap.

And it came to pass, when the people removed from their tents, to pass over Jordan, and the priests bearing the ark of the covenant before the people;

And as they that bare the ark were come unto Jordan, and the feet of the priests that bare the ark were dipped in the brim of the water, (for Jordan overfloweth all his banks all the time of harvest,)

That the waters which came down from above stood and rose up upon an heap very far from the city Adam, that is beside Zaretan: and those that came down toward the sea of the plain, even the salt sea, failed, and were cut off: and the people passed over right against Jericho.

And the priests that bare the ark of the covenant of the LORD stood firm on dry ground in the midst of Jordan, and all the Israelites passed over on dry ground, until all the people were passed clean over Jordan.

(3:8–17)

116. The Holy Ark carved on a stone fragment found at Peki'in, a small village in the Galilee, noted for its continuous Jewish settlement throughout the ages. Fragments of reliefs with Jewish symbols are found dispersed in the village, dating from the late Roman period.

117. A view of the Dead Sea region with the Mountains of Moab in the background.

And the manna ceased on the morrow after they had eaten of the old corn of the land; neither had the children of Israel manna any more; but they did eat of the fruit of the land of Canaan that year.

And it came to pass, when Joshua was by Jericho, that he lifted up his eyes and looked, and, behold, there stood a man over against him with his sword drawn in his hand: and Joshua went unto him, and said unto him, Art thou for us or for our adversaries?

(5:12–13)

118

118. Dagger and javelin-head, uncovered in archaeological excavations, dating from the period of Joshua's conquest.

119. An earthenware vessel in the shape of a man's head, from the Late Bronze Age (1500–1200 B.C.), found at Jericho. It is thought to be of Hyksos origin. (The Hyksos were an Asiatic people who invaded Egypt and Canaan in the 18th century B.C.)

119

Now Jericho was straitly shut up because of the children of Israel: none went out, and none came in.

And the LORD said unto Joshua, See, I have given into thine hand Jericho, and the king thereof, and the mighty men of valour.

And ye shall compass the city, all ye men of war, and go round about the city once. Thus shalt thou do six days.

And seven priests shall bear before the ark seven trumpets of rams' horns: and the seventh day ye shall compass the city seven times, and the priests shall blow with the trumpets.

And it shall come to pass, that when they make a long blast with the ram's horn, and when ye hear the sound of the trumpet, all the people shall shout with a great shout; and the wall of the city shall fall down flat, and the people shall ascent up every man straight before him.

And Joshua the son of Nun called the priests, and said unto them, Take up the ark of the covenant, and let seven priests bear seven trumpets of rams' horns before the ark of the LORD.

And he said unto the people, Pass on, and compass the city, and let him that is armed pass on before the ark of the LORD.

And it came to pass, when Joshua had spoken unto the people, that the seven priests bearing the seven trumpets of rams' horns passed on before the LORD, and blew with the trumpets: and the ark of the covenant of the LORD followed them.

And the armed men went before the priests that blew with the trumpets, and the rereward came after the ark, the priests going on, and blowing with the trumpets.

And Joshua had commanded the people, saying, Ye shall not shout, nor make any noise with your voice, neither shall any word proceed out of your mouth, until the day I bid you shout; then shall ye shout.

So the ark of the LORD compassed the city, going about it once: and they came into the camp, and lodged in the camp.

And Joshua rose early in the morning, and the priests took up the ark of the LORD.

And seven priests bearing seven trumpets of rams' horns before the ark of the LORD went on continually, and blew with the trumpets: and the armed men went before them; but the rereward came after the ark of the LORD, the priests going on, and blowing with the trumpets.

And the second day they compassed the city once, and returned into the camp: so they did six days.

And it came to pass on the seventh day, that they rose early about the dawning of the day, and compassed the city after the same manner seven times: only on that day they compassed the city seven times.

And it came to pass at the seventh time, when the priests blew with the trumpets, Joshua said unto the people, Shout; for the LORD hath given you the city.

And the city shall be accursed, even it, and all that are therein, to the LORD: only Rahab the harlot shall live, she and all that are with her in the house, because she hid the messengers that we sent.

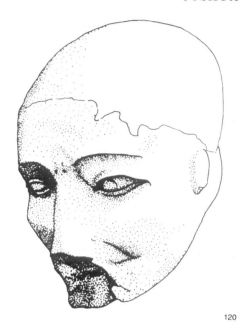

120

120. A plastered skull dating from the Neolithic (Stone) Age, found at Jericho.
The people of this culture buried their dead beneath the floors of their dwellings. The burials were very elaborate and included the molding of a clay shell over the skull into the likeness of human features, with seashell insets for the eyes.

121. A view of the site of ancient Jericho. Jericho is one of the oldest fortified cities in the Near East, and possibly the oldest city in the world to be inhabited continuously to this day.

121

And ye, in any wise keep yourselves from the accursed thing, lest ye make yourselves accursed, when ye take of the accursed thing, and make the camp of Israel a curse, and trouble it.

But all the silver, and gold, and vessels of brass and iron, are consecrated unto the LORD: they shall come into the treasury of the LORD.

So the people shouted when the priests blew with the trumpets: and it came to pass, when the people heard the sound of the trumpet, and the people shouted with a great shout, that the wall fell down flat, so that the people went up into the city, every man straight before him, and they took the city.

And they utterly destroyed all that was in the city, both man and woman, young and old, and ox, and sheep, and ass, with the edge of the sword.

But Joshua had said unto the two men that had spied out the country, Go into the harlot's house, and bring out thence the woman, and all that she hath, as ye sware unto her.

And the young men that were spies went in, and brought out Rahab, and her father, and her mother, and her brethren, and all that she had; and they brought out all her kindred, and left them without the camp of Israel.

And they burnt the city with fire, and all that was therein: only the silver, and the gold, and the vessels of brass and of iron, they put into the treasury of the house of the LORD.

(6:1–24)

122

122. Excavations at the site of the ancient city have uncovered a rock tower, and defensive walls dating back to the 10th/8th millennium B.C., the earliest thus far discovered. It was several times destroyed and rebuilt. Traces of various cultures have been brought to light at the site of ancient Jericho, which

123

And Joshua sent men from Jericho to Ai, which is beside Beth-aven, on the east side of Bethel, and spake unto them, saying, Go up and view the country. And the men went up and viewed Ai.

And they returned to Joshua, and said unto him, Let not all the people go up; but let about two or three thousand men go up and smite Ai; and make not all the people to labour thither; for they are but few.

So there went up thither of the people about three thousand men: and they fled before the men of Ai.

And the men of Ai smote of them about thirty and six men: for they chased them from before the gate even unto Shebarim, and smote them in the going down: wherefore the hearts of the people melted, and became as water.

And Joshua rent his clothes, and fell to the earth upon his face before the ark of the LORD until the eventide, he and the elders of Israel, and put dust upon their heads.

(7:2–6)

Therefore the children of Israel could not stand before their enemies, but turned their backs before their enemies, because they were accursed: neither will I be with you any more, except ye destroy the accursed from among you.

Up, sanctify the people, and say, Sanctify yourselves against to morrow: for thus saith the LORD God of Israel, There is an accursed thing in the midst of thee, O Israel: thou canst not stand before thine enemies, until ye take away the accursed thing from among you.

lies a few miles from present-day Jericho. The town is set in a valley famous for its mild climate in winter. It is 720 feet below sea level; to the south lies the Dead Sea, and beyond it the Mountains of Moab, above which rises the peak of Mount Nebo, from which Moses viewed the Promised Land.

123. The battle for Jericho, from the so-called Joshua Roll, an illuminated manuscript of the 10th century, showing seven priests blowing horns, while Joshua encourages his men entering the city. On the left are three priests bearing the Ark of the Covenant. (The Joshua Roll is now in Rome at the Vatican Library.)

124. The site of what is held to be Ai or Hai.

125

125. The Valley of Achor ("affliction" in Hebrew), northwest of Jericho, in the vicinity of Ai, is held to be the site where the Israelites stoned Achan. It is also thought to be the valley of the Brook Cherith, where Elijah was fed by the ravens.

In the morning therefore ye shall be brought according to your tribes: and it shall be, that the tribe which the LORD taketh shall come according to the families thereof; and the family which the LORD shall take shall come by households; and the household which the LORD shall take shall come man by man.

And it shall be, that he that is taken with the accursed thing shall be burnt with fire, he and all that he hath: because he hath transgressed the covenant of the LORD, and because he hath wrought folly in Israel.

So Joshua rose up early in the morning, and brought Israel by their tribes; and the tribe of Judah was taken:

And he brought the family of Judah; and he took the family of the Zarhites: and he brought the family of the Zarhites man by man; and Zabdi was taken:

And he brought his household man by man; and Achan, the son of Carmi, the son of Zabdi, the son of Zerah, of the tribe of Judah, was taken.

And Joshua said unto Achan, My son, give, I pray thee, glory to the LORD God of Israel, and make confession unto him; and tell me now what thou hast done; hide it not from me.

And Achan answered Joshua, and said, Indeed I have sinned against the LORD God of Israel, and thus and thus have I done:

When I saw among the spoils a goodly Babylonish garment, and two hundred shekels of silver, and a wedge of gold of fifty shekels weight, then I coveted them, and took them; and behold, they are hid in the earth in the midst of my tent, and the silver under it.

So Joshua sent messengers, and they ran unto the tent; and, behold, it was hid in his tent, and the silver under it.

And they took them out of the midst of the tent, and brought them unto Joshua, and unto all the children of Israel, and laid them out before the LORD.

And Joshua, and all Israel with him, took Achan the son of Zerah, and the silver, and the garment, and the wedge of gold, and his sons, and his daughters, and his oxen, and his asses, and his sheep, and his tent, and all that he had: and they brought them unto the valley of Achor.

And Joshua said, Why hast thou troubled us? the LORD shall trouble thee this day. And all Israel stoned him with stones, and burned them with fire, after they had stoned them with stones.

And they raised over him a great heap of stones unto this day. So the LORD turned from the fierceness of his anger. Wherefore the name of that place was called, The valley of Achor, unto this day.

(7:12–26)

And the LORD said unto Joshua, Fear not, neither be thou dismayed: take all the people of war with thee, and arise, go up to Ai: see, I have given into thy hand the king of Ai, and his people, and his city, and his land:

And thou shalt do to Ai and her king as thou didst unto Jericho and her king: only the spoil thereof, and the cattle thereof, shall ye take for a prey unto yourselves: lay thee an ambush for the city behind it.

(8:1–2)

And the LORD said unto Joshua, Stretch out the spear that is in thy hand toward Ai; for I will give it into thine hand. And Joshua stretched out the spear that he had in his hand toward the city.

And the ambush arose quickly out of their place, and they ran as soon as he had stretched out his hand: and they entered into the city, and took it, and hasted and set the city on fire.

And when the men of Ai looked behind them, they saw, and behold, the smoke of the city ascended up to heaven, and they had no power to flee this way or that way: and the people that fled to the wilderness turned back upon the pursuers.

And when Joshua and all Israel saw that the ambush had taken the city, and that the smoke of the city ascended, then they turned again, and slew the men of Ai.

And the other issued out of the city against them; so they were in the midst of Israel, some on this side, and some on that side: and they smote them, so that they let none of them remain or escape.

And the king of Ai they took alive and brought him to Joshua.

And it came to pass, when Israel had made an end of slaying all the inhabitants of Ai in the field, in the wilderness wherein they chased them, and when they were all fallen on the edge of the sword, until they were consumed, that all the Israelites returned unto Ai, and smote it with the edge of the sword.

And so it was, that all that fell that day, both of men and women, were twelve thousand, even all the men of Ai.

(8:18–25)

126. A clay incense stand, from the Canaanite period, found at what is believed to be the site of Ai (or Hai).
Ai was an ancient Canaanite city-state. Almost five hundred years earlier Abraham had pitched his tent in the area "having Bethel on the west and Hai on the east" (Genesis 12:8). Ai was the next objective of the Israelites after the conquest of Jericho. Joshua employed a stratagem against Ai, setting an ambush at the rear of the city, on its west side. Another body of men was deployed before the city and, pretending to retreat, lured the inhabitants out of the city in hot pursuit. He then signalled the ambush into action, took the city and burnt it down.

126

127

128

And it came to pass, when all the kings which were on this side Jordan, in the hills, and in the valleys, and in all the coasts of the great sea over against Lebanon, the Hittite, and the Amorite, the Canaanite, the Perizzite, the Hivite, and the Jebusite, heard thereof;

That they gathered themselves together, to fight with Joshua and with Israel, with one accord. (9:1–2)

Now it came to pass, when Adoni-zedek king of Jerusalem had heard how Joshua had taken Ai, and had utterly destroyed it; as he had done to Jericho and her king, so he had done to Ai and her king; and how the inhabitants of Gibeon had made peace with Israel, and were among them;

That they feared greatly, because Gibeon was a great city, as one of the royal cities, and because it was greater than Ai, and all the men thereof were mighty.

Wherefore Adoni-zedek king of Jerusalem sent unto Hoham king of Hebron, and unto Piram king of Jarmuth, and unto Japhia king of Lachish, and unto Debir king of Eglon, saying,

Come up unto me, and help me, that we may smite Gibeon: for it hath made peace with Joshua and with the children of Israel.

Therefore the five kings of the Amorites, the king of Jerusalem, the king of Hebron, the king of Jarmuth, the king of Lachish, the king of Eglon,

129

gathered themselves together, and went up, they and all their hosts, and encamped before Gibeon, and made war against it.

And the men of Gibeon sent unto Joshua to the camp to Gilgal, saying, Slack not thy hand from thy servants; come up to us quickly, and save us, and help us: for all the kings of the Amorites that dwell in the mountains are gathered together against us.

So Joshua ascended from Gilgal, he, and all the people of war with him, and all the mighty men of valour.

And the LORD said unto Joshua, Fear them not: for I have delivered them into thine hand; there shall not a man of them stand before thee.

Joshua therefore came unto them suddenly, and went up from Gilgal all night.

And the LORD discomfited them before Israel, and slew them with a great slaughter at Gibeon, and chased them along the way that goeth up to Beth-horon, and smote them to Azekah, and unto Makkedah.

And it came to pass, as they fled from before Israel, and were in the going down to Beth-horon, that the LORD cast down great stones from heaven upon them unto Azekah, and they died: they were more which died with hailstones than they whom the children of Israel slew with the sword.

Then spake Joshua to the LORD in the day when the LORD delivered

127. A glazed brick dating from the reign of Ramses III (12th century B.C.), showing a captive Syrian or Palestinian noble. Presumably, the Canaanite nobility looked like this to the Israelites at the time of the conquest of Canaan.

128. The so-called Execration Texts. These are a group of figurines which probably represent rebel leaders of city-states under Egyptian rule, inscribed with curses against the enemies of Egypt; many of the names listed are from Canaan.
In the Bible, the term "Canaan" is rather vague and applies to different parts of Palestine and Syria. At other times it is confined to the strip of land along the eastern shore of the Mediterranean.
In the Book of Joshua, Canaan includes the territory east and west of the Jordan River. The biblical term "Canaanites" refers sometimes to various peoples that lived in the land of Canaan, or to one particular group in the heterogeneous population. Sometimes it is simply a synonym for "merchant."

129. Part of a wall painting in an Egyptian tomb, showing Canaanites bringing tribute to Pharaoh Tutankhamon (14th century B.C.).

130. The Valley of Ajalon spreads below the Judean Hills. The city of Ajalon was included in the tribal lands of Dan (Joshua 21:24; I Chronicles 6:54), but the Danites were unable to subdue the Amorites, and later the region fell to the "House of Joseph" (Judges 1:34–35). The region was actually conquered by the Israelites under David.

The region was badly affected by an earthquake in the 11th century B.C. During the Crusades it was once again the scene of a battle and the Crusaders built a fortress there (now Latrun).

130

131. A Canaanite ivory plaque found at Megiddo, dating from 1500–1400 B.C., depicting a victory celebration in the palace of a Canaanite king. The king is seated on his throne; before him stands a woman wearing a crown, offering him a bouquet of flowers. Behind her stands a woman playing a lyre. A soldier armed with a shield and spear leads two prisoners with their hands behind their backs and tied to a chariot drawn by two horses. On the chariot stands a figure similar to that seated on the throne. Behind the chariot stands a warrior with a sword.

132. A fertility goddess of the Late Bronze Age, found at Lachish.

The Canaanites had many divinities, each with his or her function and authority.

up the Amorites before the children of Israel, and he said in the sight of Israel, Sun, stand thou still upon Gibeon; and thou, Moon, in the valley of Ajalon.

And the sun stood still, and the moon stayed, until the people had avenged themselves upon their enemies. Is not this written in the book of Jasher? So the sun stood still in the midst of heaven, and hasted not to go down about a whole day.

And there was no day like that before it or after it, that the LORD hearkened unto the voice of a man: for the LORD fought for Israel.

And Joshua returned, and all Israel with him, unto the camp to Gilgal.

But these five kings fled, and hid themselves in a cave at Makkedah.

And it was told Joshua, saying, The five kings are found hid in a cave at Makkedah.

And Joshua said, Roll great stones upon the mouth of the cave, and set men by it for to keep them:

And stay ye not, but pursue after your enemies, and smite the hindmost of them; suffer them not to enter into their cities: for the LORD your God hath delivered them into your hand.

And it came to pass, when Joshua and the children of Israel had made an end of slaying them with a very great slaughter, till they were consumed, that the rest which remained of them entered into fenced cities.

And all the people returned to the camp to Joshua at Makkedah in peace: none moved his tongue against any of the children of Israel.

Then said Joshua, Open the mouth of the cave, and bring out those five kings unto me out of the cave. And they did so, and brought forth those five kings unto him out of the cave, the king of Jerusalem, the king of Hebron, the king of Jarmuth, the king of Lachish, and the king of Eglon.

And it came to pass, when they brought out those kings unto Joshua, that Joshua called for all the men of Israel, and said unto the captains of the men of war which went with him, Come near, put your feet upon the necks of these kings. And they came near, and put their feet upon the necks of them.

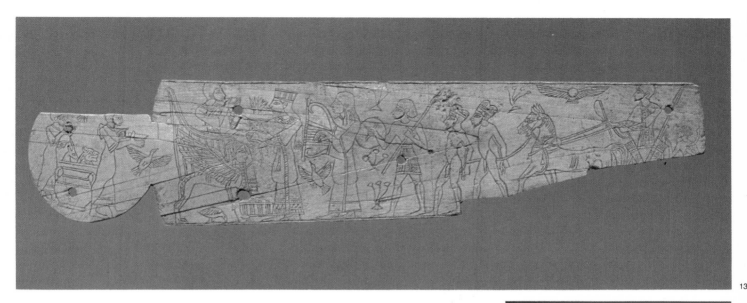

131

And Joshua said unto them, Fear not, nor be dismayed, be strong and of good courage: for thus shall the LORD do to all your enemies against whom ye fight.

And afterward Joshua smote them, and slew them, and hanged them on five trees: and they were hanging upon the trees until the evening.

And it came to pass at the time of the going down of the sun, that Joshua commanded, and they took them down off the trees, and cast them into the cave wherein they had been hid, and laid great stones in the cave's mouth, which remain until this very day.

And that day Joshua took Makkedah, and smote it with the edge of the sword, and the king thereof he utterly destroyed, them, and all the souls that were therein; he let none remain: and he did to the king of Makkedah as he did unto the king of Jericho.

Then Joshua passed from Makkedah, and all Israel with him, unto Libnah, and fought against Libnah:

And the LORD delivered it also, and the king thereof, into the hand of Israel; and he smote it with the edge of the sword, and all the souls that were therein; he let none remain in it; but did unto the king thereof as he did unto the king of Jericho.

And Joshua passed from Libnah, and all Israel with him, unto Lachish, and encamped against it, and fought against it:

And the LORD delivered Lachish into the hand of Israel, which took it on the second day, and smote it with the edge of the sword, and all the souls that were therein, according to all that he had done to Libnah.

Then Horam king of Gezer came up to help Lachish; and Joshua smote him and his people, until he had left him none remaining.

And from Lachish Joshua passed unto Eglon, and all Israel with him; and they encamped against it, and fought against it:

And they took it on that day, and smote it with the edge of the sword, and all the souls that were therein he utterly destroyed that day, according to all that he had done to Lachish.

(10:1–35)

132

133. Merom, the place where all the kings of northern Canaan foregathered under the leadership of Jabin, king of Hazor. It is known today as Meron. Rising 3940 feet above sea level, Mount Meron is the highest peak in Galilee. The present-day village of Meron stands near the remains of an ancient synagogue of the 2nd/3rd century A.D.

133

And it came to pass, when Jabin king of Hazor had heard those things, that he sent to Jobab king of Madon, and to the king of Shimron, and to the king of Achshaph,

And to the kings that were on the north of the mountains, and of the plains south of Chinneroth, and in the valley, and in the borders of Dor on the west,

And to the Canaanite on the east and on the west, and to the Amorite, and the Hittite, and the Perizzite, and the Jebusite in the mountains, and to the Hivite under Hermon in the land of Mizpeh.

And they went out, they and all their hosts with them, much people, even as the sand that is upon the sea shore in multitude, with horses and chariots very many.

And when all these kings were met together, they came and pitched together at the waters of Merom, to fight against Israel.

And the LORD said unto Joshua, Be not afraid because of them: for to morrow about this time will I deliver them up all slain before Israel: thou shalt hough their horses, and burn their chariots with fire.

So Joshua came, and all the people of war with him, against them by the waters of Merom suddenly; and they fell upon them.

And the LORD delivered them into the hand of Israel, who smote them, and chased them unto great Zidon, and unto Misrephoth-maim and unto the valley of Mizpeh eastward; and they smote them, until they left them none remaining.

And Joshua did unto them as the LORD bade him: he houghed their horses, and burnt their chariots with fire.

And Joshua at that time turned back, and took Hazor, and smote the

134

134. View of the ancient site of Hazor showing the remains of a pillared building.

135. Basalt stele from a Canaanite temple of the 13th century B.C. excavated at Hazor on which can be seen two hands raised towards a disc, probably symbolizing the moon. This is one of a row of stelae about sixteen inches high. Such groups of stones are generally found at sites associated with "high places" and temples in the Holy Land, ranging from the Neolithic Age (7500-4000 B.C.) to the end of the First Temple period (332 B.C.).

136. Nearby was a stone statuette of a man seated on a throne holding a cup-like object with the moon emblem on his chest, and believed to represent a deity.

135

king thereof with the sword: for Hazor beforetime was the head of all those kingdoms.

And they smote all the souls that were therein with the edge of the sword, utterly destroying them: there was not any left to breathe: and he burnt Hazor with fire.

And all the cities of those kings, and all the kings of them, did Joshua take, and smote them with the edge of the sword, and he utterly destroyed them, as Moses the servant of the LORD commanded.

But as for the cities that stood still in their strength, Israel burned none of them, save Hazor only; that did Joshua burn. And all the spoil of these cities, and the cattle, the children of Israel took for a prey unto themselves; but every man they smote with the edge of the sword, until they had destroyed them, neither left they any to breathe.

As the LORD commanded Moses his servant, so did Moses command Joshua, and so did Joshua; he left nothing undone of all that the LORD commanded Moses.

So Joshua took all that land, the hills, and all the south country, and all the land of Goshen, and the valley, and the plain, and the mountain of Israel, and the valley of the same;

Even from the mount Halak, that goeth up to Seir, even unto Baal-gad in the valley of Lebanon under mount Hermon: and all their kings he took, and smote them, and slew them.

Joshua made war a long time with all those kings.

There was not a city that made peace with the children of Israel, save the Hivites the inhabitants of Gibeon: all other they took in battle.

(11:1–19)

136

137

137. A view of the site of ancient Shiloh.

138. Remains of the walls of biblical Shiloh, east of Bethel, in the mountains of the territory of Ephraim, north of Jerusalem. Here lots were cast for the different tribal lands, and for the levitical cities, and here Israel assembled to settle their disputes (Joshua 21:1–12).

And the whole congregation of the children of Israel assembled together at Shiloh, and set up the tabernacle of the congregation there. And the land was subdued before them.

And there remained among the children of Israel seven tribes, which had not yet received their inheritance.

And Joshua said unto the children of Israel, How long are ye slack to go to possess the land, which the LORD God of your fathers hath given you?

Give out from among you three men for each tribe: and I will send them, and they shall rise, and go through the land, and describe it according to the inheritance of them; and they shall come again to me.

And they shall divide it into seven parts: Judah shall abide in their coast on the south, and the house of Joseph shall abide in their coasts on the north.

Ye shall therefore describe the land into seven parts, and bring the description hither to me, that I may cast lots for you here before the LORD our God.

But the Levites have no part among you; for the priesthood of the LORD is their inheritance: and Gad, and Reuben, and half the tribe of Manasseh, have received their inheritance beyond Jordan on the east, which Moses the servant of the LORD gave them.

And the men arose, and went away: and Joshua charged them that went to describe the land, saying, Go and walk through the land, and describe it, and come again to me, that I may here cast lots for you before the LORD in Shiloh.

And the men went and passed through the land, and described it by cities into seven parts in a book, and came again to Joshua to the host at Shiloh.

And Joshua cast lots for them in Shiloh before the LORD: and there Joshua divided the land unto the children of Israel according to their divisions.

(18:1–10)

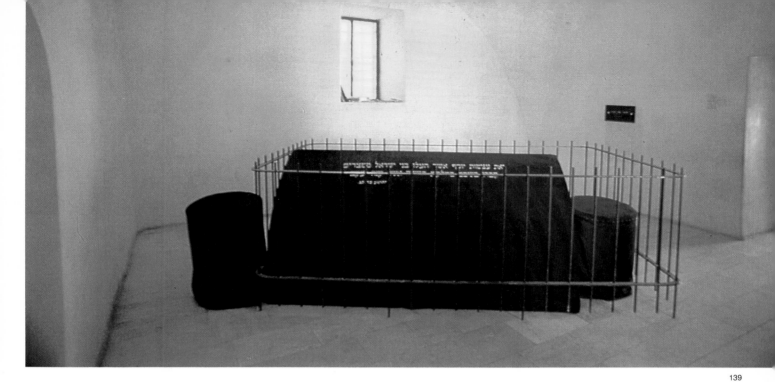

139. & 140. Between Mounts Gerizim and Ebal, not far from Shechem, there is a modest shrine which has been revered since the 4th century as the site of burial of Joseph. It is written in Exodus 13:19: "And Moses took the bones of Joseph with him: for he had straitly sworn to the children of Israel, saying, God will surely visit you; and ye shall carry up my bones away hence with you."

And the bones of Joseph, which the children of Israel brought up out of Egypt, buried they in Shechem, in a parcel of ground which Jacob bought of the sons of Hamor the father of Shechem for an hundred pieces of silver: and it became the inheritance of the children of Joseph.

And Eleazar the son of Aaron died; and they buried him in a hill that pertained to Phinehas his son, which was given him in mount Ephraim.

(24:32–33)

Neither did Asher drive out the inhabitants of Accho, nor the inhabitants of Zidon, nor of Ahlab, nor of Achzib, nor of Helbah, nor of Aphik, nor of Rehob:

But the Asherites dwelt among the Canaanites, the inhabitants of the land: for they did not drive them out.

(1:31–32)

141

142

141. Clay horse's head from a Phoenician tomb at Achzib.
The Phoenicians were a Semitic people who inhabited the coast of Syria and northern Palestine; archaeological excavations trace their presence there as far back as the 15th millennium B.C. The Phoenicians were in close contact with the Egyptian civilization from earliest times. The arrival of the "Sea Peoples" (among them the Philistines), in the middle of the second millennium B.C., coincides with the Phoenician drive across the Mediterranean.

142. A view of Achzib.
Many tombs from the Israelite period have been found north of the present village, at the site of the ancient Canaanite port, north of Acre near a promontory called "the ladder of Tyre." Most of the tombs investigated were Phoenician. They were rock-hewn and contained pottery, figurines, bronze, and silver jewelry. Other excavations in the area revealed fortification and several levels of inhabitation, ranging from the second millennium B.C. to the Roman period, and also from the Crusader period.

143. A view of the port of Acre (Accho, or Akko) on the Mediterranean coast.
It was the best and most important natural harbor in northern Palestine.
In the second century B.C. it was renamed Ptolemais, and the Crusaders called it St. Jean-d'Acre. The Crusaders left their mark on the town which is still apparent in the modern city.
It is said that glass was first made near Acre. A Phoenician ship returning from Egypt along the coast of Palestine was carrying a cargo of

And an angel of the LORD came up from Gilgal to Bochim, and said, I made you to go up out of Egypt, and have brought you unto the land which I sware unto your fathers; and I said, I will never break my covenant with you.

And ye shall make no league with the inhabitants of this land; ye shall throw down their altars: but ye have not obeyed my voice: why have ye done this?

Wherefore I also said, I will not drive them out from before you; but they shall be as thorns in your sides, and their gods shall be a snare unto you.

(2:1–3)

And the children of Israel did evil in the sight of the LORD, and served Baalim:

And they forsook the LORD God of their fathers, which brought them out of the land of Egypt, and followed other gods, of the gods of the people that were round about them, and bowed themselves unto them, and provoked the LORD to anger.

And they forsook the LORD, and served Baal and Ashtaroth.

(2:11–13)

And the children of Israel dwelt among the Canaanites, Hittites, and Amorites, and Perizzites, and Hivites, and Jebusites:

And they took their daughters to be their wives, and gave their daughters to their sons, and served their gods.

And the children of Israel did evil in the sight of the LORD, and forgat the LORD their God, and served Baalim and the groves.

(3:5–7)

146

144

large lumps of natron. As it approached Phoenicia a great storm arose. The sailors landed on the sandy shore, lit a fire and, failing to find stones on which to place their cooking pots, they brought some lumps of natron from their ships and placed their pots on these. When they had finished cooking, they saw to their astonishment that the natron had melted and combined with the sand, creating a new material which was clear and transparent.

144. & 145. Figurines of Canaanite and Phoenician goddesses dating from the period between the 20th and 14th centuries B.C.

146. Stone mold, probably of a sea goddess, the goddess of Phoenician seafarers and fishermen, found at Nahariya.
The cult of Astarte was widespread in Palestine in the Canaanite period. Thousands of Astarte figurines have been found at most of the archaeological sites of the Canaanite and Israelite periods. Some of these reveal Egyptian influence, while others bear a resemblance to Phoenician goddesses.
Astarte, or Ashtoret, is the female counterpart of Baal, the name of a god in many ancient communities in the Near East. *Baal* means "lord" or "master." The plural, *Baalim*, seems to designate local gods. Baal was the leading god of the Canaanites and in his role as rain god was responsible for the fertility of fields and cattle.
The Israelites considered the worship of Baal as idolatrous and inferior to the pure worship of God.

But when the children of Israel cried unto the LORD, the LORD raised them up a deliverer, Ehud the son of Gera, a Benjamite, a man lefthanded: and by him the children of Israel sent a present unto Eglon the king of Moab.

But Ehud made him a dagger which had two edges, of a cubit length; and he did gird it under his raiment upon his right thigh.

And he brought the present unto Eglon king of Moab: and Eglon was a very fat man.

And when he had made an end to offer the present, he sent away the people that bare the present.

But he himself turned again from the quarries that were by Gilgal, and said, I have a secret errand unto thee, O king: who said, Keep silence. And all that stood by him went out from him.

And Ehud came unto him; and he was sitting in a summer parlour, which he had for himself alone. And Ehud said, I have a message from God unto thee. And he arose out of his seat.

And Ehud put forth his left hand, and took the dagger from his right thigh, and thrust it into his belly.

(3:15–21)

147. Daggers of the 14th century B.C. from Egypt.

147

And the children of Israel cried unto the LORD: for he had nine hundred chariots of iron; and twenty years he mightily oppressed the children of Israel.

And Deborah, a prophetess, the wife of Lapidoth, she judged Israel at that time.

And she dwelt under the palm tree of Deborah between Ramah and Bethel in mount Ephraim: and the children of Israel came up to her for judgment.

And she sent and called Barak the son of Abinoam out of Kedesh-naphtali, and said unto him, Hath not the LORD God of Israel commanded, saying, Go and draw toward mount Tabor, and take with thee ten thousand men of the children of Naphtali and of the children of Zebulun?

And I will draw unto thee to the river Kishon Sisera, the captain of Jabin's army, with his chariots and his multitude; and I will deliver him into thine hand.

148. Mount Tabor. Isolated from the other mountains, it rises abruptly from the Jezreel Valley to an altitude of approximately 1840 feet, west of the Sea of Galilee and southwest of the city of Nazareth. From its summit it affords a magnificent view in all directions.

And Barak said unto her, If thou wilt go with me, then I will go: but if thou wilt not go with me, then I will not go.

And she said, I will surely go with thee: notwithstanding the journey that thou takest shall not be for thine honour; for the LORD shall sell Sisera into the hand of a woman. And Deborah arose, and went with Barak to Kedesh.

And Barak called Zebulun and Naphtali to Kedesh; and he went up with ten thousand men at his feet: and Deborah went up with him.

Now Heber the Kenite, which was of the children of Hobab the father in law of Moses, had severed himself from the Kenites, and pitched his tent unto the plain of Zaanaim, which is by Kedesh.

And they shewed Sisera that Barak the son of Abinoam was gone up to mount Tabor.

And Sisera gathered together all his chariots, even nine hundred chariots of iron, and all the people that were with him, from Harosheth of the Gentiles unto the river of Kishon.

And Deborah said unto Barak, Up; for this is the day in which the LORD hath delivered Sisera into thine hand: is not the LORD gone out before thee? So Barak went down from mount Tabor, and ten thousand men after him.

And the LORD discomfited Sisera, and all his chariots, and all his host, with the edge of the sword before Barak: so that Sisera lighted down off his chariot, and fled away on his feet.

But Barak pursued after the chariots, and after the host, unto Harosheth of the Gentiles: and all the host of Sisera fell upon the edge of the sword; and there was not a man left.

Howbeit Sisera fled away on his feet to the tent of Jael the wife of Heber the Kenite: for there was peace between Jabin the king of Hazor and the house of Heber the Kenite.

(4:3–17)

Then sang Deborah and Barak the son of Abinoam on that day, saying,

Praise ye the LORD for the avenging of Israel, when the people willingly offered themselves.

Hear, O ye kings; give ear, O ye princes; I, even I, will sing unto the LORD; I will sing praise to the LORD God of Israel.

LORD, when thou wentest out of Seir, when thou marchedst out of the field of Edom, the earth trembled, and the heavens dropped, the clouds also dropped water.

The mountains melted from before the LORD, even that Sinai from before the LORD God of Israel.

In the days of Shamgar the son of Anath, in the days of Jael, the highways were unoccupied, and the travellers walked through byways.

The inhabitants of the villages ceased, they ceased in Israel, until that I Deborah arose, that I arose a mother in Israel.

They chose new gods; then was war in the gates: was there a shield or spear seen among forty thousand in Israel?

My heart is toward the governors of Israel, that offered themselves willingly among the people. Bless ye the LORD.

149. Relief from Gozan, Mesopotamia, of the 10th century B.C., depicting charioteers.

Speak, ye that ride on white asses, ye that sit in judgment, and walk by the way.

They that are delivered from the noise of archers in the places of drawing water, there shall they rehearse the righteous acts of the LORD, even the righteous acts toward the inhabitants of his villages in Israel: then shall the people of the LORD go down to the gates.

Awake, awake, Deborah: awake, awake, utter a song: arise, Barak, and lead thy captivity captive, thou son of Abinoam.

(5:1–12)

The kings came and fought, then fought the kings of Canaan in Taanach by the waters of Megiddo; they took no gain of money.

They fought from heaven; the stars in their courses fought against Sisera.

The river of Kishon swept them away, that ancient river, the river Kishon. O my soul, thou hast trodden down strength.

Then were the horsehoofs broken by the means of the pransings, the pransings of their mighty ones.

(5:19–22)

150. The Kishon River, depicted in a colored wood-cut by C. Whymper, c. 1860 (Collection National Maritime Museum, Haifa).
The Kishon, in the western part of the Jezreel Valley, draws its waters from the mountains of Gilboa and Nazareth. It is perennial only in the last six miles of its course. But in the rainy season it becomes a rushing torrent, flooding its banks and sweeping everything in its path.

Then Jerubbaal, who is Gideon, and all the people that were with him, rose up early, and pitched beside the well of Harod: so that the host of the Midianites were on the north side of them, by the hill of Moreh, in the valley.

And the LORD said unto Gideon, The people that are with thee are too many for me to give the Midianites into their hands, lest Israel vaunt themselves against me, saying, Mine own hand hath saved me.

Now therefore go to, proclaim in the ears of the people, saying, Whosoever is fearful and afraid, let him return and depart early from mount Gilead. And there returned of the people twenty and two thousand; and there remained ten thousand.

And the LORD said unto Gideon, The people are yet too many; bring them down unto the water, and I will try them for thee there: and it shall be, that of whom I say unto thee, This shall go with thee, the same shall go with thee; and of whomsoever I say unto thee, This shall not go with thee, the same shall not go.

So he brought down the people unto the water: and the LORD said unto Gideon, Every one that lappeth of the water with his tongue, as a dog lappeth, him shalt thou set by himself; likewise every one that boweth down upon his knees to drink.

And the number of them that lapped, putting their hand to their mouth, were three hundred men: but all the rest of the people bowed down upon their knees to drink water.

And the LORD said unto Gideon, By the three hundred men that lapped will I save you, and deliver the Midianites into thine hand: and let all the other people go every man unto his place.

(7:1–7)

And he divided the three hundred men into three companies, and he put a trumpet in every man's hand, with empty pitchers, and lamps within the pitchers.

(7:16)

151. The Spring (or Well) of Harod, at the foot of Mount Gilboa, where Gideon selected his fighters to fight the Midianites.

152. Figure in glazed brick, from the mortuary temple of Ramses III, at Medinet Habu, Egypt.
The figure wearing a headdress reminiscent of the typical Philistine head covering, is thought to be a Philistine dressed in the style customary in Syria and Palestine at that period.
The Philistines were the chief enemy of the Israelites in the time of the Judges. They were among the "Sea Peoples" who invaded the Eastern Mediterranean and settled along the coast from Syria and Canaan all the way to Egypt. They were halted by Pharaoh Ramses III (1198–1166 B.C.), who later employed them as mercenaries to protect Egyptian strongholds in Canaan. Thanks to their organizational and military superiority they quickly overcame the Canaanite population. Politically they were federated in a league of city-states. The decline of Egyptian power toward the end of the 12th and beginning of 11th century B.C. encouraged the Philistines to expand the territory under their control and brought them into conflict with the Israelite tribes. The conflict lasted from 1200 B.C. to 950 B.C. approximately, until King David succeeded in driving them back into their strip of coastal plain which came to be known as Philistia, and later gave its name to the whole country.

And the three companies blew the trumpets, and brake the pitchers, and held the lamps in their left hands, and the trumpets in their right hands to blow withal: and they cried, The sword of the LORD, and of Gideon.

And they stood every man in his place round about the camp: and all the host ran, and cried, and fled.

And the three hundred blew the trumpets, and the LORD set every man's sword against his fellow, even throughout all the host: and the host fled to Beth-shittah in Zererath, and to the border of Abel-meholah, unto Tabbath.

And the men of Israel gathered themselves together out of Naphtali, and out of Asher, and out of all Manasseh, and pursued after the Midianites.

(7:20–23)

And the children of Israel did evil again in the sight of the LORD; and the LORD delivered them into the hand of the Philistines forty years.

And there was a certain man of Zorah, of the family of the Danites, whose name was Manoah; and his wife was barren, and bare not.

And the angel of the LORD appeared unto the woman, and said unto her, Behold now, thou art barren, and bearest not: but thou shalt conceive, and bear a son.

Now therefore beware, I pray thee, and drink not wine nor strong drink, and eat not any unclean thing:

For, lo, thou shalt conceive, and bear a son; and no rasor shall come on his head: for the child shall be a Nazarite unto God from the womb: and he shall begin to deliver Israel out of the hand of the Philistines.

Then the woman came and told her husband, saying, A man of God came unto me, and his countenance was like the countenance of an angel of God, very terrible: but I asked him not whence he was, neither told he me his name:

But he said unto me, Behold, thou shalt conceive, and bear a son; and now drink no wine nor strong drink, neither eat any unclean thing: for the child shall be a Nazarite to God from the womb to the day of his death.

Then Manoah intreated the LORD, and said, O my Lord, let the man of God which thou didst send come again unto us, and teach us what we shall do unto the child that shall be born.

And God hearkened to the voice of Manoah; and the angel of God came again unto the woman as she sat in the field: but Manoah her husband was not with her.

And the woman made haste, and ran, and shewed her husband, and said unto him, Behold, the man hath appeared unto me, that came unto me the other day.

And Manoah arose, and went after his wife, and came to the man, and said unto him, Art thou the man that spakest unto the woman? And he said, I am.

And Manoah said, Now let thy words come to pass. How shall we order the child, and how shall we do unto him?

And the angel of the LORD said unto Manoah, Of all that I said unto the woman let her beware.

(13:1–13)

Then went Samson to Gaza, and saw there an harlot, and went in unto her.

And it was told the Gazites, saying, Samson is come hither. And they compassed him in, and laid wait for him all night in the gate of the city, and were quiet all the night, saying, In the morning, when it is day, we shall kill him.

And Samson lay till midnight, and arose at midnight, and took the doors of the gate of the city, and the two posts, and went away with them, bar and all, and put them upon his shoulders, and carried them up to the top of an hill that is before Hebron.

And it came to pass afterward, that he loved a woman in the valley of Sorek, whose name was Delilah.   (16:1–4)

And the children of Dan sent of their family five men from their coasts, men of valour, from Zorah, and from Eshtaol, to spy out the land, and to search it; and they said unto them, Go, search the land: who when they came to mount Ephraim, to the house of Micah, they lodged there.   (18:2)

And they came unto their brethren to Zorah and Eshtaol: and their brethren said unto them, What say ye?

And they said, Arise, that we may go up against them: for we have seen the land, and, behold, it is very good: and are ye still? be not slothful to go, and to enter to possess the land.

When ye go, ye shall come unto a people secure, and to a large land: for God hath given it into your hands; a place where there is no want of any thing that is in the earth.

And there went from thence of the family of the Danites, out of Zorah and out of Eshtaol, six hundred men appointed with weapons of war.
(18:8–11)

153. View of the region of Eshtaol and Zorah, northeast of Beth Shemesh.

154. Philistine vase with geometrical designs and representations of birds. These motifs are characteristic of Philistine pottery. The outstanding survival of the material culture of the Philistines is their ceramic work. It reveals their Aegean background as well as local and Egyptian influences.

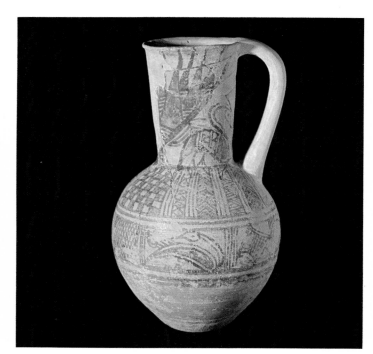

Then they said, Behold, there is a feast of the LORD in Shiloh yearly in a place which is on the north side of Bethel, on the east side of the highway that goeth up from Bethel to Shechem, and on the south of Lebonah.

Therefore they commanded the children of Benjamin, saying, Go and lie in wait in the vineyards;

And see, and, behold, if the daughters of Shiloh come out to dance in dances, then come ye out of the vineyards, and catch you every man his wife of the daughters of Shiloh, and go to the land of Benjamin.

And it shall be, when their fathers or their brethren come unto us to complain, that we will say unto them, Be favourable unto them for our sakes: because we reserved not to each man his wife in the war: for ye did not give unto them at this time, that ye should be guilty.

And the children of Benjamin did so, and took them wives, according to their number, of them that danced, whom they caught: and they went and returned unto their inheritance, and repaired the cities, and dwelt in them.

And the children of Israel departed thence at that time, every man to his tribe and to his family, and they went out from thence every man to his inheritance.

In those days there was no king in Israel: every man did that which was right in his own eyes.

(21:19–25)

155. The Plain of Lebonah, between Shechem and Jerusalem.

Now it came to pass in the days when the judges ruled, that there was a famine in the land. And a certain man of Bethlehem-judah went to sojourn in the country of Moab, he, and his wife, and his two sons.

And the name of the man was Elimelech, and the name of his wife Naomi, and the name of his two sons Mahlon and Chilion, Ephrathites of Bethlehem-judah. And they came into the country of Moab, and continued there.

And Elimelech Naomi's husband died; and she was left, and her two sons.

(1:1–3)

And Naomi said, Turn again, my daughters: why will ye go with me? are there yet any more sons in my womb, that they may be your husbands?

Turn again, my daughters, go your way; for I am too old to have an husband. If I should say, I have hope, if I should have an husband also to night, and should also bear sons;

Would ye tarry for them till they were grown? would ye stay for them from having husbands? nay, my daughters; for it grieveth me much for your sakes that the hand of the LORD is gone out against me.

And they lifted up their voice, and wept again: and Orpah kissed her mother in law; but Ruth clave unto her.

And she said, Behold, thy sister in law is gone back unto her people, and unto her gods: return thou after thy sister in law.

And Ruth said, Intreat me not to leave thee, or to return from following after thee: for whither thou goest, I will go; and where thou lodgest, I will lodge: thy people shall be my people, and thy God my God:

156. Illustration of the story of Ruth from the *Admont Bible*, c. 1130-50 (Nationalbibliothek, Vienna).
Ruth is shown gleaning after the reapers and (upper panel) in Boaz' tent.
Although Naomi had inherited from her husband a piece of land which she was later able to sell, on arriving in Judah both she and Ruth were destitute. The Law, however, had provided for such cases: "And when you reap the harvest of your land, thou shalt not wholly reap the corners of thy field, neither shalt thou gather the gleanings of thy harvest" (Leviticus 19:9). This is again repeated in Leviticus 23:22: "And when ye reap the harvest of your land, thou shalt not make clean riddance of the corners of thy harvest: thou shalt leave them unto the poor, and to the stranger."
Boaz was a kinsman of Elimelech, and hence of Ruth's dead husband, Mahlon. Naomi saw in this the possibility of a levirate marriage for Ruth. When the nearer relative refused to perform a levirate marriage, Boaz did so. Thus Ruth became the mother of Boaz' son Obed and the ancestor of King David.

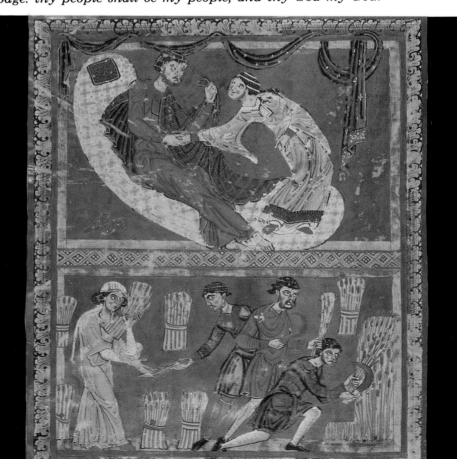

Where thou diest, will I die, and there will I be buried: the LORD do so to me, and more also, if ought but death part thee and me.   (1:11–17)

And Naomi had a kinsman of her husband's, a mighty man of wealth, of the family of Elimelech; and his name was Boaz.

And Ruth the Moabitess said unto Naomi, Let me now go to the field, and glean ears of corn after him in whose sight I shall find grace. And she said unto her, Go, my daughter.

And she went, and came, and gleaned in the field after the reapers: and her hap was to light on a part of the field belonging unto Boaz, who was of the kindred of Elimelech.

                                                                           (2:1–3)

And when Boaz had eaten and drunk, and his heart was merry, he went to lie down at the end of the heap of corn: and she came softly, and uncovered his feet, and laid her down.

And it came to pass at midnight, that the man was afraid, and turned himself: and, behold, a woman lay at his feet.

And he said, Who art thou? And she answered, I am Ruth thine handmaid: spread therefore thy skirt over thine handmaid; for thou art a near kinsman.

And he said, Blessed be thou of the LORD, my daughter: for thou hast shewed more kindness in the latter end than at the beginning, inasmuch as thou followedst not young men, whether poor or rich.

And now, my daughter, fear not; I will do to thee all that thou requirest: for all the city of my people doth know that thou art a virtuous woman.

                                                                           (3:7–11)

157. Woman gleaning in a field near Bethlehem.

And this man went up out of his city yearly to worship and to sacrifice unto the LORD of hosts in Shiloh. And the two sons of Eli, Hophni and Phinehas, the priests of the LORD, were there.

And when the time was that Elkanah offered, he gave to Peninnah his wife, and to all her sons and her daughters, portions:

But unto Hannah he gave a worthy portion; for he loved Hannah: but the LORD had shut up her womb.

And her adversary also provoked her sore, for to make her fret, because the LORD had shut up her womb.

And as he did so year by year, when she went up to the house of the LORD, so she provoked her; therefore she wept, and did not eat.

Then said Elkanah her husband to her, Hannah, why weepest thou? and why eatest thou not? and why is thy heart grieved? am not I better to thee than ten sons?

So Hannah rose up after they had eaten in Shiloh, and after they had drunk. Now Eli the priest sat upon a seat by a post of the temple of the LORD.

And she was in bitterness of soul, and prayed unto the LORD, and wept sore.

And she vowed a vow, and said, O LORD of hosts, if thou wilt indeed look on the affliction of thine handmaid, and remember me, and not forget thine handmaid, but wilt give unto thine handmaid a man child, then I will give him unto the LORD all the days of his life, and there shall no rasor come upon his head.

And it came to pass, as she continued praying before the LORD, that Eli marked her mouth.

Now Hannah, she spake in her heart; only her lips moved, but her voice was not heard: therefore Eli thought she had been drunken.

And Eli said unto her, How long wilt thou be drunken? put away thy wine from thee.

And Hannah answered and said, No, my lord, I am a woman of a sorrowful spirit: I have drunk neither wine nor strong drink, but have poured out my soul before the LORD.

Count not thine handmaid for a daughter of Belial: for out of the abundance of my complaint and grief have I spoken hitherto.

Then Eli answered and said, Go in peace: and the God of Israel grant thee thy petition that thou hast asked of him.

(1:3–17)

And when she had weaned him, she took him up with her, with three bullocks, and one ephah of flour, and a bottle of wine, and brought him unto the house of the LORD in Shiloh: and the child was young.

(1:24)

And Hannah prayed, and said, My heart rejoiceth in the LORD, mine horn is exalted in the LORD: my mouth is enlarged over mine enemies; because I rejoice in thy salvation.

There is none holy as the LORD: for there is none beside thee: neither is there any rock like our God.

158. View of the site of Shiloh.

159. Ruins of ancient Shiloh, between Jerusalem and Shechem, in the mountains of Samaria.

Shiloh was the capital of Israel in the time of the Judges.

It was the center of Israelite worship before the conquest of Jerusalem. During a religious celebration the daughters of the city danced in the vineyards, an occasion seized by the Benjamites to abduct them, as they could not get wives in any other way (Judges 21). To this day, the Arabs call the adjacent valley *Marj el-Id* – the Valley of the Feast.

It was at Shiloh that Hannah spoke the beautiful words which form what is known as the Song of Hannah (2:1–10). It is part of the reading from the Prophets in the Jewish New Year's Day festival, and the basis of the *Magnificat* (see the New Testament, Luke 1:46–55), in which the Virgin Mary rejoices that she is to be the mother of the Lord.

Talk no more so exceeding proudly; let not arrogancy come out of your mouth: for the LORD is a God of knowledge, and by him actions are weighed.

The bows of the mighty men are broken, and they that stumbled are girded with strength.

They that were full have hired out themselves for bread; and they that were hungry ceased: so that the barren hath born seven; and she that hath many children is waxed feeble.

The LORD killeth, and maketh alive: he bringeth down to the grave, and bringeth up.

The LORD maketh poor, and maketh rich: he bringeth low, and lifteth up.

He raiseth up the poor out of the dust, and lifteth up the beggar from the dunghill, to set them among princes, and to make them inherit the throne of glory: for the pillars of the earth are the LORD's, and he hath set the world upon them.

He will keep the feet of his saints, and the wicked shall be silent in darkness; for by strength shall no man prevail.

The adversaries of the LORD shall be broken to pieces; out of heaven shall he thunder upon them: the LORD shall judge the ends of the earth; and he shall give strength unto his king, and exalt the horn of his anointed.

(2:1–10)

And the word of Samuel came to all Israel. Now Israel went out against the Philistines to battle, and pitched beside Eben-ezer: and the Philistines pitched in Aphek.

And the Philistines put themselves in array against Israel: and when they joined battle, Israel was smitten before the Philistines: and they slew of the army in the field about four thousand men.

And when the people were come into the camp, the elders of Israel said, Wherefore hath the LORD smitten us to day before the Philistines? Let us fetch the ark of the covenant of the LORD out of Shiloh unto us, that, when it cometh among us, it may save us out of the hand of our enemies.

(4:1–3)

160. Aphek, at the source of the Yarkon River, was a strategically important city. The king of Aphek was one of the thirty-one rulers of Canaan vanquished by Joshua (Joshua 12:18). It later became a stronghold on the Philistines' northern border.

At this site the town of Antipatris was later built in the Roman period. Antipatris remained a way-station for travelers until the 4th century A.D., but its importance declined. In the Middle Ages the Crusaders built the castle of Toron-aux-Fontaines-Sourdes at the site – now known as Ras el-Ein. A Turkish fortress was erected in the 17th century. Its square-shaped remains are shown in this photograph.

Aphek is the name of two other sites mentioned in the Bible and named after nearby riverbeds.

161. The Holy Ark on wheels, carved on a stone found in the remains of a synagogue dating from the late 2nd or 3rd century in Capernaum, in the Galilee.

The Ark of the Covenant, or the Ark of the Lord, or the Holy Ark, are some of the names given to the chest which stood in the Holy of Holies, and in which "the Tablets of the Covenant" were kept. It is described in detail in the Book of Exodus. The Ark is said to have accompanied the children of Israel on their journey from the desert of Sinai to the land of Israel, as well as throughout the entire period of the conquest of the country, as it was believed to secure God's help. During the war against the Philistines the Ark fell into their hands, and was later restored to the Israelites. David brought it finally to the City of David – Jerusalem – and placed it in a tent which he put up for it.

162. A clay figurine of the goddess so-called by the archaeologists "Ashdoda." This Philistine statuette dating back to the 12th century B.C. was found at Ashdod. The goddess is shown seated, her body merging into a four-legged throne.

Ashdod was one of the five cities (along with Gaza, Ashkelon, Ekron, and Gath) of the Philistines, situated in the Judean Plain, a short distance from the coast. It is possible that the first reference to Ashdod is that to "the city of giants" mentioned in the Execration Texts. There is a comparable reference in Joshua 11:22, according to which the ancient inhabitants of Ashdod, Gath, and Gaza, were "Anakim," the Hebrew word for giants, which, it is believed, refers to the Philistines.

161

And the Philistines took the ark of God, and brought it from Eben-ezer unto Ashdod.

When the Philistines took the ark of God, they brought it into the house of Dagon, and set it by Dagon.

And when they of Ashdod arose early on the morrow, behold, Dagon was fallen upon his face to the earth before the ark of the LORD. And they took Dagon, and set him in his place again.

And when they arose early on the morrow morning, behold, Dagon was fallen upon his face to the ground before the ark of the LORD; and the head of Dagon and both the palms of his hands were cut off upon the threshold; only the stump of Dagon was left to him.

Therefore neither the priests of Dagon, nor any that come into Dagon's house, tread on the threshold of Dagon in Ashdod unto this day.

But the hand of the LORD was heavy upon them of Ashdod, and he destroyed them, and smote them with emerods, even Ashdod and the coasts thereof.

And when the men of Ashdod saw that it was so, they said, The ark of the God of Israel shall not abide with us: for his hand is sore upon us, and upon Dagon our god.

They sent therefore and gathered all the lords of the Philistines unto them, and said, What shall we do with the ark of the God of Israel? And they answered, Let the ark of the God of Israel be carried about unto Gath. And they carried the ark of the God of Israel about thither.

And it was so, that, after they had carried it about, the hand of the LORD was against the city with a very great destruction: and he smote the men of the city, both small and great, and they had emerods in their secret parts.

Therefore they sent the ark of God to Ekron. And it came to pass, as the ark of God came to Ekron, that the Ekronites cried out, saying, They have brought about the ark of the God of Israel to us, to slay us and our people.

So they sent and gathered together all the lords of the Philistines, and said, Send away the ark of the God of Israel, and let it go again to his own place, that it slay us not, and our people: for there was a deadly destruction throughout all the city; the hand of God was very heavy there.

And the men that died not were smitten with the emerods: and the cry of the city went up to heaven.

(5:1–12)

163

163. The Philistines returning the Ark of the Covenant to the Israelites, from a wall painting of Dura-Europos.
The Ark is on a cart pulled by two oxen which are being whipped and led by two men in Persian costume. Three men walk abreast behind the Ark. On the right, a temple, open and empty, with cult objects and fragments strewn on the ground before it. This is likely to depict the abandoned Philistine temple and the broken image of their god Dagon.

164. Beth Shemesh in Hebrew means "House of the Sun." It indicates a sun cult that was practiced there, and throws light on the name of Samson (Shimshon in Hebrew), whose root is also Shemesh.
As Ir-Shemesh, it is included among the cities of Dan (Joshua 19:41), and it is listed elsewhere as one of the cities of Judah given to the Levites (Joshua 21:16). The Book of Kings records a battle fought between the king of Israel and the king of Judah "... Therefore Jehoash king of Israel went up; and he and Amaziah king of Judah looked one another in the face at Beth-Shemesh, which belongeth to Judah" (II Kings 14:11).
Samson's birthplace, Zorah, was a few miles away from Beth Shemesh, and the stories about Samson take place in the vicinity. In the period of the monarchy it was part of Solomon's second administrative district.

And the ark of the LORD was in the country of the Philistines seven months.

And the Philistines called for the priests and the diviners, saying, What shall we do to the ark of the LORD? tell us wherewith we shall send it to his place.

And they said, If ye send away the ark of the God of Israel, send it not empty; but in any wise return him a trespass offering: then ye shall be healed, and it shall be known to you why his hand is not removed from you.
(6:1–3)

And take the ark of the LORD, and lay it upon the cart; and put the jewels of gold which ye return him for a trespass offering, in a coffer by the side thereof; and send it away, that it may go.

And see, if it goeth up by the way of his own coast to Beth-shemesh, then he hath done us this great evil: but if not, then we shall know that it is not his hand that smote us; it was a chance that happened to us.

And the men did so; and took two milch kine, and tied them to the cart, and shut up their calves at home:

And they laid the ark of the LORD upon the cart, and the coffer with the mice of gold and the images of their emerods.

And the kine took the straight way to the way of Beth-shemesh, and went along the highway, lowing as they went, and turned not aside to the right hand or to the left; and the lords of the Philistines went after them unto the border of Beth-shemesh.

And they of Beth-shemesh were reaping their wheat harvest in the valley: and they lifted up their eyes, and saw the ark, and rejoiced to see it.

And the cart came into the field of Joshua, a Beth-shemite, and stood there, where there was a great stone: and they clave the wood of the cart, and offered the kine a burnt offering unto the LORD.

And the Levites took down the ark of the LORD, and the coffer that was with it, wherein the jewels of gold were, and put them on the great stone: and the men of Beth-shemesh offered burnt offerings and sacrificed sacrifices the same day unto the LORD.
(6:8–15)

And he smote the men of Beth-shemesh, because they had looked into the ark of the LORD, even he smote of the people fifty thousand and threescore and ten men: and the people lamented, because the LORD had smitten many of the people with a great slaughter.
(6:19)

165. Kirjat-Jearim (Town of Forests, in Hebrew), was in the territory of Judah. Its ancient names were Baale Judah (II Samuel 6:2), Baalah (Joshua 15:9), attesting to the cult of Baal at this place.

The biblical site is identified with the village of Deir-el-Azar near the present-day village of Abu Gosh. Overlooking Abu Gosh and facing Jerusalem is a statue of St. Mary carrying the infant Jesus in her arms, known as Notre Dame de l'Arche de l'Alliance – Our Lady of the Ark of the Covenant. The French Sisters of St. Joseph who reside in the nearby convent maintain that it stands on the site of the house of Abinadab, where the Ark of the Covenant rested.

And the men of Kirjath-jearim came, and fetched up the ark of the LORD, and brought it into the house of Abinadab in the hill, and sanctified Eleazar his son to keep the ark of the LORD.

And it came to pass, while the ark abode in Kirjath-jearim, that the time was long; for it was twenty years: and all the house of Israel lamented after the LORD.

And Samuel spake unto all the house of Israel, saying, If ye do return unto the LORD with all your hearts, then put away the strange gods and Ashtaroth from among you, and prepare your hearts unto the LORD, and serve him only: and he will deliver you out of the hand of the Philistines.

Then the children of Israel did put away Baalim and Ashtaroth, and served the LORD only.

And Samuel said, Gather all Israel to Mizpeh, and I will pray for you unto the LORD.

And they gathered together to Mizpeh, and drew water, and poured it out before the LORD, and fasted on that day, and said there, We have sinned against the LORD. And Samuel judged the children of Israel in Mizpeh.

And when the Philistines heard that the children of Israel were gathered together to Mizpeh, the lords of the Philistines went up against Israel. And when the children of Israel heard it, they were afraid of the Philistines.

And the children of Israel said unto Samuel, Cease not to cry unto the LORD our God for us, that he will save us out of the hand of the Philistines.

And Samuel took a sucking lamb, and offered it for a burnt offering wholly unto the LORD: and Samuel cried unto the LORD for Israel; and the LORD heard him.

And as Samuel was offering up the burnt offering, the Philistines drew near to battle against Israel: but the LORD thundered with a great thunder on that day upon the Philistines, and discomfited them; and they were smitten before Israel.

(7:1–10)

And Saul said unto his uncle, He told us plainly that the asses were found. But of the matter of the kingdom, whereof Samuel spake, he told him not.

And Samuel called the people together unto the LORD to Mizpeh;

And said unto the children of Israel, Thus saith the LORD God of Israel, I brought up Israel out of Egypt, and delivered you out of the hand of the Egyptians, and out of the hand of all kingdoms, and of them that oppressed you:

And ye have this day rejected your God, who himself saved you out of all your adversities and your tribulations; and ye have said unto him, Nay, but set a king over us. Now therefore present yourselves before the LORD by your tribes, and by your thousands.

And when Samuel had caused all the tribes of Israel to come near, the tribe of Benjamin was taken.

When he had caused the tribe of Benjamin to come near by their families, the family of Matri was taken, and Saul the son of Kish was taken: and when they sought him, he could not be found.

Therefore they inquired of the LORD further, if the man should yet come thither. And the LORD answered, Behold, he hath hid himself among the stuff.

And they ran and fetched him thence: and when he stood among the people, he was higher than any of the people from his shoulders and upward.

And Samuel said to all the people, See ye him whom the LORD hath chosen, that there is none like him among all the people? And all the people shouted, and said, God save the king.

(10:16–24)

166. Mizpeh on the main road from Jerusalem to Shechem has been identified by some scholars as Tell en-Nasbeh, about six miles north of Jerusalem. Excavations at the site revealed traces of settlement as far back as the 3rd millennium B.C.
The Israelites gathered at Mizpeh, overcame their enemies, the Philistines, and forced them temporarily to withdraw to within their original borders along the coastal plain.

And Saul also went home to Gibeah; and there went with him a band of men, whose hearts God had touched.

But the children of Belial said, How shall this man save us? And they despised him, and brought him no presents. But he held his peace.

(10:26–27)

Then Nahash the Ammonite came up, and encamped against Jabesh-gilead: and all the men of Jabesh said unto Nahash, Make a covenant with us, and we will serve thee.

And Nahash the Ammonite answered them, On this condition will I make a covenant with you, that I may thrust out all your right eyes, and lay it for a reproach upon all Israel.

And the elders of Jabesh said unto him, Give us seven days' respite, that we may send messengers unto all the coasts of Israel: and then, if there be no man to save us, we will come out to thee.

Then came the messengers to Gibeah of Saul, and told the tidings in the ears of the people: and all the people lifted up their voices, and wept.

And, behold, Saul came after the herd out of the field; and Saul said, What aileth the people that they weep? And they told him the tidings of the men of Jabesh.

And the Spirit of God came upon Saul when he heard those tidings, and his anger was kindled greatly.

And he took a yoke of oxen, and hewed them in pieces, and sent them throughout all the coasts of Israel by the hands of messengers, saying, Whosoever cometh not forth after Saul and after Samuel, so shall it be done unto his oxen. And the fear of the LORD fell on the people, and they came out with one consent.

(11:1–7)

167. Gibeah, also called Gaba or Geba, was the principal town in the territory of Benjamin. The biblical site has been identified as Tell el-Ful, about three miles north of Jerusalem, on the main road to Shechem. Excavations at the site revealed five occupation periods ranging from the 12th century B.C. to Roman times. The early settlement was destroyed after the incident of the concubine narrated in Judges 19 and 20. The Philistines conquered the mountains of Benjamin and placed a garrison at Geba (the "hill of God," as it is called in I Samuel 10:5, which is the meaning of the name in Hebrew). Saul's home was there and, following his victory over the Philistines, he made it his capital and named it after himself.

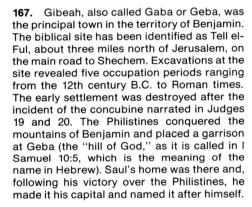

167

Saul reigned one year; and when he had reigned two years over Israel,

Saul chose him three thousand men of Israel; whereof two thousand were with Saul in Michmash and in mount Bethel, and a thousand were with Jonathan in Gibeah of Benjamin: and the rest of the people he sent every man to his tent.

And Jonathan smote the garrison of the Philistines that was in Geba, and the Philistines heard of it. And Saul blew the trumpet throughout all the land, saying, Let the Hebrews hear.

And all Israel heard say that Saul had smitten a garrison of the Philistines, and that Israel also was had in abomination with the Philistines. And the people were called together after Saul to Gilgal.

And the Philistines gathered themselves together to fight with Israel, thirty thousand chariots, and six thousand horsemen, and people as the sand which is on the sea shore in multitude: and they came up, and pitched in Michmash, eastward from Beth-aven.

When the men of Israel saw that they were in a strait, (for the people were distressed,) then the people did hide themselves in caves, and in thickets, and in rocks, and in high places, and in pits.

And some of the Hebrews went over Jordan to the land of Gad and Gilead. As for Saul, he was yet in Gilgal, and the people followed him trembling.

And he tarried seven days, according to the set time that Samuel had appointed: but Samuel came not to Gilgal; and the people were scattered from him.

And Saul said, Bring hither a burnt offering to me, and peace offerings. And he offered the burnt offering.

(13:1–9)

168. The site of Michmash, on the border of the Judean Desert, a few miles north of Jerusalem.

169. & 170. In the fields around Bethlehem. Bethlehem first appears in the Bible in connection with Rachel's death and her burial "in the way to Ephrath, which is Bethlehem" (Genesis 35:19). It was also the scene of the story of Ruth. It is the birthplace of David and the place where he was anointed by Samuel. It thus became the symbol of David's dynasty and the focus of messianic belief, for the Messiah would be a descendant of the house of David: "But thou, Bethlehem Ephratah, though thou be little among the thousands of Judah, yet out of thee shall he come forth unto me that is to be ruler in Israel; whose goings forth have been from of old, from everlasting" (Micah 5:2).

171. Horn of ivory with gold bands, made from a whole elephant's tusk, found at Megiddo; it dates from the Late Bronze Age. The horns of animals – usually rams – were sometimes used in antiquity as drinking vessels and containers. The horn found at Megiddo had its wide end sealed off, and the pointed end pierced with a hole. Held with the pointed end downwards, it was used for anointing, as the oil dripped through the hole.

169

170

And the LORD said unto Samuel, How long wilt thou mourn for Saul, seeing I have rejected him from reigning over Israel? fill thine horn with oil, and go, I will send to Jesse the Bethlehemite: for I have provided me a king among his sons.

And Samuel said, How can I go? if Saul hear it, he will kill me. And the LORD said, Take an heifer with thee, and say, I am come to sacrifice to the LORD.

And call Jesse to the sacrifice, and I will shew thee what thou shalt do: and thou shalt anoint unto me him whom I name unto thee.

And Samuel did that which the LORD spake, and came to Beth-lehem. And the elders of the town trembled at his coming, and said, Comest thou peaceably?

And he said, Peaceably: I am come to sacrifice unto the LORD: sanctify yourselves, and come with me to the sacrifice. And he sanctified Jesse and his sons, and called them to the sacrifice.

171

And it came to pass, when they were come, that he looked on Eliab, and said, Surely the LORD's anointed is before him.

But the LORD said unto Samuel, Look not on his countenance, or on the height of his stature; because I have refused him: for the LORD seeth not as man seeth; for man looketh on the outward appearance, but the LORD looketh on the heart.

Then Jesse called Abinadab, and made him pass before Samuel. And he said, Neither hath the LORD chosen this.

Then Jesse made Shammah to pass by. And he said, Neither hath the LORD chosen this.

Again, Jesse made seven of his sons to pass before Samuel. And Samuel said unto Jesse, The LORD hath not chosen these.

And Samuel said unto Jesse, Are here all thy children? And he said, There remaineth yet the youngest, and, behold, he keepeth the sheep. And Samuel said unto Jesse, Send and fetch him: for we will not sit down till he come hither.

And he sent, and brought him in. Now he was ruddy, and withal of a beautiful countenance, and goodly to look to. And the LORD said, Arise, anoint him: for this is he.

Then Samuel took the horn of oil, and anointed him in the midst of his brethren: and the Spirit of the LORD came upon David from that day forward. So Samuel rose up, and went to Ramah.

But the Spirit of the LORD departed from Saul, and an evil spirit from the LORD troubled him.

And Saul's servants said unto him, Behold now, an evil spirit from God troubleth thee.

Let our lord now command thy servants, which are before thee, to seek out a man, who is a cunning player on a harp: and it shall come to pass, when the evil spirit from God is upon thee, that he shall play with his hand, and thou shalt be well.

And Saul said unto his servants, Provide me now a man that can play well, and bring him to me.

Then answered one of the servants, and said, Behold, I have seen a son of Jesse the Bethlehemite, that is cunning in playing, and a mighty valiant man, and a man of war, and prudent in matters, and a comely person, and the LORD is with him.

Wherefore Saul sent messengers unto Jesse, and said, Send me David thy son, which is with the sheep.

And Jesse took an ass laden with bread , and a bottle of wine, and a kid, and sent them by David his son unto Saul.

And David came to Saul, and stood before him: and he loved him greatly; and he became his armourbearer.

And Saul sent to Jesse, saying, Let David, I pray thee, stand before me; for he hath found favour in my sight.

And it came to pass, when the evil spirit from God was upon Saul, that David took an harp, and played with his hand: so Saul was refreshed, and was well, and the evil spirit departed from him.

(16:1–23)

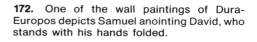

172. One of the wall paintings of Dura-Europos depicts Samuel anointing David, who stands with his hands folded.

173. David playing the harp, depicted in the mosaic floor of a synagogue of the 5th/6th century in the Byzantine style. Only the mosaic floor remains of this synagogue (Museum for Music and Ethnology, Haifa).

174. The hill of Azekah in the Valley of Elah southwest of Jerusalem extending toward the land of the Philistines, through which passed an important road from Philistia to the mountains of Judah and Jerusalem. It was here that David confronted Goliath.

174

175. Detail from the so-called Warrior's Vase showing a Mycenaean warrior armed as the description given in the Bible of Goliath's armor. Here the warrior is carrying a large spear, a round shield, a horned helmet and a leather body-armor.

Now the Philistines gathered together their armies to battle, and were gathered together at Shochoh, which belongeth to Judah, and pitched between Shochoh and Azekah, in Ephes-dammim.

And the Philistines stood on a mountain on the one side, and Israel stood on a mountain on the other side: and there was a valley between them.

And the Philistines stood on a mountain on the one side, and Israel stood on a mountain on the other side: and there was a valley between them.

And there went out a champion out of the camp of the Philistines, named Goliath, of Gath, whose height was six cubits and a span.

And he had an helmet of brass upon his head, and he was armed with a coat of mail; and the weight of the coat was five thousand shekels of brass.

And he had greaves of brass upon his legs, and a target of brass between his shoulders.

And the staff of his spear was like a weaver's beam; and his spear's head weighed six hundred shekels of iron: and one bearing a shield went before him.

And he stood and cried unto the armies of Israel, and said unto them, Why are ye come out to set your battle in array? am I not a Philistine, and ye servants to Saul? choose you a man for you, and let him come down to me.

If he be able to fight with me, and to kill me, then will we be your servants: but if I prevail against him, and kill him, then shall ye be our servants, and serve us.

And the Philistine said, I defy the armies of Israel this day; give me a man, that we may fight together.

When Saul and all Israel heard those words of the Philistine, they were dismayed, and greatly afraid.

(17:1–11)

176. Relief from Gozan showing a slinger, 10th or 9th century B.C. (British Museum, London).

The sling is popularly associated with shepherds rather than with warriors. David the shepherd used one against Goliath the warrior, which proved the efficiency of the sling when properly handled. This weapon was made of two parts: a leather or heavy cloth "pocket" with two cords or thongs for swinging it; and a stone – the missile. Using a sling required much practice and skill. A stone was placed in the pocket and then swung round and round above the head; when sufficient centrifugal force had been generated, one of the thongs was released, discharging the stone at high speed toward the distant target.

And he took his staff in his hand, and chose him five smooth stones out of the brook, and put them in a shepherd's bag which he had, even in a scrip; and his sling was in his hand: and he drew near to the Philistine.

And the Philistine came on and drew near unto David; and the man that bare the shield went before him.

And when the Philistine looked about, and saw David, he disdained him: for he was but a youth, and ruddy, and of a fair countenance.

And the Philistine said unto David, Am I a dog, that thou comest to me with staves? And the Philistine cursed David by his gods.

And the Philistine said to David, Come to me, and I will give thy flesh unto the fowls of the air, and to the beasts of the field.

Then said David to the Philistine, Thou comest to me with a sword, and with a spear, and with a shield: but I come to thee in the name of the LORD of hosts, the God of the armies of Israel, whom thou hast defied.

This day will the LORD deliver thee into mine hand; and I will smite thee, and take thine head from thee; and I will give the carcases of the host of the Philistines this day unto the fowls of the air, and to the wild beasts of the earth; that all the earth may know that there is a God in Israel.

And all this assembly shall know that the LORD saveth not with sword and spear: for the battle is the LORD's, and he will give you into our hands.

And it came to pass, when the Philistine arose, and came and drew nigh to meet David, that David hasted, and ran toward the army to meet the Philistine.

And David put his hand in his bag, and took thence a stone, and slang it, and smote the Philistine in his forehead, that the stone sunk into his forehead; and he fell upon his face to the earth.

So David prevailed over the Philistine with a sling and with a stone, and smote the Philistine, and slew him; but there was no sword in the hand of David.

Therefore David ran, and stood upon the Philistine, and took his sword and drew it out of the sheath thereof, and slew him, and cut off his head therewith. And when the Philistines saw their champion was dead, they fled.

(17:40-51)

177. The site of the tomb of the prophet Samuel has been traditionally associated with the site called Nabi-Samwil (the Prophet Samuel, in Arabic), the highest mountain overlooking Jerusalem.

In the 11th century the site was named Montjoie by the Crusaders, because it was from there that they first saw Jerusalem. A church was built there but it was destroyed in the 12th century. Moslems and Jews turned the ruins into prayer houses. In medieval times thousands of Jews used to gather at the shrine on the traditional date of Samuel's death.

In the 18th century the Turks built a mosque there. Few Jews pray here now because of the doubtfulness of the site's authenticity.

177

178. Interior of the shrine at Nabi-Samwil.

179. View of the Gilboa Range overlooking the Valley of Jezreel. Ravines divide the crescent-shaped ridge of limestone hills into several plateaus. Much of it is barren rock.

180. Beth-shean, or Beth-shan (also Beisan), a hill in the Valley of Harod at the eastern end of the Valley of Jezreel.

Situated at a main crossroads in a well-watered fertile region, 390 feet below sea level, it was an important site throughout history.

178

And Samuel died; and all the Israelites were gathered together, and lamented him, and buried him in his house at Ramah. And David arose, and went down to the wilderness of Paran.

(25:1)

Now the Philistines fought against Israel: and the men of Israel fled from before the Philistines, and fell down slain in mount Gilboa.

And the Philistines followed hard upon Saul and upon his sons; and the Philistines slew Jonathan, and Abinadab, and Malchi-shua, Saul's sons.

And the battle went sore against Saul, and the archers hit him; and he was sore wounded of the archers.

Then said Saul unto his armourbearer, Draw thy sword, and thrust me through therewith; lest these uncircumcised come and thrust me through, and abuse me. But his armourbearer would not; for he was sore afraid. Therefore Saul took a sword, and fell upon it.

And when his armourbearer saw that Saul was dead, he fell likewise upon his sword, and died with him.

So Saul died, and his three sons, and his armourbearer, and all his men, that same day together.

And when the men of Israel that were on the other side of the valley, and they that were on the other side Jordan, saw that the men of Israel fled, and that Saul and his sons were dead, they forsook the cities, and fled; and the Philistines came and dwelt in them.

And it came to pass on the morrow, when the Philistines came to strip the slain, that they found Saul and his three sons fallen in mount Gilboa.

And they cut off his head, and stripped off his armour, and sent into the land of the Philistines round about, to publish it in the house of their idols, and among the people.

And they put his armour in the house of Ashtaroth: and they fastened his body to the wall of Beth-shan.

And when the inhabitants of Jabesh-gilead heard of that which the Philistines had done to Saul;

All the valiant men arose, and went all night, and took the body of Saul and the bodies of his sons from the wall of Beth-shan, and came to Jabesh, and burnt them there.

And they took their bones, and buried them under a tree at Jabesh, and fasted seven days.

(31:1–13)

The city was a stronghold of the Egyptian empire. It seems that the Egyptians, after defeating the invading Sea Peoples (Philistines) early in the 12th century B.C., posted a garrison of mercenaries recruited from among the vanquished armies in the city. In biblical times it was one of the Canaanite towns that resisted the attack of the Israelites. The Canaanites had not been driven out but were taxed heavily (Joshua 17:11–13, 16–18; Judges 1:27–28).

Beth-shean was in the possession of the Philistines during the reign of King Saul, and following Saul's defeat at Mount Gilboa the Philistines placed Saul's armor in the "house of Ashtarot" and the bodies of Saul and his sons were displayed on the walls of Beth-shean. The city was later conquered by King David, with Megiddo and Taanach, during the expansion of his kingdom northwards.

In about 700 B.C. the site was deserted and was not reoccupied until the Hellenistic period, when it became known as Scythopolis, "City of the Scythians."

In the Roman period, it was taken by Pompey in 63 B.C. and became the capital of the Decapolis.

181. Philistine coffin-lid shaped like a man, found at Beth-shean, with the characteristic "feathered" headdress of the Philistine warriors.

181

179

And David lamented with this lamentation over Saul and over Jonathan his son:

(Also he bade them teach the children of Judah the use of the bow: behold, it is written in the book of Jasher.)

The beauty of Israel is slain upon thy high places: how are the mighty fallen!

Tell it not in Gath, publish it not in the streets of Askelon; lest the daughters of the Philistines rejoice, lest the daughters of the uncircumcised triumph.

Ye mountains of Gilboa let there be no dew, neither let there be rain, upon you, nor fields of offerings: for there the shield of the mighty is vilely cast away, the shield of Saul, as though he had not been anointed with oil.

From the blood of the slain, from the fat of the mighty, the bow of Jonathan turned not back, and the sword of Saul returned not empty.

Saul and Jonathan were lovely and pleasant in their lives, and in their death they were not divided: they were swifter than eagles, they were stronger than lions.

Ye daughters of Israel, weep over Saul, who clothed you in scarlet, with other delights, who put on ornaments of gold upon your apparel.

How are the mighty fallen in the midst of the battle! O Jonathan, thou wast slain in thine high places.

I am distressed for thee, my brother Jonathan: very pleasant hast thou been unto me: thy love to me was wonderful, passing the love of women.

How are the mighty fallen, and the weapons of war perished!

(1:17–27)

182. Egyptian archer.
Egyptians and Assyrians naturally depicted their own armies and victories, but their sources also give a good idea of the armies they fought against. Bows and arrows were the principal long-range weapons of armies in ancient times, and indeed remained so, with variations, until early modern times.

David was thirty years old when he began to reign, and he reigned forty years.

In Hebron he reigned over Judah seven years and six months: and in Jerusalem he reigned thirty and three years over all Israel and Judah.

And the king and his men went to Jerusalem unto the Jebusites, the inhabitants of the land: which spake unto David, saying, Except thou take away the blind and the lame, thou shalt not come in hither: thinking, David cannot come in hither.

Nevertheless David took the strong hold of Zion: the same is the city of David.

And David said on that day, Whosoever getteth up to the gutter, and smiteth the Jebusites, and the lame and the blind, that are hated of David's soul, he shall be chief and captain. Wherefore they said, The blind and the lame shall not come into the house.

So David dwelt in the fort, and called it the city of David. And David built round about from Millo and inward.

And David went on, and grew great, and the LORD God of hosts was with him.

And Hiram king of Tyre sent messengers to David, and cedar trees, and carpenters, and masons: and they built David an house.

And David perceived that the LORD had established him king over Israel, and that he had exalted his kingdom for his people Israel's sake.

And David took him more concubines and wives out of Jerusalem, after he was come from Hebron: and there were yet sons and daughters born to David.

(5:4–13)

183. The City of David, a view of the recent excavations, seen from northeast. In the foreground are remains of structures from the Canaanite and Israelite periods. The graded stone structure in the center dates from the 10th century B.C., that is, from the reigns of David and Solomon.

184. This typical clay figurine of a fertility goddess, found in the City of David, dates from the Israelite period, i.e., between the 8th and 6th centuries B.C.

183   184

185

185. A mural on the west wall of the 3rd-century synagogue at Dura-Europos, above the niche where presumably the Scroll of the Law was kept: it depicts the Temple in the center, with the seven-branch candelabrum on one side, and a branch of myrtle and a rough sketch showing Abraham preparing to sacrifice Isaac, on the other.

Again, David gathered together all the chosen men of Israel, thirty thousand.

And David arose, and went with all the people that were with him from Baale of Judah, to bring up from thence the ark of God, whose name is called by the name of the LORD of hosts that dwelleth between the cherubims.

And they set the ark of God upon a new cart, and brought it out of the house of Abinadab that was in Gibeah: and Uzzah and Ahio, the sons of Abinadab, drave the new cart.

And they brought it out of the house of Abinadab which was at Gibeah, accompanying the ark of God: and Ahio went before the ark.

And David and all the house of Israel played before the LORD on all manner of instruments made of fir wood, even on harps, and on psalteries, and on timbrels, and on cornets, and on cymbals.

And when they came to Nachon's threshingfloor, Uzzah put forth his hand to the ark of God, and took hold of it; for the oxen shook it.

And the anger of the LORD was kindled against Uzzah; and God smote him there for his error; and there he died by the ark of God.

And David was displeased, because the LORD had made a breach upon Uzzah: and he called the name of the place Perez-uzzah to this day.

And David was afraid of the LORD that day, and said, How shall the ark of the LORD come to me?

So David would not remove the ark of the LORD unto him into the city of David: but David carried it aside into the house of Obed-edom the Gittite.

And the ark of the LORD continued in the house of Obed-edom the Gittite three months: and the LORD blessed Obed-edom, and all his household.

And it was told king David, saying, The LORD hath blessed the house of Obed-edom, and all that pertaineth unto him, because of the ark of God. So David went and brought up the ark of God from the house of Obed-edom into the city of David with gladness.

And it was so, that when they that bare the ark of the LORD had gone six paces, he sacrificed oxen and fatlings.

(6:1–13)

186. Impression of two Ammonite seals of the 7th century B.C.
Ammon was the land of the Ammonites who settled east of the Jordan River, between the Amorites in the north and the Moabites in the south, at the beginning of the 13th century B.C. According to Genesis 19:38 the Ammonites were the descendants of Lot.
There was enmity between the Israelites and the Ammonites from early times, and war broke out when the Ammonites attempted to encroach on Israelite territory. In the reign of Saul they attempted to take Jabesh-Gilead but they were driven back (I Samuel 11:1–15).

186

And when the children of Ammon saw that they stank before David, the children of Ammon sent and hired the Syrians of Beth-rehob, and the Syrians of Zoba, twenty thousand footmen, and of king Maacah a thousand men, and of Ish-tob twelve thousand men.

And when David heard of it, he sent Joab, and all the host of the mighty men.

And the children of Ammon came out, and put the battle in array at the entering in of the gate: and the Syrians of Zoba, and of Rehob, and Ish-tob, and Maacah, were by themselves in the field.

When Joab saw that the front of the battle was against him before and behind, he chose of all the choice men of Israel, and put them in array against the Syrians:

And the rest of the people he delivered into the hand of Abishai his brother, that he might put them in array against the children of Ammon.

And he said, If the Syrians be too strong for me, then thou shalt help me: but if the children of Ammon be too strong for thee, then I will come and help thee.

Be of good courage, and let us play the men for our people, and for the cities of our God: and the LORD do that which seemeth him good.

And Joab drew nigh, and the people that were with him, unto the battle against the Syrians: and they fled before him.

And when the children of Ammon saw that the Syrians were fled, then fled they also before Abishai, and entered into the city. So Joab returned from the children of Ammon, and came to Jerusalem.

And when the Syrians saw that they were smitten before Israel, they gathered themselves together.

And Hadarezer sent, and brought out the Syrians that were beyond the river: and they came to Helam; and Shobach the captain of the host of Hadarezer went before them.

And when it was told David, he gathered all Israel together, and passed over Jordan, and came to Helam. And the Syrians set themselves in array against David, and fought with him.

(10:6–17)

187. Two Ammonite figures.

And it came to pass in an eveningtide, that David arose from off his bed, and walked upon the roof of the king's house: and from the roof he saw a woman washing herself; and the woman was very beautiful to look upon.

And David sent and inquired after the woman. And one said, Is not this Bath-sheba, the daughter of Eliam, the wife of Uriah the Hittite?

And David sent messengers, and took her; and she came in unto him, and he lay with her; for she was purified from her uncleanness: and she returned unto her house.

And the woman conceived, and sent and told David, and said, I am with child. (11:2–5)

And David said to Uriah, Tarry here to day also, and to morrow I will let thee depart. So Uriah abode in Jerusalem that day, and the morrow.

And when David had called him, he did eat and drink before him; and he made him drunk: and at even he went out to lie on his bed with the servants of his lord, but went not down to his house.

And it came to pass in the morning, that David wrote a letter to Joab, and sent it by the hand of Uriah.

And he wrote in the letter, saying, Set ye Uriah in the forefront of the hottest battle, and retire ye from him, that he may be smitten, and die.

And it came to pass, when Joab observed the city, that he assigned Uriah unto a place where he knew that valiant men were.

And the men of the city went out, and fought with Joab: and there fell some of the people of the servants of David; and Uriah the Hittite died also. (11:12–17)

188. "David espies Bath-Sheba at her bath." An illuminated initial letter "B" at the beginning of the 13th-century so-called Saint Louis Psalter (at the Bibliothèque Nationale, Paris). In the lower section, David is shown praying to God.

And it came to pass after this, that Absalom the son of David had a fair sister, whose name was Tamar; and Amnon the son of David loved her.

And Amnon was so vexed that he fell sick for his sister Tamar; for she was a virgin; and Amnon thought it hard for him to do any thing to her.

But Amnon had a friend, whose name was Jonadab, the son of Shimeah David's brother: and Jonadab was a very subtil man.

And he said unto him, Why are thou, being the king's son, lean from day to day? wilt thou not tell me? And Amnon said unto him, I love Tamar, my brother Absalom's sister.

And Jonadab said unto him, Lay thee down on thy bed, and make thyself sick: and when they father cometh to see thee, say unto him, I pray thee, let my sister Tamar come, and give me meat, and dress the meat in my sight, that I may see it, and eat it at her hand.

(13:1–5)

189

189. Women mourning, from a tomb painting from a 10th century B.C. Egyptian tomb. Mourning customs common to the peoples of the Middle East include placing ashes on one's head and rending one's clothes.

And when she had brought them unto him to eat, he took hold of her, and said unto her, Come lie with me, my sister. (13:11)

Howbeit he would not hearken unto her voice: but, being stronger than she, forced her, and lay with her.

Then Amnon hated her exceedingly; so that the hatred wherewith he hated her was greater than the love wherewith he had loved her. And Amnon said unto her, Arise, be gone.

And she said unto him, There is no cause: this evil in sending me away is greater than the other that thou didst unto me. But he would not hearken unto her.

Then he called his servant that ministered unto him, and said, Put now this woman out from me, and bolt the door after her.

And she had a garment of divers colours upon her: for with such robes were the king's daughters that were virgins apparelled. Then his servant brought her out, and bolted the door after her.

And Tamar put ashes on her head, and rent her garment of divers colours that was on her, and laid her hand on her head, and went on crying.

(13:14–19)

So the people went out into the field against Israel: and the battle was in the wood of Ephraim;

Where the people of Israel were slain before the servants of David, and there was there a great slaughter that day of twenty thousand men.

For the battle was there scattered over the face of all the country: and the wood devoured more people that day than the sword devoured.

And Absalom met the servants of David. And Absalom rode upon a mule, and the mule went under the thick boughs of a great oak, and his head caught hold of the oak, and he was taken up between the heaven and the earth; and the mule that was under him went away.

And a certain man saw it, and told Joab, and said, Behold, I saw Absalom hanged in an oak.

And Joab said unto the man that told him, And, behold, thou sawest him, and why didst thou not smite him there to the ground? and I would have given thee ten shekels of silver, and a girdle.

And the man said unto Joab, Though I should receive a thousand shekels of silver in mine hand, yet would I not put forth mine hand against the king's son: for in our hearing the king charged thee and Abishai and Ittai, saying, Beware that none touch the young man Absalom.

Otherwise I should have wrought falsehood against mine own life: for there is no matter hid from the king, and thou thyself wouldest have set thyself against me.

Then said Joab, I may not tarry thus with thee. And he took three darts in his hand, and thrust them through the heart of Absalom, while he was yet alive in the midst of the oak.

And ten young men that bare Joab's armour compassed about and smote Absalom, and slew him.

And Joab blew the trumpet, and the people returned from pursuing after Israel: for Joab held back the people.

And they took Absalom and cast him into a great pit in the wood, and laid a very great heap of stones upon him: and all Israel fled every one to his tent.

Now Absalom in his lifetime had taken and reared up for himself a pillar, which is in the king's dale: for he said, I have no son to keep my name in remembrance: and he called the pillar after his own name: and it is called unto this day, Absalom's place.

(18:6–18)

190. The death of Absalom from the *León San Isidoro Bible*, Spain, 1162 (Catedra de San Isidoro, León).

191. This remarkable edifice in the Kidron Valley is held by popular tradition to be Absalom's tomb.
Absalom was buried in the monument which he had built for himself in the Kidron Valley, also called the "Kings' Valley," because it had a royal garden watered from the Gihon Pool. It was customary for rulers in antiquity to build their tombs in their lifetime. The "pillar" erected by Absalom is believed to have been some kind of obelisk to mark the site of his tomb.
The monument shown here is a burial vault cut out of the rock, consisting of tombs and superstructures, dating from the first century B.C. in the Second Temple period. It is, thus, nearly a thousand years later than the time of Absalom.
For many centuries Jews and Moslems used to throw stones at the monument associated with Absalom, because he rebelled against his father. Jewish fathers in Jerusalem whose sons were disobedient would take them there to show them how everyone despised King David's rebellious son and threw stones at his tomb. In the course of time the stones almost hid the monument. They were removed in this century.

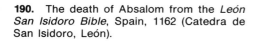

190

191

And he went through all the tribes of Israel unto Abel, and to Beth-maachah, and all the Berites: and they were gathered together, and went also after him.

And they came and besieged him in Abel of Beth-maachah, and they cast up a bank against the city, and it stood in the trench: and all the people that were with Joab battered the wall, to throw it down.

Then cried a wise woman out of the city, Hear, hear; say, I pray you, unto Joab, Come near hither, that I may speak with thee.

And when he was come near unto her, the woman said, Art thou Joab? And he answered, I am he. Then she said unto him, Hear the words of thine handmaid. And he answered, I do hear.

Then she spake, saying, They were wont to speak in old time, saying, They shall surely ask counsel at Abel: and so they ended the matter.

I am one of them that are peaceable and faithful in Israel: thou seekest to destroy a city and a mother in Israel: why wilt thou swallow up the inheritance of the LORD?

And Joab answered and said, Far be it, far be it from me, that I should swallow up or destroy.

The matter is not so: but a man of mount Ephraim, Sheba the son of Bichri by name, hath lifted up his hand against the king, even against David: deliver him only, and I will depart from the city. And the woman said unto Joab, Behold, his head shall be thrown to thee over the wall.

Then the woman went unto all the people in her wisdom. And they cut off the head of Sheba the son of Bichri, and cast it out to Joab. And he blew a trumpet, and they retired from the city, every man to his tent. And Joab returned to Jerusalem unto the king.

(20:14–22)

And David longed, and said, Oh that one would give me drink of the water of the well of Bethlehem, which is by the gate!

And the three mighty men brake through the host of the Philistines, and drew water out of the well of Bethlehem, that was by the gate, and took it, and brought it to David: nevertheless he would not drink thereof, but poured it out unto the LORD.

And he said, Be it far from me, O LORD, that I should do this: is not this the blood of the men that went in jeopardy of their lives? therefore he would not drink it. These things did these three mighty men.

(23:15–17)

192. View of the Huleh Valley, with Mount Hermon in the background. This is the region where the towns of Abel and Beth-maachah were located.

193. King David's Wells, just outside Bethlehem. These are cisterns excavated in the rock, which tradition identifies with "the well of Bethlehem, which is by the gate," from which David longed to drink.

And Jonathan answered and said to Adonijah, Verily our lord king David hath made Solomon king.

And the king hath sent with him Zadok the priest, and Nathan the prophet, and Benaiah the son of Jehoiada, and the Cherethites, and the Pelethites, and they have caused him to ride upon the king's mule:

And Zadok the priest and Nathan the prophet have anointed him king in Gihon: and they are come up from thence rejoicing, so that the city rang again. This is the noise that ye have heard.

And also Solomon sitteth on the throne of the kingdom.

And moreover the king's servants came to bless our lord king David, saying, God make the name of Solomon better than thy name, and make his throne greater than thy throne. And the king bowed himself upon the bed.

And also thus said the king, Blessed be the LORD God of Israel, which hath given one to sit on my throne this day, mine eyes even seeing it.

And all the guests that were with Adonijah were afraid, and rose up, and went every man his way.

And Adonijah feared because of Solomon, and arose, and went, and caught hold on the horns of the altar.

(1:43–50)

194. The Spring of Gihon. This is the oldest known water source in Jerusalem. Fed by sources deep in the nearby hills, it gushes out in the Kidron Valley. This spring, a rarity in the arid Judean region, attracted the Amorites and the Jebusites, who established settlements nearby.
Archaeological excavations indicate that it was probably the Jebusites who sank a shaft to the bottom of the pool in order to provide direct access to it from the city itself.

195

195. The traditional tomb of King David on Mount Zion – one of the most revered holy places in Judaism.
Although it is doubtful whether this was indeed the place of King David's burial, it must have been a hallowed site, for it was here that one of the first synagogues was erected after the fall of Jerusalem in A.D. 70. It has been called King David's Tomb since the 12th century.
A Jewish traveler from Spain, Benjamin of Tudela, who visited Jerusalem in 1173, records the story of how the tomb was revealed: Fifteen years earlier a wall of the church that was on Mount Zion collapsed and it was decided to rebuild the church with "the stones of the holy walls." The workmen lifted a stone and uncovered the entrance of a cave. Curious to see if there was a treasure in the cave, two workmen went inside and came upon a great palace. The two men rushed towards the palace when a sudden gust of wind came from the mouth of the cave crying with the voice of a man: "Rise and go hence, for God doth not desire to show it to man."

Now the days of David drew nigh that he should die; and he charged Solomon his son, saying,

I go the way of all the earth: be thou strong therefore, and shew thyself a man;

And keep the charge of the LORD thy God, to walk in his ways, to keep his statutes, and his commandments, and his judgments, and his testimonies, as it is written in the law of Moses, that thou mayest prosper in all that thou doest, and whithersoever thou turnest thyself:

That the LORD may continue his word which he spake concerning me, saying, If thy children take heed to their way, to walk before me in truth with all their heart and with all their soul, there shall not fail thee (said he) a man on the throne of Israel.

Moreover thou knowest also what Joab the son of Zeruiah did to me, and what he did to the two captains of the hosts of Israel, unto Abner the son of Ner, and unto Amasa the son of Jether, whom he slew, and shed the blood of war in peace, and put the blood of war upon his girdle that was about his loins, and in his shoes that were on his feet.

Do therefore according to thy wisdom, and let not his hoar head go down to the grave in peace.

But shew kindness unto the sons of Barzillai the Gileadite, and let them be of those that eat at thy table: for so they came to me when I fled because of Absalom thy brother.

And behold, thou hast with thee Shimei the son of Gera, a Benjamite of Bahurim, which cursed me with a grievous curse in the day when I went to Mahanaim: but he came down to meet me at Jordan, and I sware to him by the LORD, saying, I will not put thee to death with the sword.

Now therefore hold him not guiltless: for thou art a wise man, and knowest what thou oughtest to do unto him; but his hoar head bring thou down to the grave with blood.

So David slept with his fathers, and was buried in the city of David.

And the days that David reigned over Israel were forty years: seven years reigned he in Hebron, and thirty and three years reigned he in Jerusalem.

Then sat Solomon upon the throne of David his father; and his kingdom was established greatly.

(2:1–12)

And Solomon loved the LORD, walking in the statutes of David his father: only he sacrificed and burnt incense in high places.

And the king went to Gibeon to sacrifice there; for that was the great high place: a thousand burnt offerings did Solomon offer upon that altar.

In Gibeon the LORD appeared to Solomon in a dream by night: and God said, Ask what I shall give thee.

And Solomon said, Thou hast shewed unto thy servant David my father great mercy, according as he walked before thee in truth, and in righteousness, and in uprightness of heart with thee; and thou has kept for him this great kindness, that thou hast given him a son to sit on his throne, as it is this day.

And now, O LORD my God, thou hast made thy servant king instead of David my father: and I am but a little child: I know not how to go out or come in.

And thy servant is in the midst of thy people which thou hast chosen, a great people, that cannot be numbered nor counted for multitude.

Give therefore thy servant an understanding heart to judge thy people, that I may discern between good and bad: for who is able to judge this thy so great a people?

And the speech pleased the LORD, that Solomon had asked this thing.

And God said unto him, Because thou hast asked this thing, and hast not asked for thyself long life; neither hast asked riches for thyself, nor hast asked the life of thine enemies; but hast asked for thyself understanding to discern judgment;

Behold, I have done according to thy words: lo, I have given thee a wise and an understanding heart; so that there was none like thee before thee, neither after thee shall any arise like unto thee.

And I have also given thee that which thou has not asked, both riches, and honour: so that there shall not be any among the kings like unto thee all thy days.

And if thou wilt walk in my ways, to keep my statutes and my commandments, as thy father David did walk, then I will lengthen thy days.

And Solomon awoke; and, behold, it was a dream. And he came to Jerusalem, and stood before the ark of the covenant of the LORD, and offered up burnt offerings, and offered peace offerings, and made a feast to all his servants.

(3:3–15)

196. Gibeon, where there was a great high place and an altar where King Solomon offered a sacrifice and prayed for wisdom.
This was one of the most ancient Canaanite cities. The site is a short distance west of Jerusalem, on the way to Beth-Horon. It was "greater than Ai, and all the men thereof were mighty," it is told in Joshua 10:2.
The site was excavated in the 1950s and 1960s and with the exception of traces of settlement in the Late Bronze Age, all the remains at the site are of the Iron Age and later periods. The main discoveries were fortifications, a large pool, two water tunnels, wine cellars, some houses and a large amount of epigraphic material which confirms the identification of the site.

And Judah and Israel dwelt safely, every man under his vine and under his fig tree, from Dan even to Beer-sheba, all the days of Solomon.

And Solomon had forty thousand stalls of horses for his chariots, and twelve thousand horsemen.

And those officers provided victual for king Solomon, and for all that came unto king Solomon's table, every man in his month: they lacked nothing.

Barley also and straw for the horses and dromedaries brought they unto the place where the officers were, every man according to his charge.

(4:25–28)

197

197. The so-called King Solomon's Stables beneath the southeastern corner of the Temple Mount, a vaulted area of about 5000 square feet, supported by 88 pillars divided in 12 rows. The lower portion of the outer wall goes back to Herod's time, and was probably built to reinforce the structures of the Solomonic period. Whether these were Solomon's stables or not is uncertain. They were certainly used as stables by the Crusader kings of Jerusalem and the Templars in the 12th century.

198. A Phoenician coin minted in the city of Tyre, decorated with representations of owls and dolphins. Dolphins were especially popular among seafaring people, who admired them for their speed, strength, intelligence and playfulness, just as we do today.
The Phoenician god Melkart – the patron god of Tyre – is also represented on Phoenician coins. He is depicted as a bearded man holding a bow and arrow. Mounted on a winged horse with a fish's tail, he rides over the waves of the open sea. This was probably meant to symbolize the skill of the Phoenicians in seafaring.
When the ancient Hebrews began to settle in the Promised Land, about 1200 B.C., they found it inhabited by nations which were called, collectively, "Canaanites." The Canaanites were gradually subjugated by the Israelites in the north and the west. What is now Lebanon was inhabited by the Phoenicians, who built a number of great cities along the coast, the most important of which were the seaports of Tyre and Sidon. These flourishing cities were major centers of commerce. The Phoenicians were great international traders throughout the ancient Mediterranean, and Phoenician colonies were founded around its coasts – among these the most famous was Carthage.

And Hiram king of Tyre sent his servants unto Solomon; for he had heard that they had anointed him king in the room of his father: for Hiram was ever a lover of David.

And Solomon sent to Hiram, saying,

Thou knowest how that David my father could not build an house unto the name of the LORD his God for the wars which were about him on every side, until the LORD put them under the soles of his feet.

But now the LORD my God hath given me rest on every side, so that there is neither adversary nor evil occurrent.

And, behold, I purpose to build an house unto the name of the LORD my God, as the LORD spake unto David my father, saying, Thy son, whom I will set upon thy throne in thy room, he shall build an house unto my name.

Now therefore command thou that they hew me cedar trees out of Lebanon; and my servants shall be with thy servants: and unto thee will I give hire for thy servants according to all that thou shalt appoint: for thou knowest that there is not among us any that can skill to hew timber like unto the Sidonians.

198

And it came to pass, when Hiram heard the words of Solomon, that he rejoiced greatly, and said, Blessed be the LORD this day, which hath given unto David a wise son over this great people.

And Hiram sent to Solomon, saying, I have considered the things which thou sentest to me for: and I will do all thy desire concerning timber of cedar, and concerning timber of fir.

My servants shall bring them down from Lebanon unto the sea: and I will convey them by sea in floats unto the place that thou shalt appoint me, and will cause them to be discharged there, and thou shalt receive them: and thou shalt accomplish my desire, in giving food for my household.

So Hiram gave Solomon cedar trees and fir trees according to all his desire.

(5:1–10)

199

199. A view of Sidon today.

And it came to pass in the four hundred and eightieth year after the children of Israel were come out of the land of Egypt, in the fourth year of Solomon's reign over Israel, in the month Zif, which is the second month, that he began to build the house of the LORD.

And the house which king Solomon built for the LORD, the length thereof was threescore cubits, and the breadth thereof twenty cubits, and the height thereof thirty cubits.

And the porch before the temple of the house, twenty cubits was the length thereof, according to the breadth of the house: and ten cubits was the breadth thereof before the house.

And for the house he made windows of narrow lights.

And against the wall of the house he built chambers round about, against the walls of the house round about, both of the temple and of the oracle: and he made chambers round about:

The nethermost chamber was five cubits broad, and the middle was six cubits broad, and the third was seven cubits broad: for without in the wall of the house he made narrowed rests round about, that the beams should not be fastened in the walls of the house.

And the house, when it was in building, was built of stone made ready before it was brought thither: so that there was neither hammer nor axe nor any tool of iron heard in the house, while it was in building.

The door for the middle chamber was in the right side of the house: and they went up with winding stairs into the middle chamber, and out of the middle into the third.

So he built the house, and finished it; and covered the house with beams and boards of cedar.

(6:1–9)

200. Model of the First Temple according to the plans of Père Roland de Vaux (Israel Museum, Jerusalem).
The descriptions of the structure of the Temple as given in the Bible do not include enough details to enable a precise reconstruction of Solomon's Temple, and those that are given can be interpreted in various ways. Some scholars have even resorted to emendation of the biblical text to obtain a more "logical" arrangement or in order to fit their architectural notions. There have thus been several different proposals for the reconstruction of the Temple of Solomon, and that of de Vaux (one of those who emended the text) pictured here is only one.
The Temple was composed of three sections: the vestibule or porch, the Holy Place where the Lampstand and the Shewbread Table

200

(Now Hiram the king of Tyre had furnished Solomon with cedar trees and fir trees, and with gold, according to all his desire,) that then king Solomon gave Hiram twenty cities in the land of Galilee.   (9:11)

And this is the reason of the levy which king Solomon raised; for to build the house of the LORD, and his own house, and Millo, and the wall of Jerusalem, and Hazor, and Megiddo, and Gezer.

For Pharaoh king of Egypt had gone up, and taken Gezer, and burnt it with fire, and slain the Canaanites that dwelt in the city, and given it for a present unto his daughter, Solomon's wife.

And Solomon built Gezer, and Beth-horon the nether,

And Baalath, and Tadmor in the wilderness, in the land,

And all the cities of store that Solomon had, and cities for his chariots, and cities for his horsemen, and that which Solomon desired to build in Jerusalem, and in Lebanon, and in all the land of his dominion.

were placed, and the Holy of Holies where the Ark of the Covenant containing the Tables of the Law was placed.
The basic plan of Solomon's Temple has its parallels in other sanctuaries excavated in the region.
Upon Solomon's completion of the Temple, Jerusalem became the unique spiritual center for the united kingdom of Israel to which all Israel made pilgrimage three times a year. Henceforth all the kings of Judah (and Israel) are evaluated according to their attitude to the "high places" which rivalled the unity of worship at the Temple and the chosen city, Jerusalem.
Destruction of the Temple by Nebuchadnezzar and the carrying away of its vessels to Babylonia in 586 B.C. marked the end of an epoch.

201

202

203

204

And all the people that were left of the Amorites, Hittites, Perizzites, Hivites, and Jebusites, which were not of the children of Israel.

Their children that were left after them in the land whom the children of Israel also were not able utterly to destroy, upon those did Solomon levy a tribute of bondservice unto this day.

But of the children of Israel did Solomon make no bondmen: but they were men of war, and his servants, and his princes, and his captains, and rulers of his chariots, and his horsemen.

These were the chief of the officers that were over Solomon's work, five hundred and fifty, which bare rule over the people that wrought in the work.

But Pharaoh's daughter came up out of the city of David unto her house which Solomon had built for her: then did he build Millo.

And three times in a year did Solomon offer burnt offerings and peace offerings upon the altar which he built unto the LORD, and he burnt incense upon the altar that was before the LORD. So he finished the house.

And king Solomon made a navy of ships in Ezion-geber, which is beside Eloth, on the shore of the Red sea, in the land of Edom.

And Hiram sent in the navy his servants, shipmen that had knowledge of the sea, with the servants of Solomon.

And they came to Ophir, and fetched from thence gold, four hundred and twenty talents, and brought it to king Solomon.   (9:15–28)

205

206

And all king Solomon's drinking vessels were of gold, and all the vessels of the house of the forest of Lebanon were of pure gold; none were of silver: it was nothing accounted of in the days of Solomon.

For the king had at sea a navy of Tharshish with the navy of Hiram: once in three years came the navy of Tharshish, bringing gold, and silver, ivory, and apes, and peacocks.

So king Solomon exceeded all the kings of the earth for riches and for wisdom.

And all the earth sought to Solomon, to hear his wisdom, which God had put in his heart.

(10:21–24)

And the man Jeroboam was a mighty man of valour: and Solomon seeing the young man that he was industrious, he made him ruler over all the charge of the house of Joseph.

And it came to pass at that time when Jeroboam went out of Jerusalem, that the prophet Ahijah the Shilonite found him in the way; and he had clad himself with a new garment; and they two were alone in the field:

And Ahijah caught the new garment that was on him and rent it in twelve pieces:

And he said to Jeroboam, Take thee ten pieces: for thus saith the LORD, the God of Israel, Behold, I will rend the kingdom out of the hand of Solomon, and will give ten tribes to thee:

(But he shall have one tribe for my servant David's sake, and for Jerusalem's sake, the city which I have chosen out of all the tribes of Israel:)

Because that they have forsaken me, and have worshipped Ashtoreth the goddess of the Zidonians, Chemosh the god of the Moabites, and Milcom the god of the children of Ammon, and have not walked in my ways, to do that which is right in mine eyes, and to keep my statutes and my judgments, as did David his father.

Howbeit I will not take the whole kingdom out of his hand: but I will make him prince all the days of his life for David my servant's sake, whom I chose, because he kept my commandments and my statutes:

But I will take the kingdom out of his son's hand, and will give it unto thee, even ten tribes.

208

201. Remains of ancient Hazor. Commanding a pass at the point where trade routes from the north, east and west joined to enter northern Canaan, Hazor was an important city from early times. Texts of the 18th century B.C. from Mari on the river Euphrates show that Hazor had close political and economic ties with Mesopotamia; one refers to the export of tin.
Hazor was under Egyptian dominion from the 15th century B.C., but in the following centuries it was unique among the Canaanite city-states and its ruler bore the title "king" and was responsible for other cities. At the time of Joshua, it was said that "Hazor beforetime was the head of all those kingdoms" (Joshua 11:10).

202. Remains of ancient Megiddo with Mount Megiddo in the background overlooking the Valley of Jezreel.
This was an important fortress in the reign of Solomon, one of the principal bulwarks in the defense of his kingdom. Its position at the head of the most important pass through the Carmel range gave Megiddo control of the Way of the Sea, the ancient trade-route between Egypt and the east. Traders from all over the known world, as well as invading armies, passed through Megiddo. It was a strongly fortified city before 3000 B.C.
Solomon fortified the city and excavations have brought to light many relics from this period. Shown here are the remains of a columned portico, part of the fortress of the Solomonic period.
In the 7th century B.C., Megiddo inexplicably lost all importance and by the 4th century B.C. it was uninhabited and never resettled.

203. The site of ancient Gezer, another important city at the junction of two trade routes in antiquity. The Way of the Sea, the main trade link between Egypt and Mesopotamia, passed to the west, and to the north was the road between Jerusalem and the coast. The rulers of Gezer had the power to disrupt all communications.
Gezer was settled as far back as the 4th millennium B.C. and developed into a fortified

city. It was destroyed by Pharaoh Tuthmose III, c. 1468 B.C. and remained under Egyptian control.
When Solomon married the king of Egypt's daughter, Gezer was given to him as her dowry.

204. The inscription on this ostracon refers to a consignment of gold from Ophir. Where that land was nobody knows. It may have been India, an island in the Red Sea, Arabia, East Africa or even Sumatra. Most scholars, however, suggest Arabia as being the most likely.

205. A view of Jezirat Far'un – Pharaoh's Island – in the Gulf of Elath. It is also known as the Coral Island, and it has sometimes been identified as being the Ezion-geber of the Bible, the home port of King Solomon's fleet of ships voyaging to Ophir and back.

206. Canaanite merchant ship, prototype of the Tarshish Ship, c. 1400 B.C. Reconstructed according to a drawing in the tomb of Qenamon, governor of Thebes under Amenhotep III (National Maritime Museum, Haifa).

207. A Hebrew seal found at Megiddo. It shows a lion and an inscription which reads: "To Shema Servant of Jeroboam."

208. Bronze amulet showing a baboon, found at Megiddo.

209. View of the site of Samaria, the capital of the kingdom of Israel. The city was built on a hill overlooking the surrounding fertile plain at a strategic point dominating the way to the coastal plain in the west, the road east to Shechem and from there to the Jordan or to Jerusalem; and the road north, toward Megiddo and the Jezreel Valley.
The hill was purchased by Omri from a man named Shemer, hence the name of the city in Hebrew: Shomron. Ahab continued Omri's initiative, but it was Jeroboam who gave Samaria its greatest days. To the prophets Hosea and Amos, the luxuries of Samaria became the symbol of decadent arrogance.

210. The Cave of Elijah, on the slope of Mount Carmel. It is reputed to be one of the places in which the prophet took refuge to avoid persecution by the king and queen. It is a holy place to Jews, Christians and Moslems alike.
Some people believe that mental disorders can be relieved by a few days' stay in this shrine.
Elijah is a legendary hero in written and oral folk literature. He is portrayed as a heavenly emissary sent to combat social injustice. He rights wrongs and punishes the unjust, regardless of their status. In rabbinical literature he appears as the herald of the future redemption of Israel and of the messianic era. The Moslems call him "el-Khader" – the

And unto his son will I give one tribe, that David my servant may have a light alway before me in Jerusalem, the city which I have chosen me to put my name there.

And I will take thee, and thou shalt reign according to all that thy soul desireth, and shalt be king over Israel.

And it shall be, if thou wilt hearken unto all that I command thee, and wilt walk in my ways, and do that is right in my sight, to keep my statutes and my commandments, as David my servant did; that I will be with thee, and build thee a sure house, as I built for David, and will give Israel unto thee.

(11:28–38)

In the thirty and first year of Asa king of Judah began Omri to reign over Israel, twelve years: six years reigned he in Tirzah.

And he bought the hill Samaria of Shemer for two talents of silver, and built on the hill, and called the name of the city which he built, after the name of Shemer, owner of the hill, Samaria.

But Omri wrought evil in the eyes of the LORD, and did worse than all that were before him.

For he walked in all the way of Jeroboam the son of Nebat, and in his sin wherewith he made Israel to sin, to provoke the LORD God of Israel to anger with their vanities.

Now the rest of the acts of Omri which he did, and his might that he shewed, are they not written in the book of the chronicles of the kings of Israel?

So Omri slept with his fathers, and was buried in Samaria: and Ahab his son reigned in his stead.

And in the thirty and eighth year of Asa king of Judah began Ahab the son of Omri to reign over Israel: and Ahab the son of Omri reigned over Israel in Samaria twenty and two years.

And Ahab the son of Omri did evil in the sight of the LORD above all that were before him.

And it came to pass, as if it had been a light thing for him to walk in the sins of Jeroboam the son of Nebat, that he took to wife Jezebel the daughter of Ethbaal king of the Zidonians, and went and served Baal, and worshipped him.

And he reared up an altar for Baal in the house of Baal, which he had built in Samaria.

(16:23–32)

Was it not told my lord what I did when Jezebel slew the prophets of the LORD, how I hid an hundred men of the LORD's prophets by fifty in a cave, and fed them with bread and water?

And now thou sayest, Go, tell thy lord, Behold, Elijah is here: and he shall slay me.

And Elijah said, As the LORD of hosts liveth, before whom I stand, I will surely shew myself unto him to day.

So Obadiah went to meet Ahab, and told him: and Ahab went to meet Elijah.

And it came to pass, when Ahab saw Elijah, that Ahab said unto him, Art thou he that troubleth Israel?

And he answered, I have not troubled Israel; but thou, and thy father's house, in that ye have forsaken the commandments of the LORD, and thou hast followed Baalim.

Now therefore send, and gather to me all Israel unto mount Carmel, and the prophets of Baal four hundred and fifty, and the prophets of the groves four hundred, which eat at Jezebel's table.

So Ahab sent unto all the children of Israel, and gathered the prophets together unto mount Carmel.

And Elijah came unto all the people, and said, How long halt ye between two opinions? if the LORD be God, follow him: but if Baal, then follow him. And the people answered him not a word.

(18:13–21)

211

Green One — because his memory is alive and evergreen in the tradition of the people.

211. A seal made of quartzite and incised with several symbols; a sphinx and an *ankh* (Egyptian life sign) in the upper half, a winged sun below, and a falcon flanked by two serpents. The seal is inscribed in Phoenician; *izbl*, which some scholars identify as the name of Ahab's queen Jezebel. Seals bearing the owner's name were common in ancient Israel and the Near East.

210

212

212. A cave on Mount Carmel, near Haifa, a spur in the mountain range that overlooks the Bay of Haifa. On Mount Carmel, the prophet Elijah challenged the priests of Baal to a contest, to prove whose God was real.
Mount Carmel was renowned for its fertility. In ancient times it was covered with vineyards, hence its name, which is believed to be a contraction of the Hebrew *Kerem El*, "Vineyard of God."
Christian Arabs call it Jabal Mar Elias – the Mount of St. Elijah. The monastic order founded here is called Carmelite, and Elijah is its patron.
Mount Carmel, whose luxuriant green peak stands out clearly above the blue bay, was a symbol of beauty in ancient times. In the Song of Songs, the beloved is praised thus: "Thy head upon thee is like Carmel..." "And the hair of thy head like purple" also suggests Mount Carmel, for in the olden days purple dye was prepared at the foot of the mountain from the shells collected from the sea in its vicinity.

And Ahab told Jezebel all that Elijah had done, and withal how he had slain all the prophets with the sword.

Then Jezebel sent a messenger unto Elijah, saying, So let the gods do to me, and more also, if I make not thy life as the life of one of them by to morrow about this time.

And when he saw that, he arose, and went for his life, and came to Beersheba, which belongeth to Judah, and left his servant there.

But he himself went a day's journey into the wilderness, and came and sat down under a juniper tree: and he requested for himself that he might die; and said, It is enough; now, O LORD, take away my life; for I am not better than my fathers.

And as he lay and slept under a juniper tree, behold, then an angel touched him, and said unto him, Arise and eat.

And he looked, and, behold, there was a cake baken on the coals, and a cruse of water at his head. And he did eat and drink, and laid him down again. (19:1–6)

213. "The desert broom" *(Retama roetam)*, a shrub which grows in the gullies of the southern Negev and in the Sinai Peninsula. Occasionally it is tall enough to provide shade for a human being. Its thick roots are still used for fuel by the Bedouin, as in ancient times. The "juniper tree" is given as *rotem* in the Hebrew Bible and this is the bush shown here.

And it came to pass after these things, that Naboth the Jezreelite had a vineyard, which was in Jezreel, hard by the palace of Ahab king of Samaria.

And Ahab spake unto Naboth, saying, Give me thy vineyard, that I may have it for a garden of herbs, because it is near unto my house: and I will give thee for it a better vineyard than it; or, if it seem good to thee, I will give thee the worth of it in money.

And Naboth said to Ahab, The LORD forbid it me, that I should give the inheritance of my fathers unto thee.

And Ahab came into his house heavy and displeased because of the word which Naboth the Jezreelite had spoken to him: for he had said, I will not give thee the inheritance of my fathers. And he laid him down upon his bed, and turned away his face, and would eat no bread.

But Jezebel his wife came to him, and said unto him, Why is thy spirit so sad, that thou eatest no bread?

And he said unto her, Because I spake unto Naboth the Jezreelite, and said unto him, Give me thy vineyard for money; or else, if it please thee, I will give thee another vineyard for it: and he answered, I will not give thee my vineyard.

And Jezebel his wife said unto him, Dost thou now govern the kingdom of Israel? arise, and eat bread, and let thine heart be merry: I will give thee the vineyard of Naboth the Jezreelite.

(21:1–7)

Then they sent to Jezebel, saying, Naboth is stoned, and is dead.

And it came to pass, when Jezebel heard that Naboth was stoned, and was dead, that Jezebel said to Ahab, Arise, take possession of the vineyard of Naboth the Jezreelite, which he refused to give thee for money: for Naboth is not alive, but dead.

And it came to pass, when Ahab heard that Naboth was dead, that Ahab rose up to go down to the vineyard of Naboth the Jezreelite, to take possession of it.

(21:14–16)

214. A view of the Plain of Jezreel, which extends across the breadth of the country, between Mount Carmel, Mount Gilboa and the hills of lower Galilee. The Kishon River flows through its whole length to the Mediterranean.

The Plain of Jezreel takes its name from one of the important cities of the kingdom of Solomon. Ahab had a palace there. The descendants of Ahab were slain at Jezreel (II Kings 10:7).

From early times, the valley, known later as the Plain of Ezdraelon or the Great Valley, was of great importance to communications between the coast and the countries to the north and east. It is a fertile region and was the granary of Palestine in all periods.

215. A vineyard in the Plain of Jezreel.

214

215

216

Now the rest of the acts of Ahab, and all that he did, and the ivory house which he made, and all the cities that he built, are they not written in the book of the chronicles of the kings of Israel?

So Ahab slept with his fathers; and Ahaziah his son reigned in his stead.

And Jehoshaphat the son of Asa began to reign over Judah in the fourth year of Ahab king of Israel.

(22:39–41)

217

218

And the sons of the prophets that were at Jericho came to Elisha, and said unto him, Knowest thou that the LORD will take away thy master from thy head to day? And he anwered, Yea, I know it; hold ye your peace.

And Elijah said unto him, Tarry, I pray thee, here; for the LORD hath sent me to Jordan. And he said, As the LORD liveth, and as thy soul liveth, I will not leave thee. And they two went on.

And fifty men of the sons of the prophets went, and stood to view afar off: and they two stood by Jordan.

And Elijah took his mantle, and wrapped it together, and smote the waters, and they were divided hither and thither, so that they two went over on dry ground.

And it came to pass, when they were gone over, that Elijah said unto Elisha, Ask what I shall do for thee, before I be taken away from thee. And Elisha said, I pray thee, let a double portion of thy spirit be upon me.

And he said, Thou hast asked a hard thing: nevertheless, if thou see me when I am taken from thee, it shall be so unto thee; but if not, it shall not be so.

And it came to pass, as they still went on, and talked, that, behold, there appeared a chariot of fire, and horses of fire, and parted them both asunder; and Elijah went up by a whirlwind into heaven.

And Elisha saw it, and he cried, My father, my father, the chariot of Israel, and the horsemen thereof. And he saw him no more: and he took hold of his own clothes, and rent them in two pieces.

He took up also the mantle of Elijah that fell from him, and went back, and stood by the bank of Jordan;

And he took the mantle of Elijah that fell from him, and smote the waters, and said, Where is the LORD God of Elijah? and when he also had smitten the waters, they parted hither and thither: and Elisha went over.

216–218. Carved ivories from Samaria and Hazor of the 9th century B.C.
Fragments of exquisite carved ivories were found in archaeological excavations at Samaria. They were probably wall and furniture ornaments. They support the biblical reference to King Ahab's "house of ivory." The decorative motifs indicate Egyptian and Phoenician influences and some fragments bear inscriptions in ancient Hebrew script.

219. View of the Jordan Valley and Jericho area.

219

220

221

220. Elisha's Spring near Jericho.

221. Sartaba, a hill overlooking the Jordan River, which tradition identifies as the place from which Elijah "went up by a whirlwind into heaven."

And when the sons of the prophets which were to view at Jericho saw him, they said, The spirit of Elijah doth rest on Elisha. And they came to meet him, and bowed themselves to the ground before him.

And they said unto him, Behold now, there be with thy servants fifty strong men; let them go, we pray thee, and seek thy master: lest peradventure the Spirit of the LORD hath taken him up, and cast him upon some mountain, or into some valley. And he said, Ye shall not send.

And when they urged him till he was ashamed, he said, Send. They sent therefore fifty men; and they sought three days, but found him not.

And when they came again to him, (for he tarried at Jericho,) he said unto them, Did I not say unto you, Go not?

And the men of the city said unto Elisha, Behold, I pray thee, the situation of this city is pleasant, as my lord seeth: but the water is naught, and the ground barren.

And he said, Bring me a new cruse, and put salt therein. And they brought it to him.

And he went forth unto the spring of the waters, and cast the salt in there, and said, Thus saith the LORD, I have healed these waters; there shall not be from thence any more death or barren land.

So the waters were healed unto this day, according to the saying of Elisha which he spake.

(2:5–22)

222

222. The Stele of Mesha, the Moabite king, found at Dibon in the Negev.

The inscription describes Mesha's wars against Israel, and his reconstruction of the cities of Moab after the revolt (c. 852 B.C.). The inscription is in a Moabite dialect but written in the ancient Canaanite/Hebrew script, and dates from the middle of the 9th century B.C. Mesha recounts the subjection of Moab to Israel in the reign of Omri and his son, and his country's liberation after a bitter struggle. He boasts of his victorious exploits, of his savagery to his foes, and lists the cities he has built, the gates and towers he has erected, the cisterns he has dug, and the roads he has constructed.

The revolt of Mesha is one of the few events described in the Bible which are supported by non-biblical records.

The Moabites were a Semitic people that settled east of the Jordan River in the 14th century B.C., shortly before the Israelites came to Canaan. Enmity with Israel grew out of the struggle over disputed areas.

Saul fought Moab and David completed the conquest, but there were friendly relations between Moab and Israel during the reign of Solomon. Moab regained its independence after the division of Solomon's kingdom. Omri reconquered it, and Ahab (874–852 B.C.) consolidated Israelite rule over it.

And Mesha king of Moab was a sheepmaster, and rendered unto the king of Israel an hundred thousand lambs, and an hundred thousand rams, with the wool.

But it came to pass, when Ahab was dead, that the king of Moab rebelled against the king of Israel.

And king Jehoram went out of Samaria the same time, and numbered all Israel. (3:4–6)

And when all the Moabites heard that the kings were come up to fight against them, they gathered all that were able to put on armour, and upward, and stood in the border.

And they rose up early in the morning, and the sun shone upon the water, and the Moabites saw the water on the other side as red as blood:

And they said, This is blood: the kings are surely slain, and they have smitten one another: now therefore, Moab, to the spoil.

And when they came to the camp of Israel, the Israelites rose up and smote the Moabites, so that they fled before them: but they went forward smiting the Moabites, even in their country.

And they beat down the cities, and on every good piece of land cast every man his stone, and filled it; and they stopped all the wells of water, and felled all the good trees: only in Kir-haraseth left they the stones thereof; howbeit the slingers went about it, and smote it.

(3:21–25)

And it fell on a day, that Elisha passed to Shunem, where was a great woman; and she constrained him to eat bread. And so it was, that as oft as he passed by, he turned in thither to eat bread.

And she said unto her husband, Behold now, I perceive that this is an holy man of God, which passeth by us continually.

Let us make a little chamber, I pray thee, on the wall; and let us set for him there a bed, and a table, and a stool, and a candlestick: and it shall be, when he cometh to us, that he shall turn in thither.

And it fell on a day, that he came thither, and he turned into the chamber, and lay there.

And he said to Gehazi his servant, Call this Shunammite. And when he had called her, she stood before him.

And he said unto him, Say now unto her, Behold, thou hast been careful for us with all this care; what is to be done for thee? wouldest thou be spoken for to the king, or to the captain of the host? And she answered, I dwell among mine own people.

And he said, What then is to be done for her? And Gehazi answered, Verily she hath no child, and her husband is old.

And he said, Call her. And when he had called her, she stood in the door.

And he said, About this season, according to the time of life, thou shalt embrace a son. And she said, Nay, my lord, thou man of God, do not lie unto thine handmaid.

And the woman conceived, and bare a son at that season that Elisha had said unto her, according to the time of life.

(4:8–17)

And when Elisha was come into the house, behold, the child was dead, and laid upon his bed.

He went in therefore, and shut the door upon them twain, and prayed unto the LORD.

223–225. The clay models of furniture shown here are of the Israelite period: a bed, a chair and an armchair. In biblical times furniture was simple and austere. Most people slept on the floor or on a mud-brick bench with mats for mattresses and clothes for blankets (I Samuel 28:23).

223

224

225

And he went up, and lay upon the child, and put his mouth upon his mouth, and his eyes upon his eyes, and his hands upon his hands: and he stretched himself upon the child; and the flesh of the child waxed warm.

Then he returned, and walked in the house to and fro; and went up, and stretched himself upon him: and the child sneezed seven times and the child opened his eyes.

(4:32–35)

And Elisha came again to Gilgal: and there was a dearth in the land; and the sons of the prophets were sitting before him: and he said unto his servant, Set on the great pot, and seethe pottage for the sons of the prophets.

And one went out into the fields to gather herbs, and found a wild vine, and gathered there of wild gourds his lap full, and came and shred them into the pot of pottage: for they knew them not.

So they poured out for the men to eat. And it came to pass, as they were eating of the pottage, that they cried out, and said, O thou man of God, there is death in the pot. And they could not eat thereof.

But he said, Then bring meal. And he cast it into the pot; and he said, Pour out for the people, that they may eat. And there was no harm in the pot.

(4:38–41)

Now Naaman, captain of the host of the king of Syria, was a great man with his master, and honourable, because by him the LORD had given

226

226. Bitter cucumber *(Citrullus coclocynthis)*.

In time of famine Elisha's disciples found "wild gourds" and cooked them in a pot of pottage. It turned out to be poisonous, but Elisha provided an antidote by adding flour to it.

Three species of cucumber are mentioned in the Bible. The one shown here is widespread in the arid regions of Israel. It is of the same genus as the watermelon. The leaves of the bitter cucumber have an attractive shape and they were often used as a decorative motif. The oil extracted from it has medicinal properties. It is not to be confused with another variety of cucumber which was an important crop and a favorite food in Egypt for which the Israelites, tired of the daily diet of manna, yearned during the Exodus (Numbers 11:5).

227

227. Naaman, commander of the Aramean army, bathing in the Jordan to cure himself of leprosy, depicted on a 12th-century enamel plaque (British Museum, London).

deliverance unto Syria: he was also a mighty man in valour, but he was a leper.

And the Syrians had gone out by companies, and had brought away captive out of the land of Israel a little maid; and she waited on Naaman's wife.

And she said unto her mistress, Would God my lord were with the prophet that is in Samaria! for he would recover him of his leprosy.

And one went in, and told his lord, saying, Thus and thus said the maid that is of the land of Israel.

And the king of Syria said, Go to, go, and I will send a letter unto the king of Israel. And he departed, and took with him ten talents of silver, and six thousand pieces of gold, and ten changes of raiment.

And he brought the letter to the king of Israel, saying, Now when this letter is come unto thee, behold, I have therewith sent Naaman my servant to thee, that thou mayest recover him of his leprosy.

And it came to pass, when the king of Israel had read the letter, that he rent his clothes, and said, Am I God, to kill and to make alive, that this man doth send unto me to recover a man of his leprosy? wherefore consider, I pray you, and see how he seeketh a quarrel against me.

And it was so, when Elisha the man of God had heard that the king of Israel had rent his clothes, that he sent to the king, saying, Wherefore hast thou rent thy clothes? let him come now to me, and he shall know that there is a prophet in Israel.

So Naaman came with his horses and with his chariot, and stood at the door of the house of Elisha.

And Elisha sent a messenger unto him, saying, Go and wash in Jordan seven times, and thy flesh shall come again to thee, and thou shalt be clean.

But Naaman was wroth, and went away, and said, Behold, I thought, He will surely come out to me, and stand, and call on the name of the LORD

228. The Jordan River.   228

his God, and strike his hand over the place, and recover the leper.

Are not Abana and Pharpar, rivers of Damascus, better than all the waters of Israel? may I not wash in them, and be clean? So he turned and went away in a rage.

And his servants came near, and spake unto him, and said, My father, if the prophet had bid thee do some great thing, wouldest thou not have done it? how much rather then, when he saith to thee, Wash, and be clean?

Then went he down, and dipped himself seven times in Jordan, according to the saying of the man of God: and his flesh came again like unto the flesh of a little child, and he was clean.

And he returned to the man of God, he and all his company, and came, and stood before him: and he said, Behold, now I know that there is no God in all the earth, but in Israel: now therefore, I pray thee, take a blessing of thy servant.

But he said, As the LORD liveth, before whom I stand, I will receive none. And he urged him to take it; but he refused.

And Naaman said, Shall there not then, I pray thee, be given to thy servant two mules' burden of earth? for thy servant will henceforth offer neither burnt offering nor sacrifice unto other gods, but unto the LORD.

(5:1–17)

And he said, Go and spy where he is, that I may send and fetch him. And it was told him, saying, Behold, he is in Dothan.

Therefore sent he thither horses, and chariots, and a great host: and they came by night, and compassed the city about.

And when the servant of the man of God was risen early, and gone forth, behold, an host compassed the city both with horses and chariots. And his servant said unto him, Alas, my master! how shall we do?

And he answered, Fear not: for they that be with us are more than they that be with them.

And Elisha prayed, and said, LORD, I pray thee, open his eyes, that he may see. And the LORD opened the eyes of the young man; and he saw: and, behold, the mountain was full of horses and chariots of fire round about Elisha.

And when they came down to him, Elisha prayed unto the LORD, and said, Smite this people, I pray thee, with blindness. And he smote them with blindness according to the word of Elisha.

And Elisha said unto them, This is not the way, neither is this the city: follow me, and I will bring you to the man whom ye seek. But he led them to Samaria.

(6:13–19)

229. The tell of Dothan, in Samaria. Here Elisha's pursuers were struck blind. It was also at Dothan that Joseph's brothers threw him into a pit (Genesis 37:17).

And in the eleventh year of Joram the son of Ahab began Ahaziah to reign over Judah.

And when Jehu was come to Jezreel, Jezebel heard of it; and she painted her face, and tired her head, and looked out at a window.

And as Jehu entered in at the gate, she said, Had Zimri peace, who slew his master?

And he lifted up his face to the window, and said, Who is on my side? who? And there looked out to him two or three eunuchs.

And he said, Throw her down. So they threw her down: and some of her blood was sprinkled on the wall, and on the horses: and he trode her under foot.

(9:29–33)

230. An ivory carving from the 8th century B.C., representing a woman at the window. Judging from the references in the Bible, the window was a common architectural feature in ancient times: Abimelech, king of Gerar, saw Isaac and Rebecca together through a window (Genesis 26:8); Michal "let David down through a window: and he went, and fled, and escaped" (I Samuel 19:12). In the Song of Deborah, Sisera's mother is described waiting at the window for her son to return victorious from the wars (Judges 5:28). The theme of the "woman at the window" appears with some variations in ivory carvings found at Samaria and other sites. The one shown here was found at Nimrud in Mesopotamia.

230

But Jehu took no heed to walk in the law of the LORD God of Israel with all his heart: for he departed not from the sins of Jeroboam, which made Israel to sin.

In those days the LORD began to cut Israel short: and Hazael smote them in all the coasts of Israel;

From Jordan eastward, all the land of Gilead, the Gadites, and the Reubenites, and the Manassites, from Aroer, which is by the river Arnon, even Gilead and Bashan.

Now the rest of the acts of Jehu, and all that he did, and all his might, are they not written in the book of the chronicles of the kings of Israel?

And Jehu slept with his fathers: and they buried him in Samaria. And Jehoahaz his son reigned in his stead.

And the time that Jehu reigned over Israel in Samaria was twenty and eight years.

(10:31–36)

231. Landscape in Gilead.

232. Shalmaneser III (859–824 B.C.) receives tribute from Jehu. Jehu himself, or his ambassador, is shown kissing the ground at Shalmaneser's feet (British Museum).
This is a detail from the Black Obelisk of Shalmaneser.
On this stone monument, which resembles an obelisk, the king gave a brief account of his wars, and pictures various nations bringing tribute to him. On the panel shown here (one of twenty panels altogether), the "tribute of Jehu" consists chiefly of silver, gold and tin vessels, and other objects.
The inscriptions below the panels describe the scenes depicted. The obelisk ends in three steps with inscriptions.

233

And Jehoash king of Judah took all the hallowed things that Jehoshaphat, and Jehoram, and Ahaziah, his fathers, kings of Judah, had dedicated, and his own hallowed things, and all the gold that was found in the treasures of the house of the LORD, and in the king's house, and sent it to Hazael king of Syria: and he went away from Jerusalem.

And the rest of the acts of Joash, and all that he did, are they not written in the book of the chronicles of the kings of Judah?

(12:18–19)

Neither did he leave of the people to Jehoahaz but fifty horsemen, and ten chariots, and ten thousand footmen; for the king of Syria had destroyed them, and had made them like the dust by threshing.

(13:7)

But Hazael king of Syria oppressed Israel all the days of Jehoahaz.

And the LORD was gracious unto them, and had compassion on them, and had respect unto them, because of his covenant with Abraham, Isaac, and Jacob, and would not destroy them, neither cast he them from his presence as yet.

So Hazael king of Syria died; and Ben-hadad his son reigned in his stead.

And Jehoash the son of Jehoahaz took again out of the hand of Benhadad the son of Hazael the cities, which he had taken out of the hand of Jehoahaz his father by war. Three times did Joash beat him, and recovered the cities of Israel.

(13:22–25)

And Amaziah the son of Joash king of Judah lived after the death of Jehoash son of Jehoahaz king of Israel fifteen years.

And the rest of the acts of Amaziah, are they not written in the book of the chronicles of the kings of Judah?

Now they made a conspiracy against him in Jerusalem: and he fled to Lachish; but they sent after him to Lachish, and slew him there.

And they brought him on horses: and he was buried at Jerusalem with his fathers in the city of David.

And all the people of Judah took Azariah, which was sixteen years old, and made him king instead of his father Amaziah.

He built Elath, and restored it to Judah, after that the king slept with his fathers.

(14:17–22)

233. Hazael, king of Aram-Damascus; ivory sculpture.

Aram-Damascus (usually referred to simply as Aram), was the most important of the Aramean kingdoms in the 9th/8th centuries B.C. It was bordered by the kingdom of Judah to the south, Hammath in northern Syria and the Phoenician city-states to the west.

According to I Kings 19:15–16, Hazael was to be anointed king of Damascus by Elijah, as Jehu was to be anointed king of Israel.

Hazael was a royal servant who usurped the throne after murdering his master (II Kings 8:7–15). As prophesied by Elisha, Hazael began to make war on Israel. At the end of Jehu's reign, Hazael conquered all Israelite territories "from Jordan eastward, all the land of the Gadites, and the Reubenites, and the

And Pul the king of Assyria came against the land: and Menahem gave Pul a thousand talents of silver, that his hand might be with him to confirm the kingdom in his hand.

And Menahem exacted the money of Israel, even of all the mighty men of wealth, of each man fifty shekels of silver, to give to the king of Assyria. So the king of Assyria turned back, and stayed not there in the land.

(15:19–20)

In the two and fiftieth year of Azariah king of Judah Pekah the son of Remaliah began to reign over Israel in Samaria, and reigned twenty years.

And he did that which was evil in the sight of the LORD: he departed not from the sins of Jeroboam the son of Nebat, who made Israel to sin.

In the days of Pekah king of Israel came Tiglath-pileser king of Assyria, and took Ijon, and Abel-beth-maachah, and Janoah, and Kedesh, and Hazor, and Gilead, and Galilee, all the land of Naphtali, and carried them captive to Assyria.

(15:27–29)

Manassites, from Aroer, which is by the river Arnon, even Gilead and Bashan'' (II Kings 10:33). After Jehu's death he overran the entire kingdom of Israel, and even threatened Jerusalem, capital of Judah, departing only after the payment of a heavy tribute.

234. A view of the Bay of Elath, on the Red Sea.

235. Tiglath-pileser III, king of Assyria (also called Pul in the Bible – his original name was Pulu), and his ministers. Fresco from the royal palace; 8th century B.C.
He reigned from 745 to 727 B.C., warred against Syria, advanced along the Mediterranean coast, subjugating Phoenician towns as well as Gaza. Ahaz, king of Judah, turned to him for help against Pekah of Israel and his ally in Damascus. After the fall of Damascus, the entire region fell to him. He invaded Israel and subjugated several towns.

236

236. An Assyrian relief in the palace of Sennacherib at Nineveh shows captives being driven out of their destroyed city and spoils being carried off by the conquerors.

237. Inscribed ostracon uncovered at Lachish, dating from the eve of the destruction of the Kingdom of Judah by Nebuchadnezzar. The texts describe the fears in Judah in face of the imminent Babylonian invasion.

238. Glass pomegranate-shaped perfume bottle, found in Cyprus, thought to be from the 14th century B.C.
Incense and perfume spices were precious commodities in the ancient world, and were used both for religious and secular purposes. Spices were among the gifts the Queen of Sheba brought Solomon (I Kings 10:2). "The spices and precious oil" were kept in the royal treasury together with silver and gold.
The term "spices" in the Bible refers to a variety of fragrant plant products used in making anointing oils and incense. Sometimes they were in the form of granules, kept in cloth bags and sniffed from time to time (Song of Solomon 1:13). Or they were in liquid form, preserved in oil, this being the "precious oil" frequently referred to in the Bible.

239. Seal with the figure of a fighting cock, found at Tell en-Nasbeh (identified with Mizpeh), from the end of the 6th century B.C. The seal is inscribed: "[Belonging] to Jaazaniah, servant of the king".

240. The siege of Lachish shown in a relief from Sennacherib's palace at Nineveh.
The siege and capture of the city are shown in detail on a large four-panelled relief. The Assyrian infantry is assaulting the city, javelin throwers follow and behind them pairs of archers, followed by slingers whose weapon had the longest range of all.
The defenders stand on the turrets and pinnacles shooting arrows and throwing stones from behind wooden frames and shields. The Assyrian army is seen mounting its assault with battering rams.

In the twelfth year of Ahaz king of Judah began Hoshea the son of Elah to reign in Samaria over Israel nine years.

And he did that which was evil in the sight of the LORD, but not as the kings of Israel that were before him.

Against him came up Shalmaneser king of Assyria; and Hoshea became his servant, and gave him presents.

And the king of Assyria found conspiracy in Hoshea: for he had sent messengers to So king of Egypt, and brought no present to the king of Assyria, as he had done year by year: therefore the king of Assyria shut him up, and bound him in prison.

Then the king of Assyria came up throughout all the land, and went up to Samaria, and besieged it three years.

In the ninth year of Hoshea the king of Assyria took Samaria, and carried Israel away into Assyria, and placed them in Halah and in Habor by the river of Gozan, and in the cities of the Medes.

For so it was, that the children of Israel had sinned against the LORD their God, which had brought them up out of the land of Egypt, from under the hand of Pharaoh king of Egypt, and had feared other gods,

And walked in the statutes of the heathen, whom the LORD cast out from before the children of Israel, and of the kings of Israel, which they had made. (17:1–8)

And the LORD rejected all the seed of Israel, and afflicted them, and delivered them into the hand of spoilers, until he had cast them out of his sight.

For he rent Israel from the house of David; and they made Jeroboam the son of Nebat king: and Jeroboam drave Israel from following the LORD, and made them sin a great sin.

For the children of Israel walked in all the sins of Jeroboam which he did; they departed not from them;

Until the LORD removed Israel out of his sight, as he had said by all his servants the prophets. So was Israel carried away out of their own land to Assyria unto this day.

And the king of Assyria brought men from Babylon, and from Cuthah, and from Ava, and from Hamath, and from Sepharvaim, and placed them in the cities of Samaria instead of the children of Israel: and they possessed Samaria, and dwelt in the cities thereof.

(17:20–24)

And it came to pass in the fourth year of king Hezekiah, which was the seventh year of Hoshea son of Elah king of Israel, that Shalmaneser king of Assyria came up against Samaria, and besieged it.

And at the end of three years they took it: even in the sixth year of Hezekiah, that is the ninth year of Hoshea king of Israel, Samaria was taken.

And the king of Assyria did carry away Israel unto Assyria, and put them in Halah and in Habor by the river of Gozan, and in the cities of the Medes:

Because they obeyed not the voice of the LORD their God, but transgressed his covenant, and all that Moses the servant of the LORD commanded, and would not hear them, nor do them.

Now in the fourteenth year of king Hezekiah did Sennacherib king of Assyria come up against all the fenced cities of Judah, and took them.

And Hezekiah king of Judah sent to the king of Assyria to Lachish, saying, I have offended; return from me: that which thou puttest on me will I bear. And the king of Assyria appointed unto Hezekiah king of Judah three hundred talents of silver and thirty talents of gold.

(18:9–14)

237

So Rab-shakeh returned, and found the king of Assyria warring against Libnah: for he had heard that he was departed from Lachish.

And when he heard say of Tirhakah king of Ethiopia, Behold, he is come out to fight against thee: he sent messengers again unto Hezekiah, saying,

Thus shall ye speak to Hezekiah king of Judah, saying, Let not thy God in whom thou trustest deceive thee, saying, Jerusalem shall not be delivered into the hand of the king of Assyria.

Behold, thou hast heard what the kings of Assyria have done to all lands, by destroying them utterly: and shalt thou be delivered?

(19:8–11)

And Hezekiah hearkened unto them, and shewed them all the house of his precious things, the silver, and the gold, and the spices, and the precious ointment, and all the house of his armour, and all that was found in his treasures: there was nothing in his house, nor in all his dominion, that Hezekiah shewed them not. (20:13)

At that time the servants of Nebuchadnezzar king of Babylon came up against Jerusalem, and the city was besieged.

238

And Nebuchadnezzar king of Babylon came against the city, and his servants did besiege it.

And Jehoiachin the king of Judah went out to the king of Babylon, he, and his mother, and his servants, and his princes, and his officers: and the king of Babylon took him in the eighth year of his reign.

(24:10–12)

And when all the captains of the armies, they and their men, heard that the king of Babylon had made Gedaliah governor, there came to Gedaliah to Mizpah, even Ishmael the son of Nethaniah, and Johanan the son of Careah, and Seraiah the son of Tanhumeth the Netophathite, and Jaazaniah the son of a Maachathite, they and their men.

(25:23)

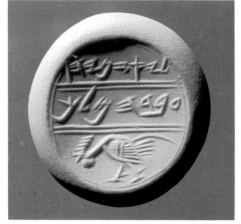

239

But Aaron and his sons offered upon the altar of the burnt offering, and on the altar of incense, and were appointed for all the work of the place most holy, and to make an atonement for Israel, according to all that Moses the servant of God had commanded. (6:49)

And the children of the Levites bare the ark of God upon their shoulders with the staves thereon, as Moses commanded according to the word of the LORD.

And David spake to the chief of the Levites to appoint their brethren to be the singers with instruments of musick, psalteries and harps and cymbals, sounding, by lifting up the voice with joy.

So the Levites appointed Heman the son of Joel; and of his brethren, Asaph the son of Berechiah; and of the sons of Merari their brethren, Ethan the son of Kushaiah;

And with them their brethren of the second degree, Zechariah, Ben, and Jaaziel, and Shemiramoth, and Jehiel, and Unni, Eliab, and Benaiah, and Maaseiah, and Mattithiah, and Elipheleh, and Mikneiah, and Obed-edom, and Jeiel, the porters.

So the singers, Heman, Asaph, and Ethan, were appointed to sound with cymbals of brass;

And Zechariah, and Aziel, and Shemiramoth, and Jehiel, and Unni, and Eliab, and Maaseiah, and Benaiah, with psalteries on Alamoth;

And Mattithiah, and Elipheleh, and Mikneiah, and Obed-edom, and Jeiel, and Azaziah, with harps on the Sheminith to excel.

And Chenaniah, chief of the Levites, was for song: he instructed about the song, because he was skilful.

And Berechiah and Elkanah were doorkeepers for the ark.

And Shebaniah, and Jehoshaphat, and Nethaneel, and Amasai, and Zechariah, and Benaiah, and Eliezer, the priests, did blow with the trumpets before the ark of God: and Obed-edom and Jehiah were doorkeepers for the ark.

So David, and the elders of Israel, and the captains over thousands, went to bring up the ark of the covenant of the LORD out of the house of Obed-edom with joy.

And it came to pass, when God helped the Levites that bare the ark of the covenant of the LORD, that they offered seven bullocks and seven rams.

And David was clothed with a robe of fine linen, and all the Levites that bare the ark, and the singers, and Chenaniah the master of the song with the singers: David also had upon him an ephod of linen.

Thus all Israel brought up the ark of the covenant of the LORD with shouting, and with sound of the cornet, and with trumpets, and with cymbals, making a noise with psalteries and harps.

(15:15–28)

Now after this it came to pass, that David smote the Philistines, and subdued them, and took Gath and her towns out of the hand of the Philistines.

(18:1)

243

241. Incense burner of the Israelite period adorned with snakes. This same symbol, in the form of Moses' rod, unleashed the plagues upon Pharaoh (Exodus 7:9–14).
Most incense and perfumes originated in tropical countries. The Land of Israel lay on the "Spice Route" which led from the Far East to the north and west. This route dates back to very early times, and the Israelites in the wilderness obtained ingredients for incense from passing caravans, which came from different parts of Asia.

242. A dancing youth, from a tomb painting at Tarquinia, Italy, 6th century B.C.

243. Philistine ritual stand made of clay, from the 10th century B.C., found at Ashdod. The openings are decorated with figures playing the cymbals, a double pipe, a frame drum and a lyre.
The Bible is a rich source of information about the music of ancient Israel. Most of the biblical evidence relates to the function of music in the cult; however, music, dancing and singing were also part of the spontaneous and organized rejoicings after a victory in war: the Song of the Sea (Exodus 15), for example, or the women's welcome to David and Saul "with tabrets, with joy and with instruments of musick" (I Samuel 18:6–7), or when the Ark of the Lord was taken to Jerusalem. Music at popular feasts is described in Judges 21:19ff. There was also musical accompaniment at the feasts of the rich and at the king's court (II Samuel 19:35; Isaiah 5:12, 6:5; etc.).

244

Apparently music was also associated with prophecy: ". . . thou shalt meet a company of prophets coming down from the high place with a psaltery, and a tabret, and a pipe, and a harp, before them and they shall prophesy" (I Samuel 10:5). Elisha is induced to prophesy "when the minstrel played, . . . the hand of the Lord came upon him" (II Kings 3:15).

The psychological effect of music was known, as shown in the story of David playing and singing to Saul to soothe him.

244. The site of ancient Gath, one of the five principal cities of the Philistines. It was originally inhabited by the "Anakim," as told in Joshua 11:22. The Philistines fled from Gath after the defeat of Goliath, "And the wounded of the Philistines fell down by the way to Shaaraim, even unto Gath and unto Ekron" (I Samuel 17:52). Here, David found refuge when he was fleeing from Saul (I Samuel 21:11).

And over the king's treasures was Azmaveth the son of Adiel: and over the storehouses in the fields, in the cities, and in the villages, and in the castles, was Jehonathan the son of Uzziah:

And over them that did the work of the field for tillage of the ground was Ezri the son of Chelub:

And over the vineyards was Shimei the Ramathite: over the increase of the vineyards for the wine cellars was Zabdi the Shiphmite:

And over the olive trees and the sycomore trees that were in the low plains was Baal-hanan the Gederite: and over the cellars of oil was Joash:

And over the herds that fed in Sharon was Shitrai the Sharonite: and over the herds that were in the valleys was Shaphat the son of Adlai:

Over the camels also was Obil the Ishmaelite: and over the asses was Jehdeiah the Meronothite:

And over the flocks was Jaziz the Hagerite. All these were the rulers of the substance which was king David's.

(27:25–31)

245. Pottery jar handle stamped and bearing the letters "Yrslm", Hebrew for Jerusalem. Such impressions, with different place-names, were stamped by royal officials as a guaranty of the capacity of the jar. Similar jar handles were found bearing seal-impressions and the words "belonging to the king" with, below, different place-names representing administrative centers where taxes were collected. The same seal-impressions were imprinted on standard-sized containers of oil and wine which were delivered to the royal treasury by way of tithes.

The rural population paid their taxes in kind, and the city dwellers in silver. Agricultural produce was delivered by the local tax collectors to the royal storehouses, situated in several places in the country.

246

247

246. Beth-Horon the Upper.

247. Beth-Horon the Lower.
These were two places adjacent to each other and distinguished by the description "upper" and "lower". The upper town was a key point on one of the main roads leading from the plain to the Judean Hills.
After Joshua defeated the five kings of the Amorites he pursued them to upper Beth-Horon, and on the descent from there the Lord cast down large stones from heaven on the fugitives (Joshua 10:10–11).

248. The sarcophagus of Ahiram, found in a tomb at Byblos (Lebanon).
The richly carved sarcophagus bears a Phoenician funerary inscription of the Sidonian king, Ahiram, on the lid. It seems that the tomb was reused, and the inscription is dated to the beginning of the 10th century B.C., although some scholars prefer to date the sarcophagus to the 12th century.
It appears that the name Hiram, Ahiram, Hirom or Hirum used in different places in the Bible refers to the same person.

249. The tomb of Ahiram at Byblos.
In the third millennium B.C., the Pharaohs of Egypt had already established commercial ties with Byblos.
Its Egyptian name was Gubla, the Gebal mentioned in Ezekiel 27:9, and this name is preserved in the modern name, Jebeil. During the first millennium Byblos was the intermediary in an active papyrus trade between Egypt and the Greek world. This is reflected in the Greek name for the city, Byblos, which in Greek also meant papyrus. It later signified a book written on papyrus and, through the Latin *biblia*, entered the European languages as the Book of Books, the Bible.

And it came to pass at the end of twenty years, wherein Solomon had built the house of the LORD, and his own house,

That the cities which Huram had restored to Solomon, Solomon built them, and caused the children of Israel·to dwell there.

And Solomon went to Hamath-zobah, and prevailed against it.

And he built Tadmor in the wilderness, and all the store cities, which he built in Hamath.

Also he built Beth-horon the upper, and Beth-horon the nether, fenced cities, with walls, gates, and bars.

(8:1–5)

248

249

250. The Tomb of Zechariah is the traditional name of a monument carved out of the rock in the Valley of Kidron, in Jerusalem. The top is shaped like a pyramid, and there are three pillars on the side. Jewish tradition holds this to be the tomb of the prophet Zechariah, although it dates from the Second Temple period.

251. Tablet recording the reburial of the remains of King Uzziah, between the first century B.C. and the first century A.D. The tablet, found on the Mount of Olives, reads: "Hither were brought the bones of Uzziah, King of Judah. Do not open."
Uzziah was the tenth king of Judah (785–754 B.C.). He was a great builder. He also waged successful campaigns against the Philistines, forced the Ammonites to pay tribute to him, and regained the port of Elath. After being stricken with leprosy, he withdrew from public affairs, appointing his son Jotham as regent.

And they left the house of the LORD God of their fathers, and served groves and idols: and wrath came upon Judah and Jerusalem for this their trespass.

Yet he sent prophets to them, to bring them again unto the LORD; and they testified against them: but they would not give ear.

And the Spirit of God came upon Zechariah the son of Jehoiada the priest, which stood above the people, and said unto them, Thus saith God, Why transgress ye the commandments of the LORD, that ye cannot prosper? because ye have forsaken the LORD, he hath also forsaken you.

And they conspired against him, and stoned him with stones at the commandment of the king in the court of the house of the LORD.

Thus Joash the king remembered not the kindness which Jehoiada his father had done to him, but slew his son. And when he died, he said, The LORD look upon it, and require it.

(24:18–22)

Then all the people of Judah took Uzziah, who was sixteen years old, and made him king in the room of his father Amaziah.

He built Eloth, and restored it to Judah, after that the king slept with his fathers.

Sixteen years old was Uzziah when he began to reign, and he reigned fifty and two years in Jerusalem. His mother's name also was Jecoliah of Jerusalem.

And he did that which was right in the sight of the LORD, according to all that his father Amaziah did.

And he sought God in the days of Zechariah, who had understanding in the visions of God: and as long as he sought the LORD, God made him to prosper.

And he went forth and warred against the Philistines, and brake down the wall of Gath, and the wall of Jabneh, and the wall of Ashdod, and built cities about Ashdod, and among the Philistines.

And God helped him against the Philistines, and against the Arabians that dwelt in Gurbaal, and the Mehunims.

And the Ammonites gave gifts to Uzziah: and his name spread abroad even to the entering in of Egypt; for he strengthened himself exceedingly.

Moreover Uzziah built towers in Jerusalem at the corner gate, and at the valley gate, and at the turning of the wall, and fortified them.

Also he built towers in the desert, and digged many wells: for he had much cattle, both in the low country, and in the plains: husbandmen also, and vine dressers in the mountains, and in Carmel: for he loved husbandry.

(26:1–10)

And Azariah the chief priest, and all the priests, looked upon him, and, behold, he was leprous in his forehead, and they thrust him out from thence; yea, himself hasted also to go out, because the LORD had smitten him.

And Uzziah the king was a leper unto the day of his death, and dwelt in a several house, being a leper; for he was cut off from the house of the LORD: and Jotham his son was over the king's house, judging the people of the land.

Now the rest of the acts of Uzziah, first and last, did Isaiah the prophet, the son of Amoz, write.

So Uzziah slept with his fathers, and they buried him with his fathers in the field of the burial which belonged to the kings; for they said, He is a leper: and Jotham his son, reigned in his stead.   (26:20–23)

252.

252. The village of Silwan (Siloam) today.

After these things, and the establishment thereof, Sennacherib king of Assyria came, and entered into Judah, and encamped against the fenced cities, and thought to win them for himself.

And when Hezekiah saw that Sennacherib was come, and that he was purposed to fight against Jerusalem,

He took counsel with his princes and his mighty men to stop the waters of the fountains which were without the city: and they did help him.

So there was gathered much people together, who stopped all the fountains, and the brook that ran through the midst of the land, saying, Why should the kings of Assyria come, and find much water?

Also, he strengthened himself, and built up all the wall that was broken, and raised it up to the towers, and another wall without, and repaired Millo in the city of David, and made darts and shields in abundance.

And he set captains of war over the people, and gathered them together to him in the street of the gate of the city, and spake comfortably to them, saying,

Be strong and courageous, be not afraid nor dismayed for the king of Assyria, nor for all the multitude that is with him: for there be more with us than with him:

With him is an arm of flesh; but with us is the LORD our God to help us, and to fight our battles. And the people rested themselves upon the words of Hezekiah king of Judah.

After this did Sennacherib king of Assyria send his servants to Jerusalem, (but he himself laid siege against Lachish, and all his power with him,) unto Hezekiah king of Judah, and unto all Judah that were at Jerusalem, saying,

Thus saith Sennacherib king of Assyria, Whereon do ye trust, that ye abide in the siege in Jerusalem?

Doth not Hezekiah persuade you to give over yourselves to die by famine and by thirst, saying, The LORD our God shall deliver us out of the hand of the king of Assyria?

(32:1–11)

And Hezekiah had exceeding much riches and honour: and he made himself treasuries for silver, and for gold, and for precious stones, and for spices, and for shields, and for all manner of pleasant jewels.

Storehouses also for the increase of corn, and wine, and oil; and stalls for all manner of beasts, and cotes for flocks.

Moreover he provided him cities, and possessions of flocks and herds in abundance: for God had given him substance very much.

This same Hezekiah also stopped the upper watercourse of Gihon, and brought it straight down to the west side of the city of David. And Hezekiah prospered in all his works.

Howbeit in the business of the ambassadors of the princes of Babylon, who sent unto him to inquire of the wonder that was done in the land, God left him, to try him, that he might know all that was in his heart.

Now the rest of the acts of Hezekiah, and his goodness, behold, they are written in the vision of Isaiah the prophet, the son of Amoz, and in the book of the kings of Judah and Israel.

And Hezekiah slept with his fathers, and they buried him in the chiefest of the sepulchres of the sons of David: and all Judah and the inhabitants of Jerusalem did him honour at his death. And Manasseh his son reigned in his stead.

(32:27–33)

253. A view of the Siloam Tunnel which skirts the village of Silwan. It was cut through the rock to carry water from the Gihon Spring, outside the walls of Jerusalem, to a pool within the city, thus ensuring a regular supply of water to Jerusalem in times of siege. The tunnel is well preserved and the water of the Gihon still flows through it.

254. The Siloam Inscription describes how King Hezekiah's tunnel was dug by two teams of miners starting at opposite ends, working toward each other and meeting in the middle. Part of the inscription reads: "... the quarrymen hewed [the rock], each man toward his fellow, axe against axe; and the water flowed from the spring toward the reservoir for 1200 cubits, and the height of the rock above the head[s] of the quarrymen was 100 cubits."

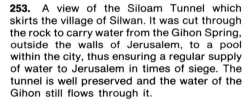

255

Now in the first year of Cyrus king of Persia, that the word of the LORD by the mouth of Jeremiah might be fulfilled, the LORD stirred up the spirit of Cyrus king of Persia, that he made a proclamation throughout all his kingdom, and put it also in writing, saying,

Thus saith Cyrus king of Persia, The LORD God of heaven hath given me all the kingdoms of the earth; and he hath charged me to build him an house at Jerusalem, which is in Judah.

Who is there among you of all his people? his God be with him, and let him go up to Jerusalem, which is in Judah, and build the house of the LORD God of Israel, (he is the God,) which is in Jerusalem.

And whosoever remaineth in any place where he sojourneth, let the men of his place help him with silver, and with gold, and with goods, and with beasts, beside the freewill offering for the house of God that is in Jerusalem.

Then rose up the chief of the fathers of Judah and Benjamin, and the priests, and the Levites, with all them whose spirit God had raised, to go up to build the house of the LORD which is in Jerusalem.

And all they that were about them strengthened their hands with vessels of silver, with gold, with goods, and with beasts, and with precious things, beside all that was willingly offered.

Also Cyrus the king brought forth the vessels of the house of the LORD; which Nebuchadnezzar had brought forth out of Jerusalem, and had put them in the house of his gods;

Even those did Cyrus king of Persia bring forth by the hand of Mithredath the treasurer, and numbered them unto Sheshbazzar, the prince of Judah.

(1:1-8)

255. The Cyrus Cylinder, 538 B.C., bears an inscription in which Cyrus represents himself as the emissary of Marduk, the chief god of Babylon.

According to the inscription, the Persian ruler showed tolerance for the conquered peoples. The records quote him as saying that he returned the ruined sanctuaries of the sacred cities "on the other side of the Tigris," and replaced the statues of their gods. He is quoted as saying: "I also gathered all their former inhabitants and returned them to their habitations."

Cyrus figures in Isaiah's prophecy concerning Jerusalem and its Temple: the Persian ruler had been chosen by God to overthrow Babylon and release the Jews who were exiled there.

256

257

256. & 257. Persian silver coin from the time of Darius, or possibly Xerxes, used by the exiles returning to Zion.

258. Ostracon from Arad, early 6th century B.C., inscribed with a letter addressed to Eliashib (Israel Museum, Jerusalem). This is the only document from the First Temple period specifically to mention the Temple – "the House of God." The inscription reads: "To my lord Eliashib: May God enquire as to thy welfare. And now: Give the Shemariahu . . . and to the Kerosite five . . . And concerning that which you commanded me, all is well. [In] the House of God he dwells."

"The children of Keros" are mentioned in the Bible as a family of Temple servants (Ezra 2:44; Nehemiah 7:47). The invasion of the Assyrian army, under Shalmaneser V, and the capture of Samaria in the year 732 B.C., brought to an end the Kingdom of Israel. A part of the population was exiled to distant lands (II Kings 17:22), and in their place came tribes from other parts of the Assyrian empire. The Kingdom of Judah remained in existence until it was invaded by Nebuchadnezzar at the head of the Babylonian army, who took Jerusalem and destroyed the Temple in 587 B.C. Many inhabitants were exiled to Babylonia. After Babylonia was conquered by the Persians in 538 B.C., Cyrus, king of Persia, permitted the exiled Israelites to return to Jerusalem and rebuild the Temple. The period of Persian rule in Palestine lasted until the conquest by Alexander the Great in 332 B.C.

258

Now when the adversaries of Judah and Benjamin heard that the children of the captivity builded the temple unto the LORD God of Israel;

Then they came to Zerubbabel, and to the chief of the fathers, and said unto them, Let us build with you: for we seek your God as ye do; and we do sacrifice unto him since the days of Esar-haddon king of Assur, which brought us up hither.

But Zerubbabel, and Jeshua, and the rest of the chief of the fathers of Israel, said unto them, Ye have nothing to do with us to build an house unto our God; but we ourselves together will build unto the LORD God of Israel, as king Cyrus the king of Persia hath commanded us.

Then the people of the land weakened the hands of the people of Judah, and troubled them in building,

And hired counsellers against them, to frustrate their purpose, all the days of Cyrus king of Persia, even until the reign of Darius king of Persia.

(4:1-5)

Then Darius the king made a decree, and search was made in the house of the rolls, where the treasures were laid up in Babylon.

And there was found at Achmetha, in the palace that is in the province of the Medes, a roll, and therein was a record thus written:

In the first year of Cyrus the king the same Cyrus the king made a decree concerning the house of God at Jerusalem, Let the house be builded, the place where they offered sacrifices, and let the foundations thereof be strongly laid; the height thereof threescore cubits, and the breadth thereof threescore cubits;

With three rows of great stones, and a row of new timber: and let the expences be given out of the king's house:

And also let the golden and silver vessels of the house of God, which Nebuchadnezzar took forth out of the temple which is at Jerusalem, and brought unto Babylon, be restored, and brought again unto the temple which is at Jerusalem, every one to his place, and place them in the house of God.

Now therefore, Tatnai, governor beyond the river, Shethar-boznai, and your companions the Apharsachites, which are beyond the river, be ye far from thence:

Let the work of this house of God alone; let the governor of the Jews and the elders of the Jews build this house of God in his place.

Moreover I make a decree what ye shall do to the elders of these Jews for the building of this house of God: that of the king's goods, even of the tribute beyond the river, forthwith expences be given unto these men, that they be not hindered.

(6:1-8)

This Ezra went up from Babylon; and he was a ready scribe in the law of Moses, which the LORD God of Israel had given: and the king granted him all his request, according to the hand of the LORD his God upon him.

And there went up some of the children of Israel, and of the priests, and the Levites, and the singers, and the porters, and the Nethinims, unto Jerusalem, in the seventh year of Artaxerxes the king.

And he came to Jerusalem in the fifth month, which was in the seventh year of the king.

For upon the first day of the first month began he to go up from Babylon, and on the first day of the fifth month came he to Jerusalem, according to the good hand of his God upon him.

For Ezra had prepared his heart to seek the law of the LORD, and to do it, and to teach in Israel statutes and judgments.

Now this is the copy of the letter that the king Artaxerxes gave unto Ezra the priest, the scribe, even a scribe of the words of the commandments of the LORD, and of his statutes to Israel.

(7:6-11)

259. Ezra the Scribe depicted on the so-called Northumbrian Bible.

260

260. The Dung Gate in Jerusalem retained its ancient name, which indicates that the city's refuse was dumped on the Valley of Hinnom located below it.

So I came to Jerusalem, and was there three days.

And I arose in the night, I and some few men with me; neither told I any man what my God had put in my heart to do at Jerusalem: neither was there any beast with me, save the beast that I rode upon.

And I went out by night by the gate of the valley, even before the dragon well, and to the dung port, and viewed the walls of Jerusalem, which were broken down, and the gates thereof were consumed with fire.

Then I went on to the gate of the fountain, and to the king's pool: but there was no place for the beast that was under me to pass.

Then went I up in the night by the brook, and viewed the wall, and turned back, and entered by the gate of the valley, and so returned.

And the rulers knew not whither I went, or what I did; neither had I as yet told it to the Jews, nor to the priests, nor to the nobles, nor to the rulers, nor to the rest that did the work.

Then said I unto them, Ye see the distress that we are in, how Jerusalem lieth waste, and the gates thereof are burned with fire: come, and let us build up the wall of Jerusalem, that we be no more a reproach.

Then I told them of the hand of my God which was good upon me; as also the king's words that he had spoken unto me. And they said, Let us rise up and build. So they strengthened their hands for this good work.

But when Sanballat the Horonite, and Tobiah the servant, the Ammonite, and Geshem the Arabian, heard it, they laughed us to scorn, and despised us, and said, What is this thing that ye do? will ye rebel against the king?

Then answered I them, and said unto them, The God of heaven, he will prosper us; therefore we his servants will arise and build: but ye have no portion, nor right nor memorial, in Jerusalem.

(2:11-20)

And Ezra blessed the LORD, the great God. And all the people answered,

261. En-rogel, a spring or well southeast of Jerusalem at the confluence of the Hinnom and Kidron valleys, is thought to be the "dragon well" mentioned by Nehemiah. It lay on the border between the tribes of Judah and Benjamin, "and the border passed toward the waters of En-shemesh and the goings out thereof were at En-rogel," according to Joshua 15:7.

When David was fleeing from Absalom, who sought to usurp the throne, he sent Jonathan and Ahimaaz "who stayed by En-rogel for they might not be seen to come into the city: and a wench went and told them and they told King David" of Absalom's plans (II Samuel 17:17).

En-rogel occurs again in connection with David's troubles with his rebellious sons. During the king's waning years, Adonijah's abortive attempt to succeed him also took place at En-rogel, where Adonijah held a feast to enlist support for his usurpation of the throne (I Kings 1:1–9).

Amen, Amen, with lifting up their hands: and they bowed their heads, and worshipped the LORD with their faces to the ground.

Also Jeshua, and Bani, and Sherebiah, Jamin, Akkub, Shabbethai, Hodijah, Maaseiah, Kelita, Azariah, Jozabad, Hanan, Pelaiah, and the Levites, caused the people to understand the law: and the people stood in their place.

(8:6–7)

And on the second day were gathered together the chief of the fathers of all the people, the priests, and the Levites, unto Ezra the scribe, even to understand the words of the law.

And they found written in the law which the LORD had commanded by Moses, that the children of Israel should dwell in booths in the feast of the seventh month:

And that they should publish and proclaim in all their cities, and in Jerusalem, saying, Go forth unto the mount, and fetch olive branches, and pine branches, and myrtle branches, and palm branches, and branches of thick trees, to make booths, as it is written.

So the people went forth, and brought them, and made themselves booths, every one upon the roof of his house, and in their courts, and in the courts of the house of God, and in the street of the water gate and in the street of the gate of Ephraim.

And all the congregation of them that were come again out of the captivity made booths, and sat under the booths: for since the days of Jeshua the son of Nun unto that day had not the children of Israel done so. And there was very great gladness.

Also day by day, from the first day unto the last day, he read in the book of the law of God. And they kept the feast seven days; and on the eighth day was a solemn assembly, according unto the manner.

(8:13-18)

262. A branch of myrtle in bloom.

263. The Festival of Tabernacles (or Booths) in Jerusalem. Fragrant branches of myrtle and branches of other trees are used to cover the huts which it is customary to erect on roofs, courtyards, gardens or even balconies in Jewish homes, during the Festival of Tabernacles.
The festival lasts a week during which families partake of their meals in the booths.
The festival is concluded by "the rejoicing of the Torah" (*Simhat Torah* in Hebrew) when the annual reading of the Pentateuch scroll in the synagogue is completed and immediately begins again. During the celebration all the Torah scrolls are removed from the Ark, and the pulpit is circled seven times. The return of the scrolls to the Ark is accompanied by joyful hymns. The children also participate in the procession, and carry flags adorned with apples in which burning candles are placed.

263

264. Illuminated Scroll of Esther, 18th century.
The Book of Esther is read as the central rite in the Purim festival.

264

Now it came to pass in the days of Ahasuerus, (this is Ahasuerus which reigned, from India even unto Ethiopia, over an hundred and seven and twenty provinces:)

That in those days, when the king Ahasuerus sat on the throne of his kingdom, which was in Shushan the palace,

In the third year of his reign, he made a feast unto all his princes and his servants; the power of Persia and Media, the nobles and princes of the provinces, being before him:

When he shewed the riches of his glorious kingdom and the honour of his excellent majesty many days, even an hundred and fourscore days.

And when these days were expired, the king made a feast unto all the people that were present in Shushan the palace, both unto great and small, seven days, in the court of the garden of the king's palace;

Where were white, green, and blue, hangings, fastened with cords of fine linen and purple to silver rings and pillars of marble: the beds were of gold and silver, upon a pavement of red, and blue, and white, and black, marble.

And they gave them drink in vessels of gold, (the vessels being diverse one from another,) and royal wine in abundance, according to the state of the king.

And the drinking was according to the law; none did compel: for so the king had appointed to all the officers of his house, that they should do according to every man's pleasure.

Also Vashti the queen made a feast for the women in the royal house which belonged to king Ahasuerus.

On the seventh day, when the heart of the king was merry with wine, he commanded Mehuman, Biztha, Harbona, Bigtha, and Abagtha, Zethar, and Carcas, the seven chamberlains that served in the presence of Ahasuerus the king,

To bring Vashti the queen before the king with the crown royal, to shew the people and the princes her beauty, for she was fair to look on.

But the queen Vashti refused to come at the king's commandment by his chamberlains: therefore was the king very wroth, and his anger burned in him.

Then the king said to the wise men, which knew the times, (for so was the king's manner toward all that knew law and judgment:

And the next unto him was Carshena, Shethar, Admatha, Tarshish, Meres, Marsena, and Memucan, the seven princes of Persia and Media, which saw the king's face, and which sat the first in the kingdom;)

What shall we do unto the queen Vashti according to law, because she hath not performed the commandment of the king Ashasuerus by the chamberlains?

And Memucan answered before the king and the princes, Vashti the queen hath not done wrong to the king only, but also to all the princes, and to all the people that are in all the provinces of the king Ahasuerus.

(1:1-16)

265. An aerial view of the ancient mount of Susa (Shushan) in the plain of modern Khuzistan. It was one of the capitals of the Persian Empire and contains the palace of Darius and his successors.

266. Bas-relief at Persepolis. King Darius is shown seated, behind him stands his son and successor Xerxes, and behind him two court officials followed by two guards. In front of Darius are a petitioner and two more attendants.

Ahasuerus-Xerxes, son of Darius I, reigned from 486 to 465 B.C. As soon as he ascended the throne, Xerxes was confronted by a revolt in Egypt. At the same time, the enemies of Judah tried to incite him against that country. Having subjugated the Egyptians and crushed a revolt in Babylon, he attempted to subjugate Greece. After the disastrous outcome of this venture, Xerxes settled down to a life of self-indulgence.

267. Scenes from the Book of Esther are represented in the cycle of paintings from the 3rd-century synagogue at Dura-Europos. In one of the scenes depicted, Ahasuerus and Esther, enthroned, receive a report on the numbers slain in Shushan.

267

Now in Shushan the palace there was a certain Jew, whose name was Mordecai, the son of Jair, the son of Shimei, the son of Kish, a Benjamite;

Who had been carried away from Jerusalem with the captivity which had been carried away with Jeconiah king of Judah, whom Nebuchadnezzar the king of Babylon had carried away.

And he brought up Hadassah, that is, Esther, his uncle's daughter: for she had neither father nor mother, and the maid was fair and beautiful; whom Mordecai, when her father and mother were dead, took for his own daughter.

So it came to pass, when the king's commandment and his decree was heard, and when many maidens were gathered together unto Shushan the palace, to the custody of Hegai, that Esther was brought also unto the king's house, to the custody of Hegai, keeper of the women.

And the maiden pleased him, and she obtained kindness of him; and he speedily gave her her things for purification, with such things as belonged to her, and seven maidens, which were meet to be given her, out of the king's house: and he preferred her and her maids unto the best place of the house of the women.

Esther had not shewed her people nor her kindred: for Mordecai had charged her that she should not shew it.

And Mordecai walked every day before the court of the women's house, to know how Esther did, and what should become of her.

Now when every maid's turn was come to go in to king Ahasuerus, after that she had been twelve months, according to the manner of the women, (for so were the days of their purifications accomplished, to wit, six months with oil of myrrh, and six months with sweet odours, and with other things for the purifying of the women;)

(2:5-12)

On the thirteenth day of the month Adar; and on the fourteenth day of

268. Haman leading Mordecai in triumph through the streets.

269. The month of Adar is represented by the zodiacal sign of Pisces, depicted here on a mosaic from Tiberias.

Adar is the name, of Assyrian origin, of the 12th month in the ancient Jewish calendar. The festival of Purim celebrates the deliverance of the Jews from Haman's plot to destroy them.

Purim (which means "lots") – so called after the lots cast by Haman to determine the month in which the slaughter of the Jews was to take place (Esther 3:7) – is observed on the 14th day of the month of Adar (February or March) in open cities, and on the 15th day of Adar in walled cities. Thus it is celebrated on the 14th in Tel Aviv and other cities, and on the 15th of Adar in Jerusalem and other formerly walled cities. The festival is marked by the reading of the Scroll of Esther in the evening and morning services in synagogues. It is also customary to exchange gifts, distribute alms to the poor and to engage in merriment.

the same rested they, and made it a day of feasting and gladness.

But the Jews that were at Shushan assembled together on the thirteenth day thereof, and the fourteenth thereof; and on the fifteenth day of the same they rested, and made it a day of feasting and gladness. (9:17–18)

But when Esther came before the king, he commanded by letters that his wicked device, which he devised against the Jews, should return upon his own head, and that he and his sons should be hanged on the gallows.

Wherefore they called these days Purim after the name of Pur. Therefore for all the words of this letter, and of that which they had seen concerning this matter, and which had come unto them,

The Jews ordained, and took upon them, and upon their seed, and upon all such as joined themselves unto them, so as it should not fail, that they would keep these two days according to their writing, and according to their appointed time every year;

And that these days should be remembered and kept throughout every generation, every family, every province, and every city; and that these days of Purim should not fail from among the Jews, nor the memorial of them perish from their seed.

Then Esther the queen, the daughter of Abihail, and Mordecai the Jew, wrote with all authority, to confirm this second letter of Purim.

And he sent the letters unto all the Jews, to the hundred twenty and seven provinces of the kingdom of Ahasuerus, with words of peace and truth.

To confirm these days of Purim in their times appointed, according as Mordecai the Jew and Esther the queen had enjoined them, and as they had decreed for themselves and for their seed, the matters of the fastings and their cry.

And the decree of Esther confirmed these matters of Purim; and it was written in the book. (9:25-32)

There was a man in the land of Uz, whose name was Job; and that man was perfect and upright, and one that feared God, and eschewed evil.

And there were born unto him seven sons and three daughters.

His substance also was seven thousand sheep, and three thousand camels, and five hundred yoke of oxen, and five hundred she asses, and a very great household; so that this man was the greatest of all the men of the east.

And his sons went and feasted in their houses, every one his day; and sent and called for their three sisters to eat and to drink with them.

And it was so, when the days of their feasting were gone about, that Job sent and sanctified them, and rose up early in the morning, and offered burnt offerings according to the number of them all: for Job said, It may be that my sons have sinned, and cursed God in their hearts. Thus did Job continually.

Now there was a day when the sons of God came to present themselves before the LORD, and Satan came also among them.

And the LORD said unto Satan, Whence comest thou? Then Satan answered the LORD, and said, From going to and fro in the earth, and from walking up and down in it.

And the LORD said unto Satan, Hast thou considered my servant Job, that there is none like him in the earth, a perfect and an upright man, one that feareth God, and escheweth evil?

Then Satan answered the LORD, and said, Doth Job fear God for nought?

Hast not thou made an hedge about him, and about his house, and about all that he hath on every side? thou hast blessed the work of his hands, and his substance is increased in the land.

But put forth thine hand now, and touch all that he hath, and he will curse thee to thy face.

And the LORD said unto Satan, Behold, all that he hath is in thy power; only upon himself put not forth thine hand. So Satan went forth from the presence of the LORD.

(1:1–12)

270. Man at a weaving loom depicted on a stone relief from Susa, 3300-3000 B.C. (Louvre, Paris).
The process of weaving, of uniting warp and woof, consists of three primary movements: shedding, or dividing the warp into two sets of odd and even threads for the passage of the weft, passing the weft through the "shed" by means of a shuttle, and beating the weft into a web of uniform consistency with the warp. Proficient weavers employ the shuttle at great speed, sending it through the warp in rapid rhythm back and forth, so that the shuttle becomes a mere blur to the eyes of an observer.

Is there not an appointed time to man upon earth? are not his days also like the days of an hireling?

As a servant earnestly desireth the shadow, and as an hireling looketh for the reward of his work:

So am I made to possess months of vanity, and wearisome nights are appointed to me.

When I lie down, I say, When shall I arise, and the night be gone? and I am full of tossings to and fro unto the dawning of the day.

My flesh is clothed with worms and clods of dust; my skin is broken, and become loathsome.

My days are swifter than a weaver's shuttle, and are spent without hope.

(7:1–6)

If I say, I will forget my complaint, I will leave off my heaviness, and comfort myself:

I am afraid of all my sorrows, I know that thou wilt not hold me innocent.

If I be wicked, why then labour I in vain?

If I wash myself with snow water, and make my hands never so clean;

Yet shalt thou plunge me in the ditch, and mine own clothes shall abhor me.

For he is not a man, as I am, that I should answer him, and we should come together in judgment.

Neither is there any daysman betwixt us, that might lay his hand upon us both.

Let him take his rod away from me, and let not his fear terrify me:

Then would I speak, and not fear him; but it is not so with me.

(9:27–35)

271. The Banias waterfalls in the Golan, fed by the melting snows from Mount Hermon. The snow of Mount Hermon as it melts seeps down into the porous ground of the mountain and later bubbles out at its foot into three main springs, one of which is the Banias. The waters of the Banias falls are very clear, cold and refreshing.

271

But now they that are younger than I have me in derision, whose fathers I would have disdained to have set with the dogs of my flock.

Yea, whereto might the strength of their hands profit me, in whom old age was perished?

For want and famine they were solitary; fleeing into the wilderness in former time desolate and waste.

Who cut up mallows by the bushes, and juniper roots for their meat.

(30:1–4)

He sealeth up the hand of every man; that all men may know his work.

(37:7)

272. Mallow *(Malva silvestris)*, thought to be the one mentioned in the Bible.
The mallow is a plant of the genus *Malva*. Several species are found in Israel. During the War of Independence and the siege of Jerusalem in 1948, the citizens of Jerusalem picked mallows and used them for a variety of dishes. The mallow is popularly known by its Arabic name, khubeiza, which means "small loaf," because its edible seeds are flat and round like the round Arab loaves of bread.

273. Drawing of a hand with chiromantic observations, from a manuscript written in Spain (or Southern France), c. 1400.
The observations are taken from a Hebrew treatise allegedly written in England in the 13th century.
The earliest evidence of chiromancy in Judaism appears in writings connected with Cabbala mysticism in the 12th century. In one of these, one can read that at the conclusion of the Sabbath "they used to examine the lines of the palms of the hands, because through the lines on the hands the sages would know a man's fate and the good things in store for him."

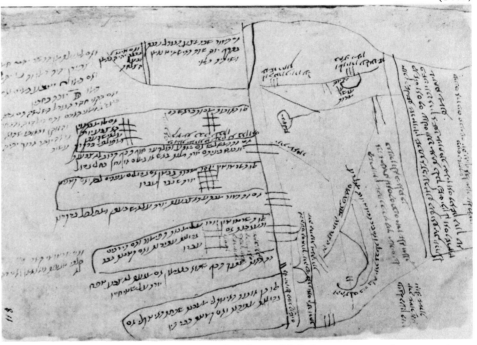

273

Hast thou with him spread out the sky, which is strong, and as a molten looking glass?

Teach us what we shall say unto him; for we cannot order our speech by reason of darkness.

Shall it be told him that I speak? if a man speak, surely he shall be swallowed up.

And now men see not the bright light which is in the clouds: but the wind passeth, and cleanseth them.

Fair weather cometh out of the north: with God is terrible majesty.

(37:18–22)

274. A brass hand mirror and its wooden case, found in the so-called Bar Kochba Caves in the Judean desert, dating back to the 1st century (Shrine of the Book, Israel Museum, Jerusalem).
The foot of the brass laver of the Tabernacle was made "of the looking-glasses of the women" (Exodus 38:8). Ancient mirrors were made of metal and had to be highly polished so as to have good reflecting surfaces.

274

275. Two ivory lions from King Ahab's "house of ivory" in Samaria, 9th century B.C.

275

Then the LORD answered Job out of the whirlwind, and said,

Who is this that darkeneth counsel by words without knowledge?

Gird up now thy loins like a man; for I will demand of thee, and answer thou me.

Where wast thou when I laid the foundations of the earth? declare, if thou hast understanding.

Who hath laid the measures thereof, if thou knowest? or who hath stretched the line upon it?

Whereupon are the foundations thereof fastened? or who laid the corner stone thereof;

When the morning stars sang together, and all the sons of God shouted for joy?

(38:1–7)

Who hath put wisdom in the inward parts? or who hath given understanding to the heart?

Who can number the clouds in wisdom? or who can stay the bottles of heaven,

When the dust groweth into hardness, and the clods cleave fast together?

Wilt thou hunt the prey for the lion? or fill the appetite of the young lions,

When they couch in their dens, and abide in the covert to lie in wait?

Who provideth for the raven his food? when his young ones cry unto God, they wander for lack of meat.

(38:36–41)

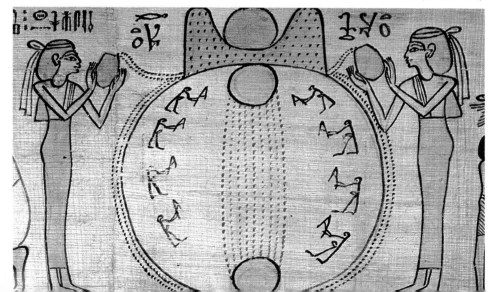

276. The creation of the world, from the papyrus of the priest of Amun Chensumose (Book of the Dead), c.1000 B.C. (Kunsthistorisches Museum, Vienna).

276

277.

277. Camels in the Negev.
In ancient times the camel was used as the principal means for transporting people and goods, especially on long journeys. It is often mentioned in the Bible in connection with the Patriarchs. King David appointed an official in charge of his camels (I Chronicles 27:30). The size of a herd of camels was an indication of its owner's wealth. The wool was used for making tent cloth and clothing.
Although the camel has lost its value as a beast of burden it still represents the principal asset of the Bedouin in desert regions. Camels are used by the Bedouin of the Negev for plowing and in some Arab villages for transporting the harvest to the threshing floor.

And the LORD turned the captivity of Job, when he prayed for his friends: also the LORD gave Job twice as much as he had before.

Then came there unto him all his brethren, and all his sisters, and all they that had been of his acquaintance before, and did eat bread with him in his house: and they bemoaned him, and comforted him over all the evil that the LORD had brought upon him: every man also gave him a piece of money, and every one an earring of gold.

So the LORD blessed the latter end of Job more than his beginning: for he had fourteen thousand sheep, and six thousand camels, and a thousand yoke of oxen, and a thousand she asses.

He had also seven sons and three daughters.

And he called the name of the first, Jemima; and the name of the second, Kezia; and the name of the third, Keren-happuch.

And in all the land were no women found so fair as the daughters of Job: and their father gave them inheritance among their brethren.

After this lived Job an hundred and forty years, and saw his sons, and his sons' sons, even four generations.

So Job died being old and full of days.

(42:10–17)

Blessed is the man that walketh not in the counsel of the ungodly, nor standeth in the way of sinners, nor sitteth in the seat of the scornful.

But his delight is in the law of the LORD; and in his law doth he meditate day and night.

And he shall be like a tree planted by the rivers of water, that bringeth forth his fruit in his season; his leaf also shall not wither; and whatsoever he doeth shall prosper.

The ungodly are not so: but are like the chaff which the wind driveth away.

Therefore the ungodly shall not stand in the judgment, nor sinners in the congregation of the righteous.

For the LORD knoweth the way of the righteous: but the way of the ungodly shall perish. (1:1–6)

Why do the heathen rage, and the people imagine a vain thing?

The kings of the earth set themselves, and the rulers take counsel together, against the LORD, and against his anointed, saying,

Let us break their bands asunder, and cast away their cords from us.

He that sitteth in the heavens shall laugh: the Lord shall have them in derision.

Then shall he speak unto them in his wrath, and vex them in his sore displeasure.

Yet have I set my king upon my holy hill of Zion.

I will declare the decree: the LORD hath said unto me, Thou art my Son: this day have I begotten thee.

Ask of me, and I shall give thee the heathen for thine inheritance, and the uttermost parts of the earth for thy possession.

Thou shalt break them with a rod of iron; thou shalt dash them in pieces like a potter's vessel.

Be wise now therefore, O ye kings: be instructed, ye judges of the earth.

Serve the LORD with fear, and rejoice with trembling.

Kiss the Son, lest he be angry, and ye perish from the way, when his wrath is kindled but a little. Blessed are all they that put their trust in him. (2:1–12)

278. Two courtiers kissing the ground, depicted on a bas-relief from Hermapolis, Egypt. (Private collection, New York).
The kiss in the Bible is a sign of affection, a token of love and, as is probable here (though not excluding the aforementioned), a sign of homage and submission, as illustrated by these Egyptian courtiers. A kiss can also be an act of idolatrous worship, as, for example, the kissing of the golden calf which the prophet Hosea condemns.

278

Preserve me, O God: for in thee do I put my trust.

O my soul, thou hast said unto the LORD, Thou art my Lord: my goodness extendeth not to thee;

But to the saints that are in the earth, and to the excellent, in whom is all my delight.

Their sorrows shall be multiplied that hasten after another god: their drink offerings of blood will I not offer, nor take up their names into my lips.

The LORD is the portion of mine inheritance and of my cup: thou maintainest my lot.

The lines are fallen unto me in pleasant places; yea, I have a goodly heritage.

I will bless the LORD, who hath given me counsel: my reins also instruct me in the night seasons.

I have set the LORD always before me: because he is at my right hand, I shall not be moved.

Therefore my heart is glad, and my glory rejoiceth: my flesh also shall rest in hope.

For thou wilt not leave my soul in hell; neither wilt thou suffer thine Holy One to see corruption.

Thou wilt shew me the path of life: in thy presence is fulness of joy; at thy right hand there are pleasures for evermore.   (16:1–11)

279. *Shiviti* from Morocco, 19th century, painted on glass and decorated with papercuts (Israel Museum, Jerusalem).
A *shiviti* is a votive tablet taking its name from the first word in Hebrew of Psalm 16:8: "I have set the Lord always before me." As part of the daily prayer, the word became an emblem for Jewish devotion in common language, and also designated a tablet containing the above verse, which hangs before those praying in the synagogue. These synagogue plaques contain other verses from the Bible, concerning the Law and the Commandments.

279

280. Assyrian war chariot with charioteer from a bas-relief from the palace of Assurbanipal in Nineveh, 7th century B.C. (Louvre, Paris).

The LORD hear thee in the day of trouble; the name of the God of Jacob defend thee;

Send thee help from the sanctuary, and strengthen thee out of Zion;

Remember all thy offerings, and accept thy burnt sacrifice; Selah.

Grant thee according to thine own heart, and fulfil all thy counsel.

We will rejoice in thy salvation, and in the name of our God we will set up our banners: the LORD fulfil all thy petitions.

Now know I that the LORD saveth his anointed; he will hear him from his holy heaven with the saving strength of his right hand.

Some trust in chariots, and some in horses: but we will remember the name of the LORD our God.

They are brought down and fallen: but we are risen, and stand upright.

Save, LORD: let the king hear us when we call. (20:1–9)

O my God, my soul is cast down within me: therefore will I remember thee from the land of Jordan, and of the Hermonites, from the hill Mizar.

Deep calleth unto deep at the noise of thy waterspouts: all thy waves and thy billows are gone over me.

Yet the LORD will command his lovingkindness in the daytime, and in the night his song shall be with me, and my prayer unto the God of my life.

I will say unto God my rock, Why hast thou forgotten me? why go I mourning because of the oppression of the enemy?

As with a sword in my bones, mine enemies reproach me; while they say daily unto me, Where is thy God?

Why art thou cast down, O my soul? and why art thou disquieted within me? hope thou in God: for I shall yet praise him, who is the health of my countenance, and my God.

(42:6–11)

281. Stag drinking water. Ivory from Samaria, 8th century B.C. (Israel Museum, Jerusalem).

The brooks do not always flow, becoming at times merely dry channels. A thirsty hart, accustomed to quench his thirst at a certain place, may find it dry and cry out by braying, which is what "panting" means here. This picture serves the poet as a metaphor for the thirsty soul who remembers at a time of "dryness" (perhaps exile) his visits to the house of God and prays, asking, "When shall I come and appear before my God?"

Have mercy upon me, O God, acccording to thy lovingkindness: according unto the multitude of thy tender mercies blot out my transgressions.

Wash me throughly from mine iniquity, and cleanse me from my sin.

For I acknowledge my transgressions: and my sin is ever before me.

Against thee, thee only, have I sinned, and done this evil in thy sight: that thou mightest be justified when thou speakest, and be clear when thou judgest.

Behold, I was shapen in iniquity; and in sin did my mother conceive me.

Behold, thou desirest truth in the inward parts: and in the hidden part thou shalt make me to know wisdom.

Purge me with hyssop, and I shall be clean: wash me, and I shall be whiter than snow.

(51:1–7)

282. Hebrew papyrus from the First Temple period, mid-7th century B.C., from Wadi Murabaat in the Judean desert.
The notion of blotting out sins derives from the practice of erasing from papyrus, which was done by a sponge and water blotting out any error. The poet, in line with prevailing concepts, conceives his transgressions as being recorded in a book. His prayer for forgiveness is thus formulated as a request that the record of his sins be blotted from the book. This idea also appears elsewhere in the Bible.

283. A fettered Nubian and an Asiatic prisoner painted on the soles of two sandals (Museo Egizio, Turin).
This scene gives expression to the notion of "putting enemies under foot."

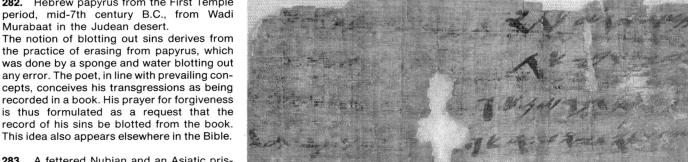

282

O God, thou hast cast us off, thou hast scattered us, thou hast been displeased; O turn thyself to us again.

Thou hast made the earth to tremble; thou hast broken it: heal the breaches thereof; for it shaketh.

Thou hast shewed thy people hard things: thou hast made us to drink the wine of astonishment.

Thou hast given a banner to them that fear thee, that it may be displayed because of the truth. Selah.

That thy beloved may be delivered; save with thy right hand, and hear me.

God hath spoken in his holiness; I will rejoice, I will divide Shechem, and mete out the valley of Succoth.

Gilead is mine, and Manasseh is mine; Ephraim also is the strength of mine head; Judah is my lawgiver;

Moab is my washpot; over Edom will I cast out my shoe: Philistia, triumph thou because of me.

Who will bring me into the strong city? who will lead me into Edom?

Wilt not thou, O God, which hadst cast us off? and thou, O God, which didst not go out with our armies?

Give us help from trouble: for vain is the help of man.

Through God we shall do valiantly: for he it is that shall tread down our enemies.

(60:1–12)

284. Three tributaries depicted on the bronze covering of a door of a palace at Balawat, Persia, 9th century B.C. (Louvre, Paris).

285. Path leading to the archaeological excavations at Shiloh.

The Lord said, I will bring again from Bashan, I will bring my people again from the depths of the sea:

That thy foot may be dipped in the blood of thine enemies, and the tongue of thy dogs in the same.

They have seen thy goings, O God; even the goings of my God, my King, in the sanctuary.

The singers went before, the players on instruments followed after; among them were the damsels playing with timbrels.

Bless ye God in the congregations, even the Lord, from the fountain of Israel.

There is little Benjamin with their ruler, the princes of Judah and their council, the princes of Zebulun, and the princes of Naphtali.

Thy God hath commanded thy strength: strengthen, O God, that which thou hast wrought for us.

Because of thy temple at Jerusalem shall kings bring presents unto thee.

(68:22–29)

He cast out the heathen also before them, and divided them an inheritance by line, and made the tribes of Israel to dwell in their tents.

Yet they tempted and provoked the most high God, and kept not his testimonies:

But turned back, and dealt unfaithfully like their fathers: they were turned aside like a deceitful bow.

For they provoked him to anger with their high places, and moved him to jealousy with their graven images.

When God heard this, he was wroth, and greatly abhorred Israel:

So that he forsook the tabernacle of Shiloh, the tent which he placed among men;

And delivered his strength into captivity, and his glory into the enemy's hand.

(78:55–61)

286

287

Sing aloud unto God our strength: make a joyful noise unto the God of Jacob.

Take a psalm, and bring hither the timbrel, the pleasant harp with the psaltery.

Blow up the trumpet in the new moon, in the time appointed, on our solemn feast day.

(81:1–3)

The LORD reigneth; let the earth rejoice; let the multitude of isles be glad thereof.

Clouds and darkness are round about him: righteousness and judgment are the habitation of his throne.

A fire goeth before him, and burneth up his enemies round about.

His lightnings enlightened the world: the earth saw, and trembled.

The hills melted like wax at the presence of the LORD, at the presence of the Lord of the whole earth.

The heavens declare his righteousness, and all the people see his glory.

Confounded be all they that boast themselves of idols: worship him, all ye gods.

Zion heard, and was glad; and the daughters of Judah rejoiced because of thy judgments, O LORD.

For thou, LORD, art high above all the earth: thou art exalted far above all gods.

Ye that love the LORD, hate evil: he preserveth the souls of his saints: he delivereth them out of the hand of the wicked.

Light is sown for the righteous, and gladness for the upright in heart.

Rejoice in the LORD, ye righteous; and give thanks at the remembrance of his holiness.

(97:1–12)

286. Large stone found on the Herodian pavement at the foot of the wall of the Temple Mount, where it had fallen when the Temple was destroyed. The inscription "To the place of trumpeting" probably refers to the place described by Josephus, in Second Temple times, from which a priest used to blow the trumpet to signal the beginning and ending of the Sabbath or holy day. It was located at the southwest corner of the Temple Mount, where the inscription was found. This corner of the Temple Mount overlooked most of the city's quarters, streets, residences and bazaars and was thus strategically located so that all could hear.

287. Trumpeter, detail of Hittite bas-relief from Carchemish, 9/8th centuries B.C. (Hittite Museum, Ankara).

288. Figurines of baked clay representing fertility goddesses; northern Syrian folk art, 2nd millennium B.C. (Louvre, Paris).

288

O God, my heart is fixed; I will sing and give praise, even with my glory.

Awake, psaltery and harp: I myself will awake early.

I will praise thee, O LORD, among the people: and I will sing praises unto thee among the nations.

For thy mercy is great above the heavens: and thy truth reacheth unto the clouds.

Be thou exalted, O God, above the heavens: and thy glory above all the earth;

That thy beloved may be delivered: save with thy right hand, and answer me.   (108:1–6)

If it had not been the LORD who was on our side, now may Israel say;

If it had not been the LORD who was on our side, when men rose up against us:

Then they had swallowed us up quick, when their wrath was kindled against us:

Then the waters had overwhelmed us, the stream had gone over our soul:

Then the proud waters had gone over our soul.

Blessed be the LORD, who hath not given us as a prey to their teeth.

Our soul is escaped as a bird out of the snare of the fowlers: the snare is broken, and we are escaped.

Our help is in the name of the LORD, who made heaven and earth.   (124:1–8)

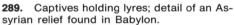

289. Captives holding lyres; detail of an Assyrian relief found in Babylon.
The relief shows an Assyrian soldier with a club and a bow slung over his shoulder conducting barefoot captives, dressed in plain long garments, carrying musical instruments.

290. Netting wild geese, from a wall painting in the tomb of Nakht, scribe and priest of Tuthmose IV.

By the rivers of Babylon, there we sat down, yea, we wept, when we remembered Zion.

We hanged our harps upon the willows in the midst thereof.

For there they that carried us away captive required of us a song; and they that wasted us required of us mirth, saying, Sing us one of the songs of Zion.

How shall we sing the LORD'S song in a strange land?

If I forget thee, O Jerusalem, let my right hand forget her cunning.

If I do not remember thee, let my tongue cleave to the roof of my mouth; if I prefer not Jerusalem above my chief joy.

Remember, O LORD, the children of Edom in the day of Jerusalem; who said, Rase it, rase it, even to the foundation thereof.

O daughter of Babylon, who art to be destroyed; happy shall he be, that rewardeth thee as thou hast served us.

Happy shall he be, that taketh and dasheth thy little ones against the stones.

(137:1–9)

Praise ye the LORD. Sing unto the LORD a new song, and his praise in the congregation of saints.

Let Israel rejoice in him that made him: let the children of Zion be joyful in their King.

Let them praise his name in the dance: let them sing praises unto him with the timbrel and harp.

For the LORD taketh pleasure in his people: he will beautify the meek with salvation.   (149:1–4)

Praise ye the LORD. Praise God in his sanctuary: praise him in the firmament of his power.

Praise him for his mighty acts: praise him according to his excellent greatness.

Praise him with the sound of the trumpet: praise him with the psaltery and harp.

Praise him with the timbrel and dance: praise him with stringed instruments and organs.

Praise him upon the loud cymbals: praise him upon the high sounding cymbals.

Let every thing that hath breath praise the LORD. Praise ye the LORD.

(150:1–6)

291

291. Willow trees grow abundantly all around watercourses in Israel, and, to be sure, most of the references to the willow in the Bible mention this tree as growing by the water.

292. Detail of a pottery incense stand from Ashdod, c. 1000 B.C., showing a figure playing a double pipe (Israel Museum, Jerusalem).

293. Clay figurine of a girl playing the tambourine, c. 8th century B.C. (Israel Museum, Jerusalem).

294. Flute player, bronze, from Byblos, 2nd millennium B.C. (Louvre, Paris).

295

The psalms abound in exhortations to praise the Lord by means of musical instruments. Levitical priests were in charge of the music connected with the Temple, instituted by David. Music also played an important part in the reforms of Hezekiah and Josiah, and in the Restoration in the days of Nehemiah. Music was often accompanied by singing and dancing.
Archaeological finds such as those shown here provide vivid examples of the various instruments employed in biblical times.

295. "This is Solomon who passes judgment over the two women." Miniature from the *British Museum Miscellany.* Written by Benjamin the Scribe, c. 1280, possibly in Troyes, France (British Museum, London). King Solomon was endowed by God, in answer to his prayer, with great wisdom, as illustrated in the story of 1 Kings 3:16-28. The book of Kings also tells that Solomon's wisdom was world-famous, and that it surpassed even that of the Wise Men of the East and of Egypt. Solomon's wisdom brought him much wealth in his commerce with Hiram of Tyre and also, no doubt, gave him guidance in the construction of the Temple. The Queen of Sheba came from afar to marvel at Solomon's wisdom and was so impressed that she fainted (1 Kings 10:5-7), saying "the half was not told me." 1 Kings 4:32-33 ascribes to Solomon the composition of three thousand proverbs and a thousand and five songs. Tradition has thus attributed to Solomon the composition of the Books of Proverbs, Ecclesiastes and the Song of Songs.
According to Jewish tradition Solomon wrote

The proverbs of Solomon the son of David, king of Israel;

To know wisdom and instruction; to perceive the words of understanding;

To receive the instruction of wisdom, justice, and judgment, and equity;

To give subtilty to the simple, to the young man knowledge and discretion.

A wise man will hear, and will increase learning; and a man of understanding shall attain unto wise counsels:

To understand a proverb, and the interpretation; the words of the wise, and their dark sayings.

The fear of the LORD is the beginning of knowledge: but fools despise wisdom and instruction.

(1:1–7)

Wisdom crieth without; she uttereth her voice in the streets:

She crieth in the chief place of concourse, in the openings of the gates: in the city she uttereth her words, saying,

How long, ye simple ones, will ye love simplicity? and the scorners delight in their scorning, and fools hate knowledge?

Turn you at my reproof: behold, I will pour out my spirit unto you, I will make known my words unto you.

(1:20–23)

296

298

the Proverbs and the Song of Songs when he was still young, optimistic and vigorous, whereas in his old age he had become so disillusioned with this world that he exclaimed, "All is vanity," the theme of the Book of Ecclesiastes.

296. Captain and mate on the bridge of a ship; detail of a limestone relief depicting "The Voyage to Punt," at the temple of the Egyptian queen Kemare-Hatshepsut, 15th century B.C.
The complex rigging of a ship makes great skill necessary to steer the vessel on its course. "Wise counsels" may refer metaphorically to the skills of a good sailor, one who "knows the ropes," as the original Hebrew implies.

297. Goddess with scales depicted on a neo-Hittite stele from Marash, Turkey, 9th century B.C.

298. Fragment of a scroll from Qumran known as "The Evil of the Strange Woman" (Shrine of the Book, Israel Museum, Jerusalem), found by Bedouin in the 1950s in a cave. This fragment, part of a poem chastising the evil woman, is an adaptation of the well-known theme of the "strange woman" mentioned several times in the Book of Proverbs. Some scholars think that this "woman" is an allegorical figure, though opinions are divided as to whether she represents Rome, the opponents of the Qumran sectarians or others. It is more likely that the poem simply warns against the enticements of a strange or foreign woman. Consequently, some have accused the members of the Qumran sect of

To deliver thee from the strange woman, even from the stranger which flattereth with her words;

Which forsaketh the guide of her youth, and forgetteth the covenant of her God.

For her house inclineth unto death, and her paths unto the dead.

None that go unto her return again, neither take they hold of the paths of life.

299

297

That thou mayest walk in the way of good men, and keep the paths of the righteous. (2:16–20)

He that gathereth in summer is a wise son: but he that sleepeth in harvest is a son that causeth shame. (10:5)

A false balance is abomination to the LORD: but a just weight is his delight. (11:1)

A righteous man regardeth the life of his beast: but the tender mercies of the wicked are cruel.   (12:10)

The fining pot is for silver, and the furnace for gold: but the LORD trieth the hearts.   (17:3)

Whoso findeth a wife findeth a good thing, and obtaineth favour of the LORD.   (18:22)

The slothful man saith, There is a lion in the way; a lion is in the streets.

As the door turneth upon his hinges, so doth the slothful upon his bed.

The slothful hideth his hand in his bosom; it grieveth him to bring it again to his mouth.

The sluggard is wiser in his own conceit than seven men that can render a reason.   (26:13–16)

300

301

302

303

misogyny, not at all uncommon among societies in which males had total control; but the attitude of the sectarians is more accurately described as gynophobia – fear of women.

299. Detail of a wall painting from the tomb of Mennah, scribe of Tuthmose IV, depicting agricultural scenes. Under the tree to the right sit two men, one of whom has fallen asleep, while, to the left, other men and two women are busy with their labors.

300. Detail of a wall painting from the tomb of Rekhmere depicting a goldsmith at his furnace.

The ancient Egyptians purified gold by placing it in clay crucibles together with lead, salt and a small quantity of tin. The crucibles were sealed and put into a furnace for five days and nights. Barley bran was used as fuel. Silver was refined by placing it in a crucible, a "fining pot," and heating it in a reverberatory furnace. As the oxide of lead – with which the silver was mixed – formed, it was blown off by bellows. The thin covering of oxide eventually became iridescent and disappeared, leaving behind the pure and shiny silver.

The prophets also make use of the metaphor of the goldsmith's furnace in order to portray the process of purification by affliction, as in Malachi 3:2 ff.

301. Egyptian official and his wife, wood carving, 4th dynasty (2650-2500 B.C.) (Louvre, Paris).

302. Men at meal in a military encampment; detail of a bas-relief from the palace of Assurbanipal in Nineveh, 7th century B.C.

One of the recurring subjects of the Book of Proverbs is slothfulness and these verses, though satirical in tone, give an incisive description of the slothful man. In verse 15 "bosom" should be, according to the Hebrew, "plate" or "bowl" such as that depicted here. The slothful man is such a slave to his vice that even the effort required to satisfy his own hunger is beyond him.

303. An Arab farmer using an ox and an ass for plowing his field. Such a scene is becoming rare nowadays as machines replace animals.

304

Ointment and perfume rejoice the heart: so doth the sweetness of a man's friend by hearty counsel.

(27:9)

The words of king Lemuel, the prophecy that his mother taught him.

What, my son? and what, the son of my womb? and what, the son of my vows?

Give not thy strength unto women, nor thy ways to that which destroyeth kings.

It is not for kings, O Lemuel, it is not for kings to drink wine; nor for princes strong drink:

Lest they drink, and forget the law, and pervert the judgment of any of the afflicted.

Give strong drink unto him that is ready to perish, and wine unto those that be of heavy hearts.

Let him drink, and forget his poverty, and remember his misery no more.

Open thy mouth for the dumb in the cause of all such as are appointed to destruction.

Open thy mouth, judge righteously, and plead the cause of the poor and needy.

(31:1–9)

This photograph illustrates an action forbidden by the Bible; as it is said in Deuteronomy 22:10: "Thou shalt not plow with an ox and an ass together," which was thought cruel since the ox is stronger than the ass, and therefore it demands a greater effort from the ass to accomplish the same work as required from the ox.

Moral and legal rules concerning the treatment of animals in the Bible are based on the principle that animals are part of God's creation for which man bears responsibility.

The Books of Exodus, Deuteronomy and Leviticus especially inculcate, in a number of verses, just and merciful treatment of animals. Among the rules given, Moses enjoins proper care of domestic animals. When found straying, these were to be returned safely to their owner; they were not to be overloaded beyond their strength; they were to be worked humanely, and they, as well as man, were to benefit from the Sabbath rest.

304. The production of perfume; relief on a sarcophagus of the Egyptian 16th dynasty, 17th century B.C. (Louvre, Paris).

Ointment generally refers to perfumed oil and perfumes were highly valued in the ancient Near East, comprising a major trade commodity and frequently included in tributary gifts. The materials used in the production of perfumes were gums, resins, roots, leaves and barks of various kinds, which were combined in different ways according to the skill of the perfumer. Nehemiah 3:8 mentions "Hananiah the son of one of the apothecaries," i.e. a member of the perfumers' guild, as one of those who helped fortify the wall of Jerusalem.

305

306

Who can find a virtuous woman? for her price is far above rubies.

The heart of her husband doth safely trust in her, so that he shall have no need of spoil.

She will do him good and not evil all the days of her life.

She seeketh wool, and flax, and worketh willingly with her hands.

She is like the merchants' ships; she bringeth her food from afar.

She riseth also while it is yet night, and giveth meat to her household, and a portion to her maidens.

She considereth a field, and buyeth it: with the fruit of her hands she planteth a vineyard.

She girdeth her loins with strength, and strengtheneth her arms.

She perceiveth that her merchandise is good: her candle goeth not out by night.

She layeth her hands to the spindle, and her hands hold the distaff.

She stretcheth out her hand to the poor; yea, she reacheth forth her hands to the needy.

She is not afraid of the snow for her household: for all her household are clothed with scarlet.

She maketh herself coverings of tapestry; her clothing is silk and purple.

Her husband is known in the gates, when he sitteth among the elders of the land.

She maketh fine linen, and selleth it; and delivereth girdles unto the merchant.

Strength and honour are her clothing; and she shall rejoice in time to come.

She openeth her mouth with wisdom; and in her tongue is the law of kindness.

She looketh well to the ways of her household, and eateth not the bread of idleness.

Her children arise up, and call her blessed; her husband also, and he praiseth her.

Many daughters have done virtuously, but thou excellest them all.

Favour is deceitful, and beauty is vain: but a woman that feareth the LORD, she shall be praised.

Give her of the fruit of her hands; and let her own works praise her in the gates.

(31:10–31)

The words of the Preacher, the son of David, king in Jerusalem.

Vanity of vanities, saith the Preacher, vanity of vanities; all is vanity.

What profit hath a man of all his labour which he taketh under the sun?

One generation passeth away, and another generation cometh: but the earth abideth for ever.

The sun also ariseth, and the sun goeth down, and hasteth to his place where he arose.

The wind goeth toward the south, and turneth about unto the north; it whirleth about continually, and the wind returneth again according to his circuits.

All the rivers run into the sea; yet the sea is not full; unto the place from whence the rivers come, thither they return again.

All things are full of labour; man cannot utter it: the eye is not satisfied with seeing, nor the ear filled with hearing.

The thing that hath been, it is that which shall be; and that which is done is that which shall be done: and there is no new thing under the sun.

Is there any thing whereof it may be said, See, this is new? it hath been already of old time, which was before us.

There is no remembrance of former things; neither shall there be any remembrance of things that are to come with those that shall come after.

I the Preacher was king over Israel in Jerusalem.

And I gave my heart to seek and search out by wisdom concerning all things that are done under heaven: this sore travail hath God given to the sons of man to be exercised therewith.

I have seen all the works that are done under the sun; and behold, all is vanity and vexation of spirit.

That which is crooked cannot be made straight: and that which is wanting cannot be numbered.

I communed with mine own heart, saying, Lo, I am come to great estate, and have gotten more wisdom than all they that have been before me in Jerusalem: yea, my heart had great experience of wisdom and knowledge.

And I gave my heart to know wisdom, and to know madness and folly: I perceived that this also is vexation of spirit.

For in much wisdom is much grief: and he that increaseth knowledge increaseth sorrow.

(1:1–18)

307. A view of one of the three water reservoirs located about three miles south of Bethlehem, known as Solomon's Pools.
This attribution is surely legendary, based on Josephus' report that Solomon frequently came here to enjoy the waters and gardens. In reality, the pools were built during the Second Temple period, probably in the reign of Herod the Great, and were part of the ancient water-supply system of Jerusalem.

I sought in mine heart to give myself unto wine, yet acquainting mine heart with wisdom; and to lay hold on folly, till I might see what was that good for the sons of men, which they should do under the heaven all the days of their life.

I made me great works; I builded me houses; I planted me vineyards:

I made me gardens and orchards, and I planted trees in them of all kind of fruits.

I made me pools of water, to water therewith the wood that bringeth forth trees: (2:3–6)

That which hath been is named already, and it is known that it is man: neither may he contend with him that is mightier than he.

Seeing there be many things that increase vanity, what is man the better?

For who knoweth what is good for man in this life, all the days of his vain life which he spendeth as a shadow? for who can tell a man what shall be after him under the sun?   (6:10–12)

A good name is better than precious ointment; and the day of death than the day of one's birth.

                                                                             (7:1)

308. Egyptian ointment jar from the tomb of Tutankhamun, 14th century B.C. (Egyptian Museum, Cairo).
The cynicism of "The Preacher" is somewhat relieved in his hinting that a good name or reputation transcends the vanity symbolized by precious ointment. The proverbial saying, "A good name is better than precious ointment," which comprises a nice word-play in Hebrew, implies that the "fragrance" of a good reputation wafts to some benefit and is sweeter than that of expensive ointments, perhaps even suggesting that a good name soothes like a salve the harshness of the world of vanity which the poet describes.

308

This is an evil among all things that are done under the sun, that there is one event unto all: yea, also the heart of the sons of men is full of evil, and madness is in their heart while they live, and after that they go to the dead.

For to him that is joined to all the living there is hope: for a living dog is better than a dead lion.

For the living know that they shall die: but the dead know not any thing, neither have they any more a reward; for the memory of them is forgotten.

Also their love, and their hatred, and their envy, is now perished; neither have they any more a portion for ever in any thing that is done under the sun.

(9:3–6)

309. A corner of the old cemetery at Safed. Here are buried several 15th-century Jewish scholars who made a considerable contribution to mystical philosophy. These sages, expelled from Spain in the 15th century, found refuge in the Holy Land.

310. Detail depicting birds in flight from a wall painting from the tomb of Nakht, scribe and priest of Tuthmose IV.

311. The almond tree blooms in the Holy Land in January or February, while other trees are still bare. Moreover, the blossoms appear before the tree is covered with leaves. It is then adorned with lovely pink and sometimes white flowers arranged in pairs. Here it is used figuratively to signify old age, the flourishing of the almond tree being likened to the white hair of old age.

Curse not the king, no not in thy thought; and curse not the rich in thy bedchamber: for a bird of the air shall carry the voice, and that which hath wings shall tell the matter.

(10:20)

Remember now thy Creator in the days of thy youth, while the evil days come not, nor the years draw nigh, when thou shalt say, I have no pleasure in them;

While the sun, or the light, or the moon, or the stars, be not darkened, nor the clouds return after the rain:

In the day when the keepers of the house shall tremble, and the strong men shall bow themselves, and the grinders cease because they are few, and those that look out of the windows be darkened,

And the doors shall be shut in the streets, when the sound of the grinding is low, and he shall rise up at the voice of the bird, and all the daughters of musick shall be brought low;

Also when they shall be afraid of that which is high, and fears shall be in the way, and the almond tree shall flourish, and the grasshopper shall be a burden, and desire shall fail: because man goeth to his long home, and the mourners go about the streets.

(12:1–5)

The song of songs, which is Solomon's.

Let him kiss me with the kisses of his mouth: for thy love is better than wine.

Because of the savour of thy good ointments thy name is as ointment poured forth, therefore do the virgins love thee.

Draw me, we will run after thee: the king hath brought me into his chambers: we will be glad and rejoice in thee, we will remember thy love more than wine: the upright love thee.

I am black, but comely, O ye daughters of Jerusalem, as the tents of Kedar, as the curtains of Solomon.

Look not upon me, because I am black, because the sun hath looked upon me: my mother's children were angry with me; they made me the keeper of the vineyards; but mine own vineyard have I not kept.

Tell me, O thou whom my soul loveth, where thou feedest, where thou makest thy flock to rest at noon: for why should I be as one that turneth aside by the flocks of thy companions?

If thou know not, O thou fairest among women, go thy way forth by the footsteps of the flock, and feed thy kids beside the shepherds' tents.

I have compared thee, O my love, to a company of horses in Pharaoh's chariots.

Thy cheeks are comely with rows of jewels, thy neck with chains of gold.

We will make thee borders of gold with studs of silver.

While the king sitteth at his table, my spikenard sendeth forth the smell thereof.

A bundle of myrrh is my wellbeloved unto me; he shall lie all night betwixt my breasts.

My beloved is unto me as a cluster of camphire in the vineyards of En-gedi.

Behold, thou art fair, my love; behold, thou art fair; thou hast doves' eyes.

Behold, thou art fair, my beloved, yea, pleasant: also our bed is green.

The beams of our house are cedar, and our rafters of fir.   (1:1–17)

312. The Fountain of the Kids, also called David's Fountain, a beautiful spring sparkling in the wild, luxuriant gorge at En-gedi, foams over the rocks in a picturesque waterfall. En-gedi was one of the cities of Judah, where David found shelter from Saul who "took three thousand chosen men out of all Israel, and went to seek David and his men upon the rocks of the wild goats..." (I Samuel 24:2). En-gedi was famed for its fruitful vineyards which covered the slopes of the surrounding mountains. To Ezekiel it was a symbol of fertility and abundance (Ezekiel 47:10).

313. The Song of Solomon has been interpreted in different ways. The original setting of the beautiful love poetry of the book may have been secular songs sung at wedding feasts in praise of the bride and groom. Both Jewish and Christian tradition have had reservations concerning its explicit references to erotic love and have allegorized it by interpretation: the former as an allegory of God and his love for the Children of Israel, the latter as an allegory of Christ and the Church.

312   313

I am the rose of Sharon, and the lily of the valleys.
As the lily among thorns, so is my love among the daughters.

(2:1–2)

The flowers appear on the earth; the time of the singing of birds is come, and the voice of the turtle is heard in our land.

(2:12)

314

315

316

317

Thy teeth are like a flock of sheep that are even shorn, which came up from the washing; whereof every one bear twins, and none is barren among them.

Thy lips are like a thread of scarlet, and thy speech is comely: thy temples are like a piece of a pomegranate within thy locks.

(4:2–3)

Spikenard and saffron; calamus and cinnamon, with all trees of frankincense; myrrh and aloes, with all the chief spices:

314. Narcissus.
The "lily of the valley" may be one of the following four flowers: the narcissus, the wild tulip, the crocus or the anemone.
The narcissus grows in the generally monotonous landscape of the swamplands. It has white petals with an orange crown in the center and is the first flower to bloom in winter.

315. The wild tulip of Israel, deep red in color, cannot compete with its cultivated relatives in hues, though in beauty and form it is their equal.

316. Sea daffodils.
All along the Mediterranean shore in Israel, large white flowers shoot up from the sand among the rocks in the dry summer months: these are the sea daffodils which some scholars identify with the "rose of Sharon."

317. The anemones bloom over hill and dale, everywhere from the Negev to the Galilee.

318. A flock of sheep beside a pond at the foot of Mount Hermon.

318

A fountain of gardens, a well of living waters, and streams from Lebanon.

Awake, O north wind; and come, thou south; blow upon my garden, that the spices thereof may flow out. Let my beloved come into his garden, and eat his pleasant fruits.

(4:14–16)

319

319. View of the Dan Spring, one of the three sources of the Jordan River. It is fed by the waters of the melting snows of Mount Hermon, "Lebanon," which seep into the ground and later bubble up in a multitude of springs which join together to form the Dan River. At the source of the Dan there is lush vegetation.

320. Branch of myrrh (*Commiphora abyssinia*) with fruit, a shrub which also grows in Africa and in the Arabian peninsula. This plant contains a fragrant sap under the bark. It was one of the most important perfumes of ancient times. It was used to prepare the holy anointing oil in the Tabernacle (Exodus 30:23). In the Book of Esther (2:12) the maidens were treated with myrrh for six months before being presented to the king.

321. Mandrake plant with fruit. It grows in all regions of Israel.

Come, my beloved, let us go forth into the field; let us lodge in the villages.

Let us get up early to the vineyards; let us see if the vine flourish, whether the tender grape appear, and the pomegranates bud forth: there will I give thee my loves.

The mandrakes give a smell, and at our gates are all manner of pleasant fruits, new and old, which I have laid up for thee, O my beloved.

(7:11–13)

322. Just as the ibex is king of the rocks, the gazelle reigns over the plains and hills. The ancient Hebrew had good reason to see the gazelle as a symbol of beauty and love. No one observing this shy, wild animal with its graceful neck and slender legs, and the gentle expression upon its face, could think otherwise.

320

321

322

Solomon had a vineyard at Baal-hamon; he let out the vineyard unto keepers; every one for the fruit thereof was to bring a thousand pieces of silver.

My vineyard, which is mine, is before me: thou, O Solomon, must have a thousand, and those that keep the fruit thereof two hundred.

Thou that dwellest in the gardens, the companions hearken to thy voice: cause me to hear it.

Make haste, my beloved, and be thou like to a roe or to a young hart upon the mountains of spices.

(8:11–14)

To what purpose is the multitude of your sacrifices unto me? saith the LORD: I am full of the burnt offerings of rams, and the fat of fed beasts; and I delight not in the blood of bullocks, or of lambs, or of he goats.

When ye come to appear before me, who hath required this at your hand, to tread my courts?

Bring no more vain oblations; incense is an abomination unto me; the new moons and sabbaths, the calling of assemblies, I cannot away with; it is iniquity, even the solemn meeting.

Your new moons and your appointed feasts my soul hateth: they are a trouble unto me; I am weary to bear them.

And when ye spread forth your hands, I will hide mine eyes from you: yea, when ye make many prayers, I will not hear: your hands are full of blood.

Wash you, make you clean; put away the evil of your doings from before mine eyes; cease to do evil;

Learn to do well; seek judgment, relieve the oppressed, judge the fatherless, plead for the widow.

Come now, and let us reason together, saith the LORD: though your sins be as scarlet, they shall be as white as snow; though they be red like crimson, they shall be as wool.

If ye be willing and obedient, ye shall eat the good of the land:

But if ye refuse and rebel, ye shall be devoured with the sword: for the mouth of the LORD hath spoken it.

(1:11–20)

323. Memorial stone of the prince general Sebeki; limestone relief, c. 1970 B.C. (Staatliche Sammlung Aegyptischer Kunst, Munich).
The scene depicts the extreme religiosity of an Egyptian prince, whose anxious desire to find favor in the eyes of his gods is indicated by the table piled high with offerings and sacrifices.
The prophets of Israel frequently condemn such an approach to God and give vivid expression to their conviction that "rite" without "right" is abominable to the Lord.

324. Two winged genii on an ivory plaque from Arslan Tash, Northern Syria, 8th century B.C. (Louvre, Paris).
The Seraphim were part of the divine assembly in the heavens, seen by Isaiah in his vision on the occasion of his divine commission as a prophet. Such heavenly visions as recorded in the Bible always retain an air of mystery and inspire much speculation as to the character and appearance of divine beings and even the Godhead himself. Portrayals of winged beings are quite common in the art of the ancient Near East.
Though the Seraphim are described here as having six wings (and, indeed, depictions have been found of six-winged creatures!), the beings depicted here could illustrate the creatures described in Isaiah's vision.

323

In the year that king Uzziah died I saw also the Lord sitting upon a throne, high and lifted up, and his train filled the temple.

Above it stood the seraphims: each one had six wings; with twain he covered his face, and with twain he covered his feet, and with twain he did fly.

And one cried unto another, and said, Holy, holy, holy, is the LORD of hosts: the whole earth is full of his glory.

(6:1–3)

324

325. Detail from a wall painting in the tomb of Mennah, scribe of Tuthmose IV, depicting a scribe recording the harvest on a "roll". Scribes were employed by ancient Near Eastern kings to record not only harvest yields, as here, but especially to record the spoils taken from conquered enemies. The Lord's command to Isaiah here makes him essentially such a scribe, recording not the actual spoils, but the prophecy that Samaria will be subjugated and plundered by the king of Assyria. This prophecy is also expressed when the Lord commands Isaiah to give his son a name with a prophetic portent: Maher-shalal-hashbaz, meaning "Hurry, spoil! He has come quickly to the plunder," or, "Hastening to the spoil, he has come quickly to the plunder."

326. Copper saw found near Nahariya, Israel (Israel Museum, Jerusalem).
Israel's prophets often referred to everyday objects in their prophecies. Here Isaiah points out the limitations of the king of Assyria's power by referring to the purely utilitarian use of an axe or a saw or rod, inquiring rhetorically and not without irony whether a mere tool can raise itself against its wielder, thus highlighting the Lord's sovereignty over the affairs of the world.

Moreover the LORD said unto me, Take thee a great roll, and write in it with a man's pen concerning Maher-shalal-hash-baz.

And I took unto me faithful witnesses to record, Uriah the priest, and Zechariah the son of Jeberechiah.

And I went unto the prophetess; and she conceived, and bare a son. Then said the LORD to me, Call his name Maher-shalal-hash-baz.

For before the child shall have knowledge to cry, My father, and my mother, the riches of Damascus and the spoil of Samaria shall be taken away before the king of Assyria.   (8:1–4)

Shall the axe boast itself against him that heweth therewith? or shall the saw magnify itself against him that shaketh it? as if the rod should shake itself against them that lift it up, or as if the staff should lift up itself, as if it were no wood.

Therefore shall the Lord, the Lord of hosts, send among his fat ones leanness; and under his glory he shall kindle a burning like the burning of a fire.

And the light of Israel shall be for a fire, and his Holy One for a flame: and it shall burn and devour his thorns and his briers in one day;

And shall consume the glory of his forest, and of his fruitful field, both soul and body: and they shall be as when a standardbearer fainteth.

And the rest of the trees of his forest shall be few, that a child may write them.   (10:15–19)

325

326

Thus saith the LORD GOD of hosts, Go, get thee unto this treasurer, even unto Shebna, which is over the house, and say,

What hast thou here? and whom hast thou here, that thou hast hewed thee out a sepulchre here, as he that heweth him out a sepulchre on high, and that graveth an habitation for himself in a rock?

Behold, the LORD will carry thee away with a mighty captivity, and will surely cover thee.

(22:15–17)

327. Rock hewn tomb thought to be that of Shebna, chief minister of Hezekiah, king of Judah. This is one of several caves on the eastern scarp of the Kidron Valley, now in the village of Silwan.
The tomb is identified on the basis of an inscription mentioning "...yahu which is over the house," the biblical title equivalent to "prime minister," appearing on the tomb, itself identified on the basis of this verse in Isaiah. The partly missing name can easily be reconstructed as Shebnayahu.

328. Detail from a wall painting in the tomb of Nakht, scribe and priest of Tuthmose IV, depicting a blind harpist playing for the deceased.
Blindness was a fairly common affliction in the Near East, and it is mentioned a number of times in the Bible and in ancient Near Eastern sources. The prophet refers to the blind recovering their sight just as those who "erred in spirit" attain understanding.

327

328

Surely your turning of things upside down shall be esteemed as the potter's clay: for shall the work say of him that made it, He made me not? or shall the thing framed say of him that framed it, He had no understanding?

Is it not yet a very little while, and Lebanon shall be turned into a fruitful field, and the fruitful field shall be esteemed as a forest?

And in that day shall the deaf hear the words of the book, and the eyes of the blind shall see out of obscurity, and out of darkness.

The meek also shall increase their joy in the LORD, and the poor among men shall rejoice in the Holy One of Israel.

For the terrible one is brought to nought, and the scorner is consumed, and all that watch for iniquity are cut off:

That make a man an offender for a word, and lay a snare for him that reproveth in the gate, and turn aside the just for a thing of nought.

Therefore thus saith the LORD, who redeemed Abraham, concerning the house of Jacob, Jacob shall not now be ashamed, neither shall his face now wax pale.

But when he seeth his children, the work of mine hands, in the midst of him, they shall sanctify my name, and sanctify the Holy One of Jacob, and shall fear the God of Israel.

They also that erred in spirit shall come to understanding, and they that murmured shall learn doctrine.

(29:16–24)

329

329. Wall painting from the tomb of Rekhmere depicting carpenters and goldsmiths at work.
Isaiah compares God's care for the seed of Abraham with the collaboration of craftsmen in the creation of a perfect work.

So the carpenter encouraged the goldsmith, and he that smootheth with the hammer him that smote the anvil, saying, It is ready for the sodering: and he fastened it with nails, that it should not be moved.

But thou, Israel, art my servant, Jacob whom I have chosen, the seed of Abraham my friend.

Thou whom I have taken from the ends of the earth, and called thee from the chief men thereof, and said unto thee, Thou art my servant; I have chosen thee, and not cast thee away. (41:7–9)

Hearken to me, ye that follow after righteousness, ye that seek the LORD: look unto the rock whence ye are hewn, and to the hole of the pit whence ye are digged.

Look unto Abraham your father, and unto Sarah that bare you: for I called him alone, and blessed him, and increased him.

For the LORD shall comfort Zion: he will comfort all her waste places; and he will make her wilderness like Eden, and her desert like the garden of the LORD; joy and gladness shall be found therein, thanksgiving, and the voice of melody. (51:1–3)

330. Wall painting of a lush garden, from the tomb of Sennutem, 13th century B.C.
A bountiful land, watered by irrigation channels, was the picture of the blissful afterlife for the ancient Egyptians. The same motif is found in Mesopotamia and Israel. Isaiah refers here to the comforting of Zion as a restoration of the Garden of Eden, proclaiming that God's salvation and righteousness shall be forever.

331. The village of Anata today is about three miles north of Jerusalem and near the site of ancient Anathoth. This was a city of the Levites in the territory of Benjamin (Joshua 21:18) and the birthplace of two of David's mighty men (II Samuel 23:27). King Solomon banished the high priest Abiathar to his own fields at Anathoth. It was resettled after the Jews returned from exile (Ezra 2:23; Nehemiah 7:27: 11:32).

332. The deep and narrow Valley of Hinnom is a continuation of the Kidron Valley in Jerusalem. It has become known as Gehenna, the Greek form of the Hebrew Gei-Hinnom. There, at a place called Tophet, the Judean kings Ahaz and Manasseh engaged in idolatrous worship involving the burning of children (II Kings 23:10). This was strictly forbidden by the Law as enjoined in Deuteronomy 18:10 : "There shall not be found among you any one that maketh his son or his daughter to pass through fire . . ." Jeremiah repeatedly condemned this cult and predicted that on this account Tophet and the Valley of Hinnom would be called the "Valley of the Slaughter." Because it was a place of depravity and abomination, the name Gehinnom (Gehenna) came to be given to the place prepared for the wicked in the world to come – as opposed to the Garden of Eden, where the just and righteous shall dwell in everlasting happiness. The sages of Israel said: "There are three entrances to Gehinnom-hell: one in the wilderness, one in the sea, and one in Jerusalem." They based this interpretation on the verse of Isaiah: "Saith the Lord, whose fire is Zion, and his furnace in Jerusalem."

333. The site of Lachish today. One of the cities of Judah destroyed by Nebuchadnezzar, king of Babylon, was Lachish. More than a hundred years earlier the city had been besieged by Assyrian King Sennacherib who recorded his victory in a relief in his palace at Nineveh.

The words of Jeremiah the son of Hilkiah, of the priests that were in Anathoth in the land of Benjamin.

To whom the word on the LORD came in the days of Josiah the son of Amon king of Judah, in the thirteenth year of his reign.

It came also in the days of Jehoiakim the son of Josiah king of Judah, unto the end of the eleventh year of Zedekiah the son of Josiah king of Judah, unto the carrying away of Jerusalem captive in the fifth month.

Then the word of the LORD came unto me saying,

Before I formed thee in the belly I knew thee; and before thou camest forth out of the womb I sanctified thee, and I ordained thee a prophet unto the nations.

Then said I, Ah, Lord God! behold, I cannot speak: for I am a child.

But the LORD said unto me, Say not, I am a child: for thou shalt go to all that I shall send thee, and whatsoever I command thee thou shalt speak.

Be not afraid of their faces: for I am with thee to deliver thee, saith the LORD.

Then the LORD put forth his hand, and touched my mouth. And the LORD said unto me, Behold, I have put my words in thy mouth.

See, I have this day set thee over the nations and over the kingdoms, to root out, and to pull down, and to destroy, and to throw down, to build, and to plant.   (1:1–10)

And they have built the high places of Tophet, which is in the valley of the son of Hinnom, to burn their sons and their daughters in the fire; which I commanded them not, neither came it into my heart.

Therefore, behold, the days come, saith the LORD, that it shall no more be called Tophet, nor the valley of the son of Hinnom, but the valley of slaughter: for they shall bury in Tophet, till there be no place.

And the carcases of this people shall be meat for the fowls of the heaven, and for the beasts of the earth; and none shall fray them away.

(7:31–33)

*Can the Ethiopian change his skin, or the leopard his spots? then may
ye also do good, that are accustomed to do evil.*

(13:23)

And I charged Baruch before them, saying,
*Thus saith the LORD of hosts, the God of Israel; Take these evidences,
this evidence of the purchase, both which is sealed, and this evidence which
is open; and put them in an earthen vessel, that they may continue many
days.*

*For thus saith the LORD of hosts, the God of Israel; Houses and fields
and vineyards shall be possessed again in this land.*

(32:13–15)

*Then Jeremiah the prophet spake all these words unto Zedekiah king of
Judah in Jerusalem,*
*When the king of Babylon's army fought against Jerusalem, and
against all the cities of Judah that were left, against Lachish, and against
Azekah: for these defenced cities remained of the cities of Judah.*

(34:6–7)

*And I will give the men that have transgressed my covenant, which have
not performed the words of the covenant which they had made before me,
when they cut the calf in twain, and passed between the parts thereof,*
*The princes of Judah, and the princes of Jerusalem, the eunuchs, and
the priests, and all the people of the land, which passed between the parts of
the calf;*
*I will even give them into the hand of their enemies, and into the hand of
them that seek their life: and their dead bodies shall be for meat unto the
fowls of the heaven, and to the beasts of the earth.*

*And Zedekiah king of Judah and his princes will I give into the hand of
their enemies, and into the hand of them that seek their life, and into the
hand of the king of Babylon's army, which are gone up from you.*

*Behold, I will command, saith the LORD, and cause them to return to
this city; and they shall fight against it, and take it, and burn it with fire:
and I will make the cities of Judah a desolation without an inhabitant.*

(34:18–22)

334

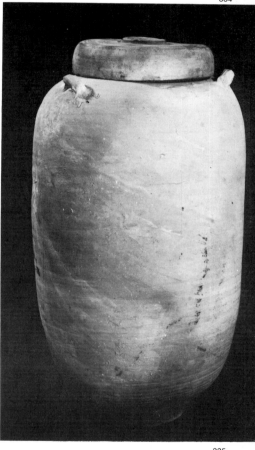

335

334. Although several leopards have been
seen not far from Jerusalem in recent years,
they are the last survivors of the large beasts
of prey that roamed the countryside in ancient
times.

335. Clay jar in which the famous Qumran
Scrolls were discovered.
This passage in Jeremiah reflects both the
legal practice of real estate transactions and
the depositing of the "evidences" in an
earthen vessel for their preservation. The fact
that the Qumran Scrolls were preserved for
nearly 2000 years illustrates the purpose of
the earthen vessel – "that they may continue
for many days."

333

336

Then Jeremiah called Baruch the son of Neriah: and Baruch wrote from the mouth of Jeremiah all the words of the LORD, which he had spoken unto him, upon a roll of a book.

And Jeremiah commanded Baruch, saying, I am shut up; I cannot go into the house of the LORD:

Therefore go thou, and read in the roll, which thou hast written from my mouth, the words of the LORD in the ears of the people in the LORD'S house upon the fasting day: and also thou shalt read them in the ears of all Judah that come out of their cities.

It may be they will present their supplication before the LORD, and will return every one from his evil way: for great is the anger and the fury that the LORD hath pronounced against this people.

And Baruch the son of Neriah did according to all that Jeremiah the prophet commanded him, reading in the book the words of the LORD in the LORD'S house.

(36:4–8)

336. Seal with the name "Be(rachaiah) the son of Neriahu the scribe," found in Judah. It may actually have belonged to Jeremiah's scribe. Baruch is a shorter version of the name Berachaiah. The Book of Jeremiah is the only book of the Bible which describes the writing down of a prophet's words (Israel Museum, Jerusalem).

337. Weapons believed to have been brought to Punt by Egyptian ships, 15th century B.C.
The instrument of God's punishment of Babylon was now Jacob, just as Babylon was formerly God's instrument against Israel.
The judgment against Babylon was particularly severe. It is contained in whole chapters (110 verses) and concludes the Book of Jeremiah (except for the historical account in Chapter 52). Such a severe judgment is dealt, no doubt, because Babylon despoiled and destroyed the Temple.

337

The portion of Jacob is not like them; for he is the former of all things: and Israel is the rod of his inheritance: the LORD of hosts is his name.

Thou art my battle axe and weapons of war: for with thee will I break in pieces the nations, and with thee will I destroy kingdoms;

And with thee will I break in pieces the horse and his rider; and with thee will I break in pieces the chariot and his rider;

With thee also will I break in pieces man and woman; and with thee will I break in pieces old and young; and with thee will I break in pieces the young man and the maid;

I will also break in pieces with thee the shepherd and his flock; and with thee will I break in pieces the husbandman and his yoke of oxen; and with thee will I break in pieces captains and rulers.

And I will render unto Babylon and to all the inhabitants of Chaldea all their evil that they have done in Zion in your sight, saith the LORD.

(51:19–24)

How doth the city sit solitary, that was full of people! how is she become as a widow! she that was great among the nations, and princess among the provinces, how is she become tributary!

She weepeth sore in the night, and her tears are on her cheeks: among all her lovers she hath none to comfort her: all her friends have dealt treacherously with her, they are become her enemies.

Judah is gone into captivity because of affliction, and because of great servitude: she dwelleth among the heathen, she findeth no rest: all her persecutors overtook her between the straits.

The ways of Zion do mourn, because none come to the solemn feasts: all her gates are desolate: her priests sigh, her virgins are afflicted, and she is in bitterness.

Her adversaries are the chief, her enemies prosper; for the LORD hath afflicted her for the multitude of her transgressions: her children are gone into captivity before the enemy.

(1:1–5)

338. Warriors trampling enemies under foot, depicted on Stele of the Vultures, Lagash, c. 2450 B.C. (Louvre, Paris).

339. Praying at the Western Wall or Wailing Wall on the 9th of Ab.
On the ninth day of the Jewish month of Ab, which is the anniversary date of the destruction of the Temple, pious Jews come to pray at the Western Wall.
On that day, the Scroll of Lamentations is read as well as the Book of Job, some verses of Leviticus (26:12–16), and some chapters of the Book of Jeremiah (Chapter 39 for example).
For many generations Jews from all corners of the earth have come here to pray at this sad relic of departed glory and to mourn the destruction of their Temple first built by Solomon, destroyed in 586 B.C., rebuilt fifty years later, and destroyed a second time by the Romans in A.D. 70. When Jerusalem was defeated by the Romans, four commanders

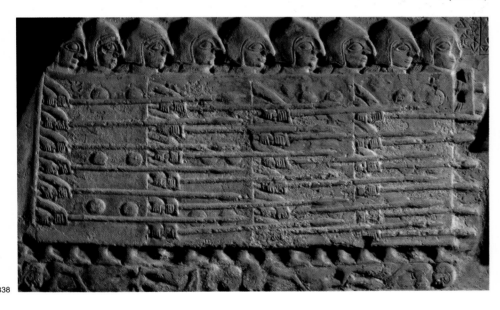

338

339

The yoke of my transgressions is bound by his hand: they are wreathed, and come up upon my neck: he hath made my strength to fall, the LORD hath delivered me into their hands, from whom I am not able to rise up.

The LORD hath trodden under foot all my mighty men in the midst of me: he hath called an assembly against me to crush my young men: the LORD hath trodden the virgin, the daughter of Judah, as in a winepress.

For these things I weep; mine eye, mine eye runneth down with water, because the comforter that should relieve my soul is far from me: my children are desolate, because the enemy prevailed.

Zion spreadeth forth her hands, and there is none to comfort her: the LORD hath commanded concerning Jacob, that his adversaries should be round about him: Jerusalem is as a menstruous woman among them.

The LORD is righteous; for I have rebelled against his commandment: hear, I pray you, all people, and behold my sorrow: my virgins and my young men are gone into captivity.

(1:14–18)

were assigned to destroy one wall each of the Temple. Three of the walls were destroyed, but the fourth commander failed to carry out the instructions to destroy his part. When the Roman emperor reproved him, it is told, the commander replied: "Had I destroyed my wall as the others did, none of the nations coming after you could have known how glorious was the work that you have destroyed . . ." Legend says that this wall which was not destroyed is the Western Wall.

He hath filled me with bitterness, he hath made me drunken with wormwood.

He hath also broken my teeth with gravel stones, he hath covered me with ashes.

And thou hast removed my soul far off from peace: I forgat prosperity.

And I said, My strength and my hope is perished from the LORD:

Remembering mine affliction and my misery, the wormwood and the gall.

My soul hath them still in remembrance, and is humbled in me.

This I recall to my mind, therefore have I hope.

(3:15–21)

340 & 341. Gall, identified as hemlock *(Conium maculatum)* and wormwood *(Artemisia herba-alba)*. Both plants are known for their extremely bitter taste and are mentioned in the Bible as metaphors for bitter affliction.

342. Stairs of the procession way along the southern wall of the Temple Mount, uncovered in excavations. The large stones were probably toppled down from the walls above during the destruction of the Temple by Titus in A.D. 70.

342

How is the gold become dim! how is the most fine gold changed! the stones of the sanctuary are poured out in the top of every street.

The precious sons of Zion, comparable to fine gold, how are they esteemed as earthen pitchers, the work of the hands of the potter!

Even the sea monsters draw out the breast, they give suck to their young ones: the daughter of my people is become cruel, like the ostriches in the wilderness.

The tongue of the sucking child cleaveth to the roof of his mouth for thirst: the young children ask bread, and no man breaketh it unto them.

They that did feed delicately are desolate in the streets: they that were brought up in scarlet embrace dunghills.

For the punishment of the iniquity of the daughter of my people is greater than the punishment of the sin of Sodom, that was overthrown as in a moment, and no hands stayed on her.

(4:1–6)

The LORD hath accomplished his fury; he hath poured out his fierce anger, and hath kindled a fire in Zion, and it hath devoured the foundations thereof.

The kings of the earth, and all the inhabitants of the world, would not have believed that the adversary and the enemy should have entered into the gates of Jerusalem.

(4:11–12)

And thou, son of man, be not afraid of them, neither be afraid of their words, though briers and thorns be with thee, and thou dost dwell among scorpions: be not afraid of their words, nor be dismayed at their looks, though they be a rebellious house.

And thou shalt speak my words unto them, whether they will hear, or whether they will forbear: for they are most rebellious.

But thou, son of man, hear what I say unto thee; Be not thou rebellious like that rebellious house: open thy mouth; and eat that I give thee.

(2:6–8)

And he brought me to the door of the court; and when I looked, behold a hole in the wall.

Then said he unto me, Son of man, dig now in the wall: and when I had digged in the wall, behold a door.

And he said unto me, Go in, and behold the wicked abominations that they do here.

So I went in and saw; and behold every form of creeping things, and abominable beasts, and all the idols of the house of Israel, pourtrayed upon the wall round about.

And there stood before them seventy men of the ancients of the house of Israel, and in the midst of them stood Jaazaniah the son of Shaphan, with every man his censer in his hand; and a thick cloud of incense went up.

Then said he unto me, Son of man, hast thou seen what the ancients of the house of Israel do in the dark, every man in the chambers of his imagery? for they say, The LORD seeth us not; the LORD hath forsaken the earth.

He said also unto me, Turn thee yet again, and thou shalt see greater abominations that they do.

(8:7–13)

343

343. The scorpion belongs to the Arachnidae or spider family and is found in abundance in Israel, where fifteen species are known. It is a nocturnal creature and feeds on small insects, killing them by means of the poisonous sting at the end of its tail. The poison causes severe pain to human beings and may be fatal especially to young children. In the daytime the scorpion hides under stones.

344. Detail of a relief on a large sacrificial basalt basin of the Middle Bronze period, found at Ebla, northern Syria (Aleppo Museum). The relief shows mythological figures, a dragon spurting water, and a hunting scene beneath.

345. Incense burners from Tel Zafit, 11/10th century B.C. and Tel Amal, 10/9th century B.C. (Israel Museum, Jerusalem).

344

345

346.

346. Seal depicting a winged cherub with a crown, found in Jerusalem (Hecht Museum, University of Haifa).
The cherubim are closely associated with the presence of God in the Old Testament and as guardians of the way to the Tree of Life in Genesis after the fall of mankind. There is no clear or consistent description of them in the Bible, where their main features seem to be faces and wings. Ezekiel provides the most detailed description of the cherubim and identifies them with the vision of the living creatures in Chapter 1 who had four wings and four faces: of a man, of a lion, of an ox, and of an eagle, and human hands under their wings. They appear in Ezekiel and elsewhere as a kind of throne for God and their being four in number signifies the four corners of the earth and their ability to move in all directions. Cherubim of gold overhung the "mercy-seat" of the Ark of the Covenant and were embroidered and carved as decoration in the rich hangings and panelling of the Tabernacle and Solomon's Temple.

347. A group of deportees – two men and a boy – carrying packs, and an Assyrian soldier urging them along, with a staff in his hand. From a relief in Sennacherib's palace at Nineveh (Louvre, Paris).

348. Model of a cow's liver made of clay with inscribed omens. It was found at Hazor and is dated to c. 1400 B.C.
The appearance of the liver of animals was used for divination and foretelling the future, in ancient times, particularly by the Babylonians.
The birthplace of occult practices was Babylonia; first used by the Chaldeans they spread around the world through the migrations of mankind. Divination was strictly forbidden by the Bible: "neither shall ye use enchantment, nor observe time" it is said in Leviticus 19:26, and the injunction is again repeated in Deuteronomy 18:9-12.
Those who practice divination believe that the

Then I looked, and behold, in the firmament that was above the head of the cherubims there appeared over them as it were a sapphire stone, as the appearance of the likeness of a throne.

And he spake unto the man clothed with linen, and said, Go in between the wheels, even under the cherub, and fill thine hand with coals of fire from between the cherubims, and scatter them over the city. And he went in in my sight.

Now the cherubims stood on the right side of the house, when the man went in; and the cloud filled the inner court.

Then the glory of the LORD went up from the cherub, and stood over the threshold of the house; and the house was filled with the cloud, and the court was full of the brightness of the LORD's glory.

And the sound of the cherubims' wings was heard even to the outer court, as the voice of the Almighty God when he speaketh.

(10:1–5)

The word of the LORD also came unto me, saying,

Son of man, thou dwellest in the midst of a rebellious house, which have eyes to see, and see not; they have ears to hear, and hear not: for they are a rebellious house.

Therefore, thou son of man, prepare thee stuff for removing, and remove by day in their sight; and thou shalt remove from thy place to another place in their sight: it may be they will consider, though they be a rebellious house.

Then shalt thou bring forth thy stuff by day in their sight, as stuff for removing: and thou shalt go forth at even in their sight, as they that go forth into captivity.

(12:1–4)

Also, thou son of man, appoint thee two ways, that the sword of the king of Babylon may come: both twain shall come forth out of one land: and choose thou a place, choose it at the head of the way to the city.

Appoint a way, that the sword may come to Rabbath of the Ammonites, and to Judah in Jerusalem the defenced.

For the king of Babylon stood at the parting of the way, at the head of the two ways, to use divination: he made his arrows bright, he consulted with images, he looked in the liver.

At his right hand was the divination for Jerusalem, to appoint captains, to open the mouth in the slaughter, to lift up the voice with shouting, to appoint battering rams against the gates, to cast a mount , and to build a fort.

And it shall be unto them as a false divination in their sight, to them that have sworn oaths: but he will call to remembrance the iniquity, that they may be taken.

(21:19–23)

The word of the LORD came again unto me, saying,

Now, thou son of man, take up a lamentation for Tyrus;

And say unto Tyrus, O thou that art situate at the entry of the sea, which art a merchant of the people for many isles, Thus saith the Lord God; O Tyrus, thou hast said, I am of perfect beauty.

Thy borders are in the midst of the seas, thy builders have perfected thy beauty.

They have made all thy ship boards of fir trees of Senir: they have taken cedars from Lebanon to make masts for thee.

Of the oaks of Bashan have they made thine oars; the company of the Ashurites have made thy benches of ivory, brought out the isles of Chittim.

Fine linen with broidered work from Egypt was that which thou spreadest forth to be thy sail; blue and purple from the isles of Elishah was that which covered thee.

The inhabitants of Zidon and Arvad were thy mariners: thy wise men, O Tyrus, that were in thee, were thy pilots.

The ancients of Gebal and the wise men thereof were in thee thy calkers: all the ships of the sea with their mariners were in thee to occupy thy merchandise.

(27:1–9)

348

future is revealed to people trained to interpret certain signs which are communicated in various ways: by celestial phenomena, by terrestrial physical forces such as the winds, storms, fire, and also by the behavior of animals (for example, the howling of dogs, the flight of birds, the movement of snakes, etc.), and by reading the lines of the hands, by the direction of falling arrows, and by the appearance of the entrails and liver of sacrificial animals.

The model of the cow's liver shown here consists of two broken fragments bearing inscriptions that were pressed into their face and back. The temple priests held the knowledge of these evil or good omens, and announced the tidings to the king as they saw fit.

349

349. Bas-relief from Sargon's palace in Khorsabad, 8th century B.C., depicting the transportation of timber from Lebanon by sea (Louvre, Paris).

The cedars of Lebanon were highly valued as building material for luxurious buildings such as palaces and temples. The forests of Lebanon were exploited not only by the Assyrian king Sargon, but also by the Egyptians and Israel, thanks to King Solomon's relations with Hiram, king of Tyre. The trees were cut down in Lebanon and carried to the coast where they were tied together onto barges. The barges were towed by ships and the logs put ashore upon reaching the desired destination, whereupon they were carried on land or further floated as far as possible on inland rivers.

Thou hast been in Eden the garden of God; every precious stone was thy covering, the sardius, topaz, and the diamond, the beryl, the onyx, and the jasper, the sapphire, the emerald, and the carbuncle, and gold: the workmanship of thy tabrets and of thy pipes was prepared in thee in the day that thou wast created.

(28:13)

350. Canaanite jewelry (Israel Museum, Jerusalem).
In biblical times, the term "precious stones" did not apply as it does today to diamond, emerald, ruby or sapphire, but had a broader application to minerals that were rare and beautiful.

350

351. Man watching from a tower, bas-relief from the palace of Khorsabad, 8th century B.C. (Louvre, Paris).

Again the word of the LORD came unto me, saying,
Son of man, speak to the children of thy people, and say unto them, When I bring the sword upon a land, if the people of the land take a man of their coasts, and set him for their watchman:
If when he seeth the sword come upon the land, he blow the trumpet, and warn the people;
Then whosoever heareth the sound of the trumpet, and taketh not warning; if the sword come, and take him away, his blood shall be upon his own head.
He heard the sound of the trumpet, and took not warning; his blood shall be upon him. But he that taketh warning shall deliver his soul.
But if the watchman see the sword come, and blow not the trumpet, and the people be not warned; if the sword come, and take any person from among them, he is taken away in his iniquity; but his blood will I require at the watchman's hand.
So thou, O son of man, I have set thee a watchman unto the house of Israel; therefore thou shalt hear the word at my mouth, and warn them from me.

(33:1–7)

Again he said unto me, Prophesy upon these bones, and say unto them, O ye dry bones, hear the word of the LORD.

Thus saith the Lord God unto these bones; Behold, I will cause breath to enter into you, and ye shall live:

And I will lay sinews upon you, and will bring up flesh upon you, and cover you with skin, and put breath in you, and ye shall live; and ye shall know that I am the LORD.

So I prophesied as I was commanded: and as I prophesied, there was a noise, and behold a shaking, and the bones came together, bone to his bone.

And when I beheld, lo, the sinews and the flesh came up upon them, and the skin covered them above: but there was no breath in them.

Then said he unto me, Prophesy unto the wind, prophesy, son of man, and say to the wind, Thus saith the Lord God; Come from the four winds, O breath, and breathe upon these slain, that they may live.

So I prophesied as he commanded me, and the breath came into them, and they lived, and stood up upon their feet, an exceeding great army.

Then he said unto me, Son of man, these bones are the whole house of Israel: behold, they say, Our bones are dried, and our hope is lost: we are cut off for our parts.

Therefore prophesy and say unto them, Thus saith the Lord God; Behold, O my people, I will open your graves, and cause you to come up out of your graves, and bring you into the land of Israel.

And ye shall know that I am the LORD, when I have opened your graves, O my people, and brought you up out of your graves,

And shall put my spirit in you, and ye shall live, and I shall place you in your own land: then shall ye know that I the LORD have spoken it, and performed it, saith the LORD.

(37:4–14)

352. Panel from the synagogue at Dura-Europos portraying Ezekiel's vision.

In this, one of the most striking images of restoration to be found in biblical prophecy, the condition of exiled Israel is described as a valley of dry bones. Once again, the energizing factor of the restoration is the Spirit, the "breath" which upon entering the dry bones will bring them to life.

In verse 11 the interpretation of the vision is given: "Son of man, these bones are the whole house of Israel: behold, they say, our bones are dried, and our hope is lost: we are cut off for our parts." Ezekiel is probably quoting a popular saying which circulated among the exiles, and which provided the stimulus for his prophecy.

353. Fragment of the Babylonian Epic of Gilgamesh found at Megiddo, 15th century B.C. (Israel Museum, Jerusalem).
The Epic of Gilgamesh, which tells the story of the deeds of a legendary hero who sought eternal life, was quite popular in the ancient Near East and achieved the status of classic literature. As such it served as a text for aspiring scribes and uneducated courtiers. Its great popularity is attested by the fact that a fragment of the Epic was found at far-off Megiddo. Daniel, in Babylon, where the Epic of Gilgamesh surely comprised part of the national literature, probably read the legend as part of the "learning and the tongue of the Chaldeans."

354. Silver statuette of either a Mede or Persian dignitary from the court of Artaxerxes I (464-424 B.C.) (Staatliche Museen, East Berlin).

And the king spake unto Ashpenaz the master of his eunuchs, that he should bring certain of the children of Israel, and of the king's seed, and of the princes;

Children in whom was no blemish, but well favoured, and skilful in all wisdom and cunning in knowledge, and understanding science, and such as had ability in them to stand in the king's palace, and whom they might teach the learning and the tongue of the Chaldeans.

And the king appointed them a daily provision of the king's meat, and of the wine which he drank: so nourishing them three years, that at the end thereof they might stand before the king.

Now among these were of the children of Judah, Daniel, Hananiah, Mishael, and Azariah:

Unto whom the prince of the eunuchs gave names: for he gave unto Daniel the name of Belteshazzar: and to Hananiah, of Shadrach; and to Mishael, of Meshach; and to Azariah, of Abed-nego.

But Daniel purposed in his heart that he would not defile himself with the portion of the king's meat, nor with the wine which he drank: therefore he requested of the prince of the eunuchs that he might not defile himself.

(1:3—8)

353

354

And this is the writing that was written, Mene, Mene, Tekel, Upharsin.

This is the interpretation of the thing: Mene; God hath numbered thy kingdom, and finished it.

Tekel; Thou art weighed in the balances, and art found wanting.

Peres; Thy kingdom is divided, and given to the Medes and Persians.

Then commanded Belshazzar, and they clothed Daniel with scarlet, and put a chain of gold about his neck, and made a proclamation concerning him, that he should be the third ruler in the kingdom.

In that night was Belshazzar the king of the Chaldeans slain.

And Darius the Median took the kingdom, being about threescore and two years old.

(5:25—31)

355

355. Winged lion with ram's head and griffin's hind legs, depicted on glazed tiles from the palace of Darius the Great, Susa, c. 500 B.C. (Louvre, Paris).

Glazed bricks furnished brilliant color for the palace of Darius the Great at Susa, and some complete panels have been reconstructed, such as the one pictured here. The colors of the glaze, blue, white, green and yellow, and the subjects of the reliefs, processions of lions, winged "bulls" (actually composite creatures, like those of Daniel's vision), and dragons, were all figures of old-established tradition.

Daniel here plays the role of an apocalyptist who has a disturbing dream and writes an account of it. Daniel's dreams, like those of Nebuchadnezzar, are symbolic, and Daniel is as much at a loss to explain his own dreams as Nebuchadnezzar and his counselors were to interpret the latter's. The meaning of Daniel's dream is given in the dream itself by an angel. The structure of Daniel's dream is also similar to that of Nebuchadnezzar's: a succession of four passing kingdoms with a lasting fifth one. Here, however, is an additional element of judgment, as the beasts representing the first and fourth kingdoms are annihilated. The fifth, world-wide and everlasting empire will be ruled by "the saints of the Most High" (verse 27).

In the first year of Belshazzar king of Babylon Daniel had a dream and visions of his head upon his bed: then he wrote the dream, and told the sum of the matters.

Daniel spake and said, I saw in my vision by night, and, behold, the four winds of the heaven strove upon the great sea.

And four great beasts came up from the sea, diverse one from another.

The first was like a lion, and had eagle's wings: I beheld till the wings thereof were plucked, and it was lifted up from the earth, and made stand upon the feet as a man, and a man's heart was given to it.

And behold another beast, a second, like to a bear, and it raised up itself on one side, and it had three ribs in the mouth of it between the teeth of it: and they said thus unto it, Arise, devour much flesh.

After this I beheld, and lo another, like a leopard, which had upon the back of it four wings of a fowl; the beast had also four heads; and dominion was given to it.

After this I saw in the night visions, and behold a fourth beast, dreadful and terrible, and strong exceedingly; and it had great iron teeth: it devoured and brake in pieces, and stamped the residue with the feet of it: and it was diverse from all the beasts that were before it; and it had ten horns.

I considered the horns, and behold, there came up among them another little horn, before whom there were three of the first horns plucked up by the roots: and, behold, in this horn were eyes like the eyes of man, and a mouth speaking great things. (7:1–8)

In the third year of the reign of king Belshazzar a vision appeared unto me, even unto me Daniel, after that which appeared unto me at the first.

And I saw in a vision; and it came to pass, when I saw, that I was at Shushan in the palace, which is in the province of Elam; and I saw in a

356. Mosaic from Pompeii depicting Alexander the Great fighting the Persians.
In Daniel's vision of a battle between a ram and a he-goat, these are believed to symbolize the Persian and the Greek Empires respectively. The two tall horns of the ram that sprout successively represent the Median and Persian monarchies. The Medes and Persians under command of Cyrus the Great put an end to the Babylonian Empire. Some two hundred years later Persian domination of Babylonia came to an end when Alexander the Great conquered Babylon. The goat with one great horn symbolizes the united Greek kingdoms of Alexander the Great. After his death his empire became the scene of a long struggle among his generals who aimed at creating realms of their own (the successor kingdoms are symbolized by the four great horns that sprout instead of the one great horn). The smaller horn which branches off from one of the successor horns is a particular king of one of the successor kingdoms, the Seleucid Antiochus IV Epiphanes who desecrated the Temple in Jerusalem (167 B.C.) and attempted to Hellenize the Jews.

vision, and I was by the river of Ulai.

Then I lifted up mine eyes, and saw, and, behold, there stood before the river a ram which had two horns: and the two horns were high; but one was higher than the other, and the higher came up last.

I saw the ram pushing westward, and northward, and southward; so that no beasts might stand before him, neither was there any that could deliver out of his hand; but he did according to his will, and became great.

And as I was considering, behold, an he goat came from the west on the face of the whole earth, and touched not the ground: and the goat had a notable horn between his eyes. (8:1–5)

For the ships of Chittim shall come against him: therefore he shall be grieved, and return, and have indignation against the holy covenant: so shall he do; he shall even return, and have intelligence with them that forsake the holy covenant.

And arms shall stand on his part, and they shall pollute the sanctuary of strength, and shall take away the daily sacrifice, and they shall place the abomination that maketh desolate.

And such as do wickedly against the covenant shall he corrupt by flatteries: but the people that do know their God shall be strong, and do exploits. (11:30–32)

357. Breakwater of the ancient harbor of New Paphos, Cyprus.
Chittim or Kittim is identified with the island of Cyprus. The name is based on the name of the settlement of Kition, modern Larnaka, which was the first trading port of the Phoenicians in the Mediterranean. The use of the term Chittim is rather vague, here apparently referring to the Romans.

357

Israel is swallowed up: now shall they be among the Gentiles as a vessel wherein is no pleasure.

For they are gone up to Assyria, a wild ass alone by himself: Ephraim hath hired lovers.

Yea, though they have hired among the nations, now will I gather them, and they shall sorrow a little for the burden of the king of princes.

Because Ephraim hath made many altars to sin, altars shall be unto him to sin.

I have written to him the great things of my law, but they were counted as a strange thing.

They sacrifice flesh for the sacrifices of mine offerings, and eat it; but the LORD accepteth them not; now will he remember their iniquity, and visit their sins: they shall return to Egypt.

For Israel hath forgotten his Maker, and buildeth temples; and Judah hath multiplied fenced cities: but I will send a fire upon his cities, and it shall devour the palaces thereof.   (8:8–14)

O Israel, thou hast sinned from the days of Gibeah: there they stood: the battle in Gibeah against the children of iniquity did not overtake them.

It is in my desire that I should chastise them; and the people shall be gathered against them, when they shall bind themselves in their two furrows.

And Ephraim is as an heifer that is taught, and loveth to tread out the corn; but I passed over upon her fair neck: I will make Ephraim to ride; Judah shall plow, and Jacob shall break his clods.

Sow to yourselves in righteousness, reap in mercy; break up your fallow ground: for it is time to seek the LORD, till he come and rain righteousness upon you.

Ye have plowed wickedness, ye have reaped iniquity; ye have eaten the fruit of lies: because thou didst trust in thy way, in the multitude of thy mighty men.

Therefore shall a tumult arise among thy people, and all thy fortresses shall be spoiled, as Shalman spoiled Beth-arbel in the day of battle: the mother was dashed in pieces upon her children.

So shall Beth-el do unto you because of your great wickedness: in a morning shall the king of Israel utterly be cut off.

(10:9–15)

358

358. Small domestic shrine from Megiddo in the form of a clay model of a temple with two pillars, c. 11th century B.C. (Israel Department of Antiquities, Jerusalem).
One of the most persistent shortcomings of Israel condemned by the prophets is the practice of idolatry. In the case of the northern kingdom of Israel, Hosea indicts them for making the golden calves ostensibly in worship of the One God of Israel but viewed by the prophet as plain idolatry - Israel had forgotten its Maker. The divisive presumptuousness of the northern kingdom, to set up their own kings and to build their own temples, perhaps similar to the one modeled here, and erect their own altars, is severely judged, Israel having become "a vessel wherein is no pleasure."

359. Farmer and two oxen plowing; terracotta from Byblos; 2nd millennium B.C. (National Museum of Archaeology, Beirut).

359

360. Locusts: frightening and unwelcome visitors, "strong and without number, whose teeth are the teeth of a lion..."
The vivid description of the habits of locusts given by Joel attests to the hold this creature had on the imagination of the Hebrews. Up to modern times the arrival of a swarm of locusts meant famine for thousands of people. Even today, in spite of a highly efficient international exchange of information on the movements of the locusts, and effective means of control, a swarm of locusts is still regarded as a real danger to crops.

The word of the LORD that came to Joel the son of Pethuel.

Hear this, ye old men, and give ear, all ye inhabitants of the land. Hath this been in your days, or even in the days of your fathers?

Tell ye your children of it, and let your children tell their children, and their children another generation.

That which the palmerworm hath left hath the locust eaten; and that which the locust hath left hath the cankerworm eaten; and that which the cankerworm hath left hath the caterpiller eaten.

Awake, ye drunkards, and weep; and howl, all ye drinkers of wine, because of the new wine; for it is cut off from your mouth.

For a nation is come up upon my land, strong, and without number, whose teeth are the teeth of a lion, and he hath the cheek teeth of a great lion.

He hath laid my vine waste, and barked my fig tree: he hath made it clean bare, and cast it away; the branches thereof are made white.

Lament like a virgin girded with sackcloth for the husband of her youth.

The meat offering and the drink offering is cut off from the house of the LORD; the priests, the LORD'S ministers, mourn.

The field is wasted, the land mourneth; for the corn is wasted: the new wine is dried up, the oil languisheth.

(1:1–10)

Blow ye the trumpet in Zion, and sound an alarm in my holy mountain: let all the inhabitants of the land tremble: for the day of the LORD cometh, for it is nigh at hand;

A day of darkness and of gloominess, a day of clouds and of thick darkness, as the morning spread upon the mountains: a great people and a strong; there hath not been ever the like, neither shall be any more after it, even to the years of many generations.

A fire devoureth before them; and behind them a flame burneth: the land is as the garden of Eden before them, and behind them a desolate wilderness; yea, and nothing shall escape them.

The appearance of them is as the appearance of horses; and as horsemen, so shall they run.

361. Detail of a relief on a sacrificial basalt basin from Ebla showing soldiers in strict rank (Aleppo Museum).
The locusts are likened to soldiers methodically destroying everything as they advance in ranks.

Like the noise of chariots on the tops of mountains shall they leap, like the noise of a flame of fire that devoureth the stubble, as a strong people set in battle array.

Before their face the people shall be much pained: all faces shall gather blackness.

They shall run like mighty men; they shall climb the wall like men of war; and they shall march every one on his ways, and they shall not break their ranks:

Neither shall one thrust another; they shall walk every one in his path: and when they fall upon the sword, they shall not be wounded.

They shall run to and fro in the city; they shall run upon the wall, they shall climb up upon the houses; they shall enter in at the windows like a thief.

The earth shall quake before them; the heavens shall tremble: the sun and the moon shall be dark, and the stars shall withdraw their shining.

(2:1–10)

For, behold, in those days, and in that time, when I shall bring again the captivity of Judah and Jerusalem.

I will also gather all nations, and will bring them down into the valley of Jehoshaphat, and will plead with them there for my people and for my heritage Israel, whom they have scattered among the nations, and parted my land.

And they have cast lots for my people; and have given a boy for an harlot, and sold a girl for wine, that they might drink.

362. Detail of the tomb believed to be that of Jehoshaphat in the valley bearing his name. It has an impressive entrance whose decorated tympanum is engraved with acanthus leaves, vines and fruit motifs, all of them typical of Jewish art in the Second Temple period.

363. The Valley of Jehoshaphat is part of the brook of Kidron; it spreads east of Jerusalem, between the Mount of Olives and Mount Moriah. Its slopes are dotted with burial caves and tomb-monuments of the Second Temple period, which already show the popularity of the site as a burial place, apparently from the belief that the soul would not have to travel so far to the "Valley of Judgment" in order to be judged. The two monuments shown are the tomb of the Bnei Hezir and the so-called Tomb of Zechariah, from the Second Temple period.

The name Jehoshaphat means "God is Judge" and the Valley of Jehoshaphat is the valley where the Last Judgment is to take place, according to the prophecy in the Book of Joel. It is also called the "valley of decision" in Joel 3:14.

A popular Jewish folk tale tells that on the day of resurrection, all human beings will be gathered on the Mount of Olives, and the Seat of Judgment will be on Mount Moriah. Over the Valley of Jehoshaphat, which is between these two mountains, two bridges will appear for the resurrected to pass over for judgment on Mount Moriah. One bridge will be of massive iron and stone, and the second, parallel to the first, will be of paper and will be light and frail. All the heathens will cross over the iron bridge, which will collapse under them; they will fall into the depths of the abyss beneath, none will remain. All the righteous will cross the bridge of paper safely and will enjoy eternal life.

According to an Arab legend, when the Arab dead are resurrected at the end of days, Mohammed will sit on top of the Pillar of Mohammed (a round pillar which stands opposite the Mount of Olives facing the Moslem cemetery on the slopes of Mount Moriah) and the Moslems will pass before him. A bridge will then appear between Mount Moriah and the Mount of Olives, spanning the Valley. This bridge will be as thin as a hair and as sharp as a sword. The righteous will cross the bridge safely; the wicked will fall into the depths of the valley and will be shattered to pieces.

362

Yea, and what have ye to do with me, O Tyre, and Zidon, and all the coasts of Palestine? will ye render me a recompence? and if ye recompense me, swiftly and speedily will I return your recompence upon your own head.

Because ye have taken my silver and my gold, and have carried into your temples my goodly pleasant things.

The children also of Judah and the children of Jerusalem have ye sold unto the Grecians, that ye might remove them far from their border.

Behold, I will raise them out of the place whither ye have sold them, and will return your recompence upon your own head:

And I will sell your sons and your daughters into the hand of the children of Judah, and they shall sell them to the Sabeans, to a people far off: for the LORD hath spoken it.

Proclaim ye this among the Gentiles; Prepare war, wake up the mighty men, let all the men of war draw near; let them come up.

Beat your plowshares into swords, and your pruninghooks into spears: let the weak say, I am strong.

Assemble yourselves, and come, all ye heathen, and gather yourselves together round about: thither cause thy mighty ones to come down, O LORD.

Let the heathen be wakened up, and come up to the valley of Jehoshaphat: for there will I sit to judge all the heathen round about.

(3:1–12)

364. Seal depicting a man harvesting with a sickle (Hecht Museum, University of Haifa).

365

365. The Valley of Shittim is identified with the lower course of the Kidron. This same valley is mentioned in Ezekiel and in Zechariah as the valley through which the waters coming forth from the Temple in the last days flow all the way to the Dead Sea whose brackish waters, Ezekiel prophesies, will then be healed.

Put ye in the sickle, for the harvest is ripe: come, get you down; for the press is full, the fats overflow; for their wickedness is great.

Multitudes, multitudes in the valley of decision: for the day of the LORD is near in the valley of decision.

The sun and the moon shall be darkened, and the stars shall withdraw their shining.

The LORD also shall roar out of Zion, and utter his voice from Jeruslem; and the heavens and the earth shall shake: but the LORD will be the hope of his people, and the strength of the children of Israel.

So shall ye know that I am the LORD your God dwelling in Zion, my holy mountain: then shall Jeruslem be holy, and there shall no strangers pass through her any more.

And it shall come to pass in that day, that the mountains shall drop down new wine, and the hills shall flow with milk, and all the rivers of Judah shall flow with waters, and a fountain shall come forth of the house of the LORD, and shall water the valley of Shittim.

Egypt shall be a desolation, and Edom shall be a desolate wilderness, for the violence against the children of Judah, because they have shed innocent blood in their land.

But Judah shall dwell for ever, and Jerusalem from generation to generation.

For I will cleanse their blood that I have not cleansed: for the LORD dwelleth in Zion.

(3:13–21)

366. Tekoa is identified with Khirbet Taqu'a, about ten miles south of Jerusalem, at an elevation of some 2,700 feet. The wilderness of Judea stretches to the east, the region by the settlement of Tekoa being called, apparently, the "wilderness of Tekoa" (II Chronicles 20:20, 24), where the Ammonites, Moabites and forces from Mount Seir were routed by Jehoshaphat. David's grandson Rehoboam rebuilt and fortified Tekoa and the city evidently served thereafter as a Judean defense outpost. The wise woman who appealed to King David for Joab on behalf of Absalom came from Tekoa (II Samuel 14:1-21). After the return from the Babylonian exile the people of Tekoa participated in rebuilding the walls of Jerusalem (Nehemiah 3:5), but "their nobles did not put their necks to the work of their Lord." In that period Tekoa was the capital of a small district.

During the Hasmonaean uprising it was fortified by Bacchides (Josephus, *Jewish Antiquities*). Josephus relates that he was sent by Titus to the village of Tekoa to see whether a camp could be pitched there, and that it was the scene of some battles during the revolt against the Romans.

The words of Amos, who was among the herdmen of Tekoa, which he saw concerning Israel in the days of Uzziah king of Judah, and in the days of Jeroboam the son of Joash king of Israel, two years before the earthquake.

And he said, The LORD will roar from Zion, and utter his voice from Jerusalem; and the habitations of the shepherds shall mourn, and the top of Carmel shall wither. (1:1-2)

366

Thus saith the LORD; For three transgressions of the children of Ammon, and for four, I will not turn away the punishment therof; because they have ripped up the women with child of Gilead, that they might enlarge their border;

But I will kindle a fire in the wall of Rabbah, and it shall devour the palaces thereof, with shouting in the day of battle, with a tempest in the day of the whirlwind.

And their king shall go into captivity, he and his princes together, saith the LORD. (1:13-15)

367. View of Gilead, the central part of the territory east of the Jordan River, which consisted of three regions: the plain, Gilead and the Bashan (Deuteronomy 3:10). Gilead extended from the Sea of Galilee in the north to the Dead Sea in the south. After the Israelite conquest it was divided between the tribes of Reuben and Gad and half of the tribe of Manasseh (Deuteronomy 3:12-13). The name Gilead is sometimes applied to certain portions of this region, which was rich in pasture and therefore a place for cattle-raising (Numbers 32:1). It was also famous for its balm (Jeremiah 8:22).

Thus saith the LORD; For three transgressions of Israel, and for four, I will not turn away the punishment thereof; because they sold the righteous for silver, and the poor for a pair of shoes;

That pant after the dust of the earth on the head of the poor, and turn aside the way of the meek: and a man and his father will go in unto the same maid, to profane my holy name:

And they lay themselves down upon clothes laid to pledge by every altar, and they drink the wine of the condemned in the house of their god.

Yet destroyed I the Amorite before them, whose height was like the height of the cedars, and he was strong as the oaks; yet I destroyed his fruit from above, and his roots from beneath.

Also I brought you up from the land of Egypt, and led you forty years through the wilderness, to possess the land of the Amorite.

And I raised up of your sons for prophets, and of your young men for Nazarites. Is it not even thus, O ye children of Israel? saith the LORD.

But ye gave the Nazarites wine to drink; and commanded the prophets, saying, Prophesy not.

Behold, I am pressed under you, as a cart is pressed that is full of sheaves.

Therefore the flight shall perish from the swift, and the strong shall not strengthen his force, neither shall the mighty deliver himself:

Neither shall he stand that handleth the bow; and he that is swift of foot shall not deliver himself: neither shall he that rideth the horse deliver himself.

And he that is courageous among the mighty shall flee away naked in that day, saith the LORD.

(2:6–16)

368. Wagon with two oxen; bronze from Anatolia, 2nd millennium B.C. (Dagon Museum, Haifa).

The cart was invented in Asia, the earliest ones consisting of a light framework set on an axle with solid wheels. The Assyrian relief of the Siege of Lachish depicts a cart which was probably in use in Israel in monarchic times, with a low wooden body and spoked wheels. Carts were normally drawn by a pair of oxen yoked to a pole, and were used for transporting persons and goods, and particularly for transporting sheaves of grain to the threshing floor.

Amos employs the image of an overloaded cart to express the "pressing" of Israel's transgressions, which hastens the Lord's judgment. Israel commanding the Prophet not to prophesy (verse 12) is evidently the "last straw" which brings about their punishment.

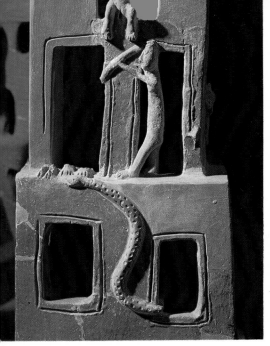

369

369. Rectangular incense stand in the form of a house with two stories and windows, decorated with snakes; from Beth-shean (Rockefeller Museum, Jerusalem).

The most dangerous of all the poisonous snakes in Israel is the Palestine viper, being responsible for most cases of snake-poisoning and fatalities. It inhabits the part of the country most thickly settled and even makes its home in dwelling-places, feeding on the mice and birds that frequent farmyards. The viper, fortunately, is quite slow in its movements, except for its final lunge when it strikes like lightning in self-defense if one inadvertently steps too close or stretches out one's hand towards it.

The serpents depicted on the cultic stand

370

Woe unto you that desire the day of the LORD! to what end is it for you? the day of the LORD is darkness, and not light.

As if a man did flee from a lion, and a bear met him; or went into the house, and leaned his hand on the wall, and a serpent bit him.

Shall not the day of the LORD be darkness, and not light? even very dark, and no brightness in it? (5:18–20)

Also Amaziah said unto Amos, O thou seer, go, flee thee away into the land of Judah, and there eat bread, and prophesy there:

But prophesy not again any more at Beth-el: for it is the king's chapel, and it is the king's court.

Then answered Amos, and said to Amaziah, I was no prophet, neither was I a prophet's son; but I was an herdman, and a gatherer of sycomore fruit.

And the LORD took me as I followed the flock, and the LORD said unto me, Go, prophesy unto my people Israel. (7:12–15)

Hear this, O ye that swallow up the needy, even to make the poor of the land to fail,

Saying, When will the new moon be gone, that we may sell corn? and the sabbath, that we may set forth wheat, making the ephah small, and the shekel great, and falsifying the balances by deceit?

That we may buy the poor for silver, and the needy for a pair of shoes; yea, and sell the refuse of the wheat?

The LORD hath sworn by the excellency of Jacob, Surely I will never forget any of their works.

Shall not the land tremble for this, and every one mourn that dwelleth therein? and it shall rise up wholly as a flood; and it shall be cast out and drowned, as by the flood of Egypt.

And it shall come to pass in that day, saith the Lord GOD, that I will cause the sun to go down at noon, and I will darken the earth in the clear day:

And I will turn your feasts into mourning, and all your songs into lamentation; and I will bring up sackcloth upon all loins, and baldness upon every head; and I will make it as the mourning of an only son, and the end thereof as a bitter day.

(8:4–10)

371

The pride of thine heart hath deceived thee, thou that dwellest in the clefts of the rock, whose habitation is high; that saith in his heart, Who shall bring me down to the ground?

Though thou exalt thyself as the eagle, and though thou set thy nest among the stars, thence will I bring thee down, saith the LORD.

If thieves came to thee, if robbers by night, (how art thou cut off!) would they not have stolen till they had enough? if the grapegatherers came to thee, would they not leave some grapes?

How are the kings of Esau searched out! how are his hidden things sought up!

All the men of thy confederacy have brought thee even to the border: the men that were at peace with thee have deceived thee, and prevailed against thee; they that eat thy bread have laid a wound under thee: there is none understanding in him.

Shall I not in that day, saith the LORD, even destroy the wise men out of Edom, and understanding out of the mount of Esau?

(1:3–8)

here may have been venerated in hope of gaining some protection from snake-bite. Amos employs the image in his prophecy as an expression of the inescapability from the Day of the Lord, a recurring theme in the Book of Amos.

370. The fruit of the sycamore.
The sycamore (*Ficus sycomorus*) is of the same genus as the fig tree.
Nowadays, it grows wild in Israel, but the fruit is rarely eaten. It was appreciated for its wood which was used as building timber as it does not absorb damp and withstands rot. The fruit was less valued than the timber, and special care had to be taken for it to be edible: a few days before it ripened it had to be punctured with a sharp instrument. If this is not done the fruit will not ripen and will fall prematurely.

371. Grain measuring-cup from Benaya in the Negev, c. 2200-1900 B.C. (Dagon Museum, Haifa).

372. Edom (also called Seir) is the mountainous region east of the Dead Sea. The Edomites are traditionally thought to be the descendants of Esau. They are believed to have settled in the area as early as the 14th century B.C.
The Israelites' first troubles with Edom began when they were still in the wilderness. Their first armed opposition came from an Edomite tribe: the Amalekite. Hostility between Israel and Edom runs though the Bible.
The first Israelite king to conquer Edom was David (II Samuel 8:14). Edom revolted in the days of Joram (II Kings 8:20). About a hundred years later, King Amaziah of Judah (798-769 B.C.) took Sela in Edom. The reconquest of Edom was completed later by Uzziah. It was not until the reign of Ahaz that the country finally regained its independence.
The prophetic poem here, if not genuinely predictive, may reflect an actual event, and thus may have been written while the Israelites still recalled the role played by the Edomites at the time of the fall of Judah in 586 B.C.

373. Detail from a bas-relief from Sennacherib's palace at Khorsabad, 8th century B.C. (Louvre, Paris).

374. The port of Jaffa today, a few miles from the site of ancient Joppa. The meaning of the name Jaffa (Yaffo) in Hebrew is "lovely" or "pretty," and indeed, the town today is very picturesque.
According to tradition Jaffa was named after Japheth, the son of Noah, who founded the town when he left the ark after the waters subsided. One legend narrates that after his death Noah was buried in one of the rocks which rise above the waters in front of the old harbor.
Jaffa is one of the oldest ports and one of the most important on the Mediterranean coast in the ancient world.
Before the Israelites had yet entered the Land, Joppa was conquered by the king of Egypt Tuthmose III in the 15th century B.C. It is told that in order to capture the city Egyptian soldiers were smuggled into Joppa in baskets.
King Solomon brought timber to Joppa from Lebanon for the construction of his Temple (II Chronicles 2:16; Ezra 3:7).
In the 8th century B.C. Joppa was conquered by Sennacherib, king of Assyria, who took it from the Philistine king of Ashkelon.
In the Persian period (587-332 B.C.) it was held

Now the word of the LORD came unto Jonah the son of Amittai, saying,

Arise, go to Nineveh, that great city, and cry against it; for their wickedness is come up before me.

But Jonah rose up to flee unto Tarshish from the presence of the LORD, and went down to Joppa; and he found a ship going to Tarshish: so he paid the fare thereof, and went down into it, to go with them unto Tarshish from the presence of the LORD.

But the LORD sent out a great wind into the sea, and there was a mighty tempest in the sea, so that the ship was like to be broken.

Then the mariners were afraid, and cried every man unto his god, and cast forth the wares that were in the ship into the sea, to lighten it of them. But Jonah was gone down into the sides of the ship; and he lay, and was fast asleep.

So the shipmaster came to him, and said unto him, What meanest thou, O sleeper? arise, call upon thy God, if so be that God will think upon us, that we perish not.

And they said every one to his fellow, Come, and let us cast lots, that we may know for whose cause this evil is upon us. So they cast lots, and the lot fell upon Jonah.

Then said they unto him, Tell us, we pray thee, for whose cause this evil is upon us; What is thine occupation? and whence comest thou? what is thy country? and of what people art thou?

And he said unto them, I am an Hebrew; and I fear the LORD, the God of heaven, which hath made the sea and the dry land.

Then were the men exceedingly afraid, and said unto him, Why hast thou done this? For the men knew that he fled from the presence of the LORD, because he had told them.

Then said they unto him, What shall we do unto thee, that the sea may be calm unto us? for the sea wrought, and was tempestuous.

And he said unto them, Take me up, and cast me forth into the sea; so shall the sea be calm unto you: for I know that for my sake this great tempest is upon you.

Nevertheless the men rowed hard to bring it to the land: but they could not: for the sea wrought, and was tempestuous against them.

Wherefore they cried unto the LORD, and said, We beseech thee, O LORD, we beseech thee, let us not perish for this man's life, and lay not upon us innocent blood: for thou, O LORD, hast done as it pleased thee.

So they took up Jonah, and cast him forth into the sea; and the sea ceased from her raging.

Then the men feared the LORD exceedingly, and offered a sacrifice unto the LORD, and made vows.

Now the LORD had prepared a great fish to swallow up Jonah. And Jonah was in the belly of the fish three days and three nights.

(1:1–17)

Then said the LORD, Doest thou well to be angry?

So Jonah went out of the city, and sat on the east side of the city, and there made him a booth, and sat under it in the shadow, till he might see what would become of the city.

And the LORD God prepared a gourd, and made it to come up over Jonah, that it might be a shadow over his head, to deliver him from his grief. So Jonah was exceeding glad of the gourd.

(4:4–6)

by the Sidonians with the support of the Persian rulers.

There are many legends related to Jaffa. One of them tells that a fearsome monster lived in the sea of Jaffa and cast dread over all the sailors. He caused great storms, sank ships, and destroyed many lives. But if a human sacrifice of the most beautiful maiden was made to the monster he would hold the tempests for a year and protect the sailors and their ships. The beautiful Andromeda, the daughter of Cepheus, king of Ethiopia, was taken to a rock near Joppa and chained there as an offering to this "lord of the sea." But when the monster approached to receive his gift, Perseus (the mythological Greek hero) appeared wearing winged sandals, and slew the monster. He broke Andromeda's chains and delivered her.

For many years the relics of these chains were shown on a rock in Jaffa. The Roman historian Pliny writes: "It (Joppa) is situated on a hill, and in front of it is a rock on which they point out marks made by the chains with which Andromeda was fettered."

375. A castor-oil plant. It has been identified by tradition with the gourd (*kikayon* in Hebrew) in the shade of which Jonah sat outside Nineveh.

The castor plant grows wild in various parts of the Holy Land. It grows quickly and produces large, shady leaves. A medicinal oil is extracted from its seeds.

The "gourd" in the Bible has also sometimes been identified with the calabash gourd.

376. A view of Bethlehem.
Bethlehem is located five miles south of Jerusalem. Genesis 35:19 relates that Rachel was buried nearby. Bethlehem, together with the surrounding towns, became the center of the tribe of Judah and was settled by a clan descending from Perez, the son of Judah and Tamar, whose later descendants were Boaz and Jesse, the father of David. David himself was born in Bethlehem and it was there that he was anointed king by Samuel (I Samuel 16:1–13).
On the basis of this passage from the Book of Micah, the early Christians identified Jesus' birthplace with Bethlehem (Matthew 2:1,5; Luke 2:4,15; John 7:42).

377. Relief on one side of a basalt ritual basin found in a temple at Ebla, depicting warriors embracing as if to conclude a peace treaty, Middle Bronze Period (Aleppo Museum, Syria).

Now gather thyself in troops, O daughter of troops: he hath laid siege against us: they shall smite the judge of Israel with a rod upon the cheek.

But thou, Beth-lehem Ephratah, though thou be little among the thousands of Judah, yet out of thee shall he come forth unto me that is to be ruler in Israel; whose goings forth have been from of old, from everlasting.

Therefore will he give them up, until the time that she which travaileth hath brought forth: then the remnant of his brethren shall return unto the children of Israel.

And he shall stand and feed in the strength of the LORD, in the majesty of the name of the LORD his God; and they shall abide: for now shall he be great unto the ends of the earth.

And this man shall be the peace, when the Assyrian shall come into our land: and when he shall tread in our palaces, then shall we raise against him seven shepherds, and eight principal men.

And they shall waste the land of Assyria with the sword, and the land of Nimrod in the entrances thereof: thus shall he deliver us from the Assyrian, when he cometh into our land, and when he treadeth within our borders.

(5:1–6)

377

376

Trust ye not in a friend, put ye not confidence in a guide: keep the doors of thy mouth from her that lieth in thy bosom.

For the son dishonoureth the father, the daughter riseth up against her mother, the daughter in law against her mother in law; a man's enemies are the men of his own house.

Therefore I will look unto the LORD; I will wait for the God of my salvation: my God will hear me.

(7:5–7)

The burden of Nineveh. The book of the vision of Nahum the Elkoshite.

God is jealous, and the LORD revengeth, and is furious; the LORD will take vengeance on his adversaries, and he reserveth wrath for his enemies.

The LORD is slow to anger, and great in power, and will not at all acquit the wicked: the LORD hath his way in the whirlwind and in the storm, and the clouds are the dust of his feet.

He rebuketh the sea, and maketh it dry, and drieth up all the rivers: Bashan languisheth, and Carmel, and the flower of Lebanon languisheth.

The mountains quake at him, and the hills melt, and the earth is burned at his presence, yea, the world, and all that dwell therein.

Who can stand before his indignation? and who can abide in the fierceness of his anger? his fury is poured out like fire, and the rocks are thrown down by him.

The LORD is good, a strong hold in the day of trouble; and he knoweth them that trust in him.

But with an overrunning flood he will make an utter end of the place thereof, and darkness shall pursue his enemies.

What do ye imagine against the LORD? he will make an utter end: affliction shall not rise up the second time.

For while they be folden together as thorns, and while they are drunken as drunkards, they shall be devoured as stubble fully dry.

There is one come out of thee, that imagineth evil against the LORD, a wicked counseller.

(1:1–11)

Woe to the bloody city! it is all full of lies and robbery; the prey departeth not.

The noise of a whip, and the noise of the rattling of the wheels, and of the pransing horses, and of the jumping chariots.

The horseman lifteth up both the bright sword and the glittering spear: and there is a multitude of slain, and a great number of carcases; and there is none end of their corpses; they stumble upon their corpses.

(3:1–3)

378

378. Thicket of thorny burnet *(Sarcopoterium spinosum)* which grows profusely in the countryside of the Holy Land. It burns readily and is used by the Bedouin for fuel.

379

379. Detail of the giant bronze doors in a 9th-century palace at Balawat, Assyria, showing a military expedition with chariots and galloping horsemen, and people trampled on the ground (British Museum).

Judah suffered long under Assyria. Nahum preached at about the end of the 7th century B.C. and prophesied the fall of Nineveh, the capital of the Assyrian Empire which was captured, looted and destroyed, at the hands of the Babylonians and the Medes in 612 B.C, never to be rebuilt again. The prophet calls it a "bloody city" because of the many wars waged by the Assyrians and their cruelty towards their captives.

What profiteth the graven image that the maker thereof hath graven it; the molten image, and a teacher of lies, that the maker of his work trusteth therein, to make dumb idols?

Woe unto him that saith to the wood, Awake; to the dumb stone, Arise, it shall teach! Behold, it is laid over with gold and silver, and there is no breath at all in the midst of it.

But the LORD is in his holy temple: let all the earth keep silence before him.

(2:18–20)

380. Gold-plated bronze figurine from a Canaanite sanctuary in the district of El-Hamah near the junction of the Jordan and Yarmuk rivers, 14th/13th century B.C. (Archaeological Collections, R.E.H. Rishumim, Haifa).

381. Painted relief from the Akhenaton temple at Karnak, Egypt, c. 1350 B.C. showing Akhenaton and his wife Nefertiti making an offering to the sun. (Centre Franco-Egyptien, Karnak).
The rays of the sun are depicted as lines radiating from the sun. This is, in fact, what the word "horns" refers to here, describing the brightness radiating from the Holy One.

A prayer of Habakkuk the prophet upon Shigionoth.

O LORD, I have heard thy speech, and was afraid: O LORD, revive thy work in the midst of the years, in the midst of the years make known; in wrath remember mercy.

God came from Teman, and the Holy One from mount Paran. Selah. His glory covered the heavens, and the earth was full of his praise.

And his brightness was as the light; he had horns coming out of his hand: and there was the hiding of his power.

(3:1–4)

Although the fig tree shall not blossom, neither shall fruit be in the vines; the labour of the olive shall fail, and the fields shall yield no meat; the flock shall be cut off from the fold, and there shall be no herd in the stalls: Yet I will rejoice in the LORD, I will joy in the God of my salvation.

The LORD God is my strength, and he will make my feet like hinds' feet, and he will make me to walk upon mine high places. To the chief singer on my stringed instruments.

(3:17–19)

382. Ibex from En-gedi.
The ibex was regarded as a symbol of beauty, such as the "pleasant roe" of Proverbs 5:19 in the description of a beautiful maiden. The ibex has long been in danger of extinction from the firearms of the Bedouin in the Negev, but in recent years, after the enacting of nature conservation laws in Israel, many grace the desert by their presence. Scores of them can be found at the oasis of En-gedi, nimbly scaling the cliff walls of the *wadi* and peering down at the visitors.

Gather yourselves together, yea, gather together, O nation not desired;

Before the decree bring forth, before the day pass as the chaff, before the fierce anger of the Lord come upon you, before the day of the Lord's anger come upon you.

Seek ye the Lord, all ye meek of the earth, which have wrought his judgment; seek righteousness, seek meekness: it may be ye shall be hid in the day of the Lord's anger.

For Gaza shall be forsaken, and Ashkelon a desolation: they shall drive out Ashdod at the noon day, and Ekron shall be rooted up.

Woe unto the inhabitants of the sea coast, the nation of the Cherethites! the word of the Lord is against you; O Canaan, the land of the Philistines, I will even destroy thee, that there shall be no inhabitant.

And the sea coast shall be dwellings and cottages for shepherds, and folds for flocks.

And the coast shall be for the remnant of the house of Judah; they shall feed thereupon: in the houses of Ashkelon shall they lie down in the evening: for the Lord their God shall visit them, and turn away their captivity.

I have heard the reproach of Moab, and the revilings of the children of Ammon, whereby they have reproached my people, and magnified themselves against their border.

Therefore as I live, saith the Lord of hosts, the God of Israel, Surely Moab shall be as Sodom, and the children of Ammon as Gomorrah, even the breeding of nettles, and saltpits, and a perpetual desolation: the residue of my people shall spoil them, and the remnant of my people shall possess them.

This shall they have for their pride, because they have reproached and magnified themselves against the people of the Lord of hosts.

The Lord will be terrible unto them: for he will famish all the gods of the earth; and men shall worship him, every one from his place, even all the isles of the heathen.

Ye Ethiopians also, ye shall be slain by my sword.

And he will stretch out his hand against the north, and destroy Assyria; and will make Nineveh a desolation, and dry like a wilderness.

(2:1–13)

383. Relief from the palace of Sargon II showing the siege of Ekron by the Assyrian army.

The book of Zephaniah is primarily a prophecy of judgment against both Judah and the surrounding nations of Philistia, Moab and Ammon, and also against the Ethiopians and Assyria, itself the executor of the judgment against the Philistines as depicted here. Chapter 2 begins with a warning to the "nation not desired," possibly Judah itself, to "seek ye the Lord . . . seek righteousness, seek meekness," hinting that a remnant might be saved. This is supported by the prophecy against the Philistines, whose destruction would mean salvation and pasturage for the remnant of Judah.

384. Ammonite clay figurine (Israel Department of Antiquities).

The Ammonites inhabited the Transjordanian territory south of the Jabbok River and north of Moab. They were conquered by David but apparently regained their independence after the reign of Solomon. According to II Chronicles 20:1–10 they joined Moab and Edom in invading Judah during the reign of Jehoshaphat and later attempted to take over Gilead. Their relations with Judah were ambivalent, at times siding with Judah against the Assyrians, at other times harassing Judah and seeking to enlarge their territory.

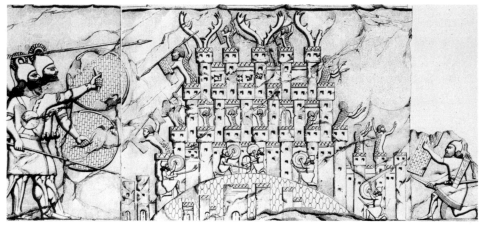

383

384

In the second year of Darius the king, in the sixth month, in the first day of the month, came the word of the Lord by Haggai the prophet unto Zerubbabel the son of Shealtiel, governor of Judah, and to Joshua the son of Josedech, the high priest, saying,

Thus speaketh the Lord of hosts, saying, This people say, The time is not come, the time that the Lord's house should be built.

Then came the word of the Lord by Haggai the prophet, saying,

Is it time for you, O ye, to dwell in your cieled houses, and this house lie waste?

Now therefore thus saith the Lord of hosts; Consider your ways.

Ye have sown much, and bring in little; ye eat, but ye have not enough; ye drink, but ye are not filled with drink; ye clothe you, but there is none warm; and he that earneth wages earneth wages to put it into a bag with holes.

Thus saith the Lord of hosts; Consider your ways.

385. Assyrians carrying cedar wood for the construction of the palace of Khorsabad, bas-relief from the palace of Khorsabad, 8th century B.C. (Louvre, Paris).
Haggai's prophecies deal mainly with the rebuilding of the Temple in the days of the return to Zion from the Babylonian exile. The prophet is mentioned in Ezra 5:1 and 6:14 as playing an important part in the rebuilding of the Temple: "And the elders of the Jews builded, and they prospered through the prophesying of Haggai the prophet and Zechariah the son of Iddo . . ." (6:14). Haggai encourages the returnees not to postpone the building or to remain content in their own houses, "and this house lie waste," but to "consider your ways" and to "go up to the mountain, and bring wood, and build the house." He explains all the tribulations of the people as being caused by delaying the building work. Despite their fears, the people obey, led by Zerubbabel and Joshua, the king and the High Priest, whose spirits were stirred by the Lord, together with all the people, to "do work in the house of the Lord of Hosts, their God."

385

Go up to the mountain, and bring wood, and build the house; and I will take pleasure in it, and I will be glorified, saith the Lord.

Ye looked for much, and, lo, it came to little; and when ye brought it home, I did blow upon it. Why? saith the Lord of hosts. Because of mine house that is waste, and ye run every man unto his own house.

Therefore the heaven over you is stayed from dew, and the earth is stayed from her fruit.

And I called for a drought upon the land, and upon the mountains, and upon the corn, and upon the new wine, and upon the oil, and upon that which the ground bringeth forth, and upon men, and upon cattle, and upon all the labour of the hands.

Then Zerubbabel the son of Shealtiel, and Joshua the son of Josedech, the high priest, with all the remnant of the people, obeyed the voice of the Lord their God, and the words of Haggai the prophet, as the Lord their God had sent him, and the people did fear before the Lord.

Then spake Haggai the Lord's messenger in the Lord's message unto the people, saying, I am with you, saith the Lord.

And the Lord, stirred up the spirit of Zerubbabel the son of Shealtiel, governor of Judah, and the spirit of Joshua the son of Josedech, the high priest, and the spirit of all the remnant of the people; and they came and did work in the house of the Lord of hosts, their God.

In the four and twentieth day of the sixth month, in the second year of Darius the king.

(1:1–15)

In the seventh month, in the one and twentieth day of the month, came the word of the LORD by the prophet Haggai, saying,

Speak now to Zerubbabel the son of Shealtiel, governor of Judah, and to Joshua the son of Josedech, the high priest, and to the residue of the people, saying,

386

386. Proto-Aeolic capital from the citadel of the kings of Judah at Ramat Rachel near Jerusalem, from the period of the Judean monarchy. The design is essentially that of a stylized palm tree.

A capital such as this may possibly have been a part of the "first glory" of the Temple of Solomon. The design is of Phoenician origin. Phoenician artisans were employed by Solomon in the building of the First Temple. The style of the capital shown here is thought by some to have inspired the later classical Greek Ionic capital.

Haggai prophesies that even though the new Temple might seem "as nothing," especially in the eyes of those who had seen the Temple of Solomon, "the glory of this latter house shall be greater than that of the former." The people and the two leaders, Zerubbabel and Joshua, are exhorted to be strong and to work, "for I am with you, saith the Lord of Hosts." The rebuilding of the house is according to the Covenant after the Exodus and God's spirit remains with them. There is thus no reason to fear. Furthermore, the people are encouraged by a prophecy foretelling the shaking of all nations, who will then come to the house bearing tribute. Thus the house will be filled with glory and this glory will be even greater than that of the "former house."

Who is left among you that saw this house in her first glory? and how do ye see it now? is it not in your eyes in comparison of it as nothing?

Yet now be strong, O Zerubbabel, saith the LORD; and be strong, O Joshua, son of Josedech, the high priest; and be strong, all ye people of the land, saith the LORD, and work: for I am with you, saith the LORD of hosts:

According to the word that I covenanted with you when ye came out of Egypt, so my spirit remaineth among you: fear ye not.

For thus saith the LORD of hosts; Yet once, it is a little while, and I will shake the heavens, and the earth, and the sea, and the dry land;

And I will shake all nations, and the desire of all nations shall come: and I will fill this house with glory, saith the LORD of hosts.

The silver is mine, and the gold is mine, saith the LORD of hosts.

The glory of this latter house shall be greater than of the former, saith the LORD of hosts: and in this place will I give peace, saith the LORD of hosts.

(2:1–9)

387. The "candlestick all of gold" described in Zechariah's vision depicted in a miniature from the *Cervera Bible*, Spain c. 1300 (Biblioteca Nacional de Lisboa, Portugal). Two olive trees flank the *menorah* (candelabrum) and, through two spouts, pour oil into a bowl from which it is distributed to the *menorah* lamps by seven pipes.

The Book of Zechariah can be divided into two parts, Chapters 1–8 written against the background of the return from the Babylonian Exile, and Chapters 9–14 which are eschatological in nature, referring to events of the Last Days. Chapters 1–6 contain eight visions, the fifth of which being that of the golden lampstand.

The angel explains that the seven lamps are the "eyes of the Lord which run to and fro through the whole earth" signifying not only God's watching over the earth, but his searching, examining and measuring the spiritual condition and readiness of his people, exposing and illuminating all the darkened corners of their character and supplying the "oil which ministers to their need." The two olive trees represent "the two anointed ones, that stand by the Lord of the whole earth," referring, no doubt, to Joshua and Zerubbabel, the high priest and the king of the restored Jewish state. On a deeper level, one can see here the attainment of the twofold ideal of a "holy nation" and "royal priesthood," the two anointed ones. Moreover, it is especially clear in this vision that the oil signifies the spirit of God, as mentioned in verse 6: "Not by might, nor by power, but by my spirit, saith the Lord of Hosts."

It is interesting to note the emphasis here, and in the Book of Zechariah in general (as in 4:6 in the vision of the golden candlestick), on the matter of the spirit, which plays an important part in the prophecies related to the coming age of fulfillment described by other prophets as well. This outpouring of a new spirit inspires the people to repentance, to prophesy (as Joel describes), and to walk in God's statutes (as in Ezekiel). Here, in Zechariah 12, two spirits are mentioned in conjunction: first of all, verse 1 – "the Lord . . . (who) formeth the spirit of man within him," and in verse 10 "the spirit of grace and supplications," implying that the spirit of man is the organ or vessel to contain, and be inspired by, the new spirit. Chapter 13 continues Zechariah's vision of the age of fulfillment, telling of a fountain of purification of sin which will be opened to the house of David and the dwellers of Jerusalem "in that day," which will also be free from idolatry and unclean spirits and false prophecy. The prophet mentions again, as in Chapter 10, the punishment of a shepherd and his flock. A third of the nation will be left as a remnant and this third will pass "through the fire" to be refined and tried as silver and gold are tested for purity. The result of this process will be that "they shall call on my name and I will hear them."

387

And the angel that talked with me came again, and waked me, as a man that is wakened out of his sleep,

And said unto me, What seest thou? And I said, I have looked, and behold a candlestick all of gold, with a bowl upon the top of it, and his seven lamps thereon, and seven pipes to the seven lamps, which are upon the top thereof:

And two olive trees by it, one upon the right side of the bowl, and the other upon the left side thereof.

So I answered and spake to the angel that talked with me, saying, What are these, my lord?

Then the angel that talked with me answered and said unto me, Knowest thou not what these be? And I said, No, my lord.

Then he answered and spake unto me, saying, This is the word of the Lord unto Zerubbabel, saying, Not by might, nor by power, but by my spirit, saith the Lord of hosts.

Who art thou, O great mountain? before Zerubbabel thou shalt become a plain: and he shall bring forth the headstone thereof with shoutings, crying, Grace, grace unto it.

(4:1–7)

In that day, saith the LORD, I will smite every horse with astonishment, and his rider with madness: and I will open mine eyes upon the house of Judah, and will smite every horse of the people with blindness.

And the governors of Judah shall say in their heart, The inhabitants of Jerusalem shall be my strength in the LORD of hosts their God.

In that day will I make the governors of Judah like an hearth of fire among the wood, and like a torch of fire in a sheaf; and they shall devour all the people round about, on the right hand and on the left: and Jerusalem shall be inhabited again in her own place, even in Jerusalem.

The LORD also shall save the tents of Judah first, that the glory of the house of David and the glory of the inhabitants of Jerusalem do not magnify themselves against Judah.

In that day shall the LORD defend the inhabitants of Jerusalem; and he that is feeble among them at that day shall be as David; and the house of David shall be as God, as the angel of the LORD before them.

And it shall come to pass in that day, that I will seek to destroy all the nations that come against Jerusalem.

And I will pour upon the house of David, and upon the inhabitants of Jerusalem, the spirit of grace and of supplications: and they shall look upon me whom they have pierced, and they shall mourn for him, as one mourneth for his only son, and shall be in bitterness for him, as one that is in bitterness for his firstborn.

In that day shall there be a great mourning in Jerusalem, as the mourning of Hadadrimmon in the valley of Megiddon.

And the land shall mourn, every family apart; the family of the house of David apart, and their wives apart; the family of the house of Nathan apart, and their wives apart;

The family of the house of Levi apart, and their wives apart; the family of Shimei apart, and their wives apart; (12:4–13)

388. Bone inlay representing a man in an attitude of prayer, 1600–1200 B.C., from Bethshean (Israel Museum, Jerusalem).

In Chapter 12 the "burden" refers to Israel, prophesying that Jerusalem will be besieged by many nations, but that "in that day" every horse will be smitten with astonishment and every rider will be driven mad, and the "governors" of Judah will devour "all the people round about, on the right hand and on the left." The result will be that Jerusalem will be inhabited again. In that day, it is written, the house of David and the dwellers in Jerusalem, as a result of the pouring out of the spirit of grace and supplications, will "look upon me whom they have pierced, and they shall mourn for him . . . as one that is in bitterness for his firstborn," a famous prophecy which Christian tradition has taken to refer to the recognition of a crucified Messiah (see also Isaiah 6).

388

In that day there shall be a fountain opened to the house of David and to the inhabitants of Jerusalem for sin and for uncleanness.

And it shall come to pass in that day, saith the LORD of hosts, that I will cut off the names of the idols out of the land, and they shall no more be remembered: and also I will cause the prophets and the unclean spirit to pass out of the land.

And it shall come to pass, that when any shall yet prophesy, then his father and his mother that begat him shall say unto him, Thou shalt not live; for thou speakest lies in the name of the LORD: and his father and his mother that begat him shall thrust him through when he prophesieth.

And it shall come to pass in that day, that the prophets shall be ashamed every one of his vision, when he hath prophesied; neither shall they wear a rough garment to deceive:

But he shall say, I am no prophet, I am an husbandman; for man taught me to keep cattle from my youth.

And one shall say unto him, What are these wounds in thine hands? Then he shall answer, Those with which I was wounded in the house of my friends.

Awake, O sword, against my shepherd, and against the man that is my fellow, saith the LORD of hosts: smite the shepherd, and the sheep shall be scattered: and I will turn mine hand upon the little ones.

And it shall come to pass, that in all the land, saith the LORD, two parts therein shall be cut off and die; but the third shall be left therein.

And I will bring the third part through the fire, and will refine them as silver is refined, and will try them as gold is tried: they shall call on my name, and I will hear them: I will say, It is my people: and they shall say, The LORD is my God.

(13:1–9)

389. View of the archaeological site and valley of Megiddo.
Zechariah likens the mourning of the house of Judah and the dwellers in Jerusalem to that of the "valley of Megiddon," long known as the scene of historic battles and later (in the New Testament) coming to symbolize the final battle between the forces of good and evil. An ancient tradition holds that Zechariah refers here to the mourning for King Josiah, who was killed by Pharaoh Neco at Megiddo (II Kings 23:29ff.).

Bring ye all the tithes into the storehouse, that there may be meat in mine house, and prove me now herewith, saith the Lord of hosts, if I will not open you the windows of heaven, and pour you out a blessing, that there shall not be room enough to receive it.

And I will rebuke the devourer for your sakes, and he shall not destroy the fruits of your ground; neither shall your vine cast her fruit before the time in the field, saith the Lord of hosts.

And all nations shall call you blessed: for ye shall be a delightsome land, saith the Lord of hosts.

(3:10–12)

390

390. Model of a granary with twelve silos from El Kab, Upper Egypt, 2600–2500 B.C. (Dagon Museum, Haifa).
The institution of offering the first fruits of the field and of the flock is prescribed in Leviticus 27:30–33 and Deuteronomy 14:22–29, and is a symbol of gratitude to the Creator for his blessings. Malachi asks rhetorically in verse 8: "Will a man rob God?" and reminds the sinful people of the mutuality of the relationship between the people's thankful offering of tithes and God's "pouring-out" of super-abundant blessing.

Behold, I will send you Elijah the prophet before the coming of the great and dreadful day of the Lord:

And he shall turn the heart of the fathers to the children, and the heart of the children to their fathers, lest I come and smite the earth with a curse.

(4:5-6)

391. The coming of Elijah on Passover Eve – carrying a family on his donkey. Illustration from the so-called Washington Haggadah, written and illuminated in 1478 in northern Italy (Library of Congress, Washington).
The revolutionary ministry and miraculous translation of the prophet Elijah left a strong impression already on the later biblical prophets, such as Malachi, who closes his book by mentioning Elijah as the harbinger of the Day of the Lord. This became the point of departure for the subsequent association of Elijah with the messianic age.
In Jewish tradition, Elijah is not only a precursor but an active partner of the Messiah, and both are occupied with recording the good deeds of the righteous with a view to hastening the day of Redemption. He is also accorded the privilege of resurrecting the dead, having shown his power in reviving the son of the widow (I Kings 17:17ff.).

MAPS

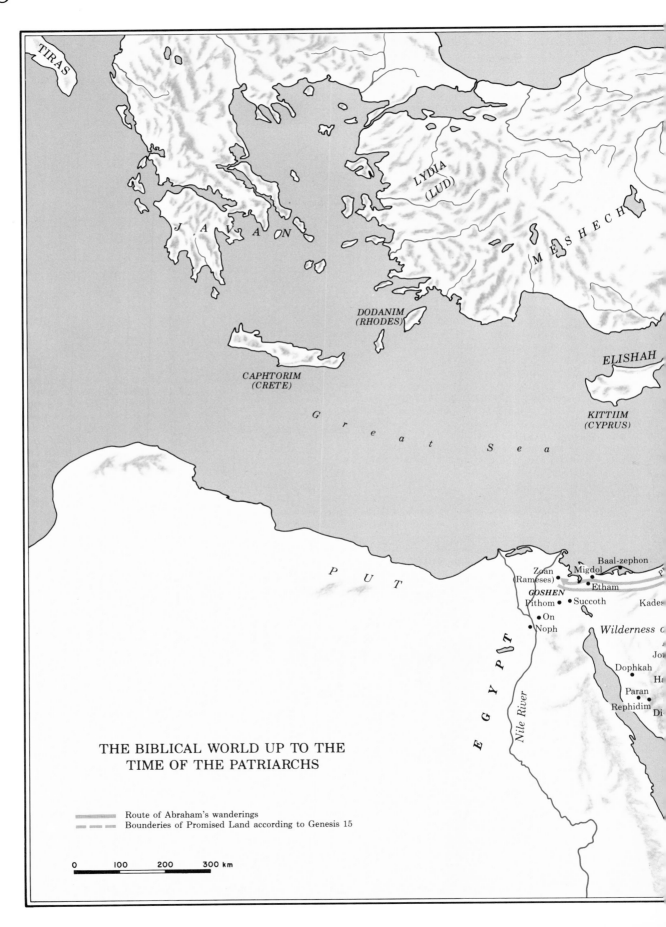

TIRAS

LYDIA
(LUD)

MESHECH

J A V A ON

DODANIM
(RHODES)

ELISHAH

CAPHTORIM
(CRETE)

KITTIIM
(CYPRUS)

G r e a t   S e a

P U T

Baal-zephon

Zoan
(Rameses)
Migdol

GOSHEN
Etham

Pithom   Succoth

Kades

On

Noph   Wilderness o

E G Y P T   Nile River

Jo

Dophkah   Ha

Paran

Rephidim   Di

THE BIBLICAL WORLD UP TO THE
TIME OF THE PATRIARCHS

━━━━━ Route of Abraham's wanderings
─ ─ ─ Bounderies of Promised Land according to Genesis 15

0   100   200   300 km

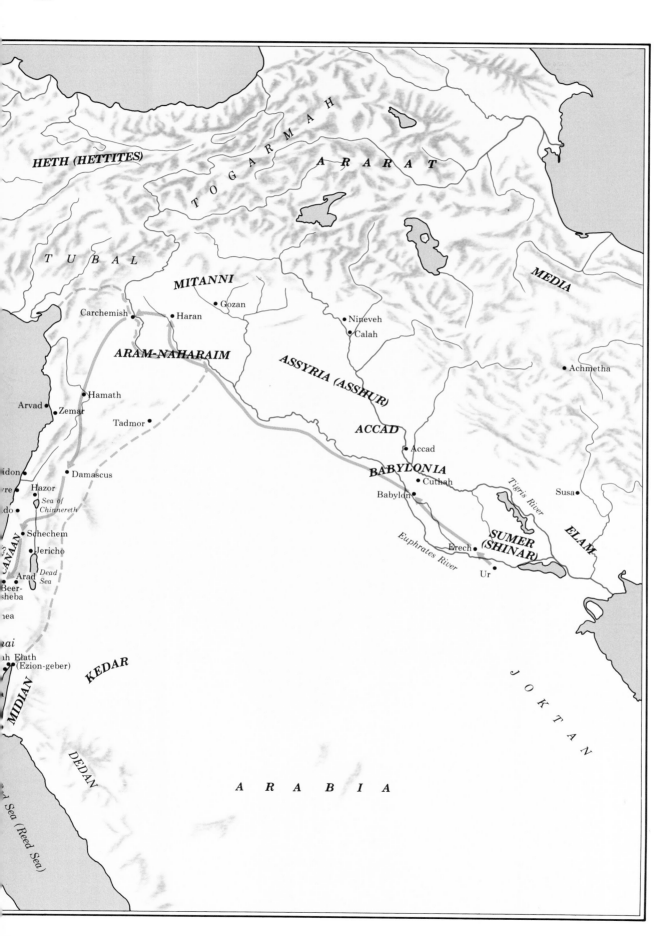

HETH (HETTITES)

T O G A R M A H

A R A R A T

T U B A L

MITANNI

MEDIA

Carchemish   • Haran   • Gozan

• Nineveh
• Calah

ARAM-NAHARAIM

ASSYRIA (ASSHUR)

• Achmetha

Arvad •   • Hamath
• Zemar

Tadmor •

ACCAD

• Accad

idon   • Damascus

BABYLONIA

re •   • Hazor

• Cuthah

do   Sea of
Chinnereth

Babylon •

Tigris River

• Susa

SUMER
(SHINAR)

ELAM

ANAAN   • Schechem

• Jericho

Euphrates River   Erech •

Arad • Dead
Sea

Ur •

• Beer-
sheba

nea

ai

ah Elath
(Ezion-geber)

KEDAR

J O K T A N

MIDIAN

DEDAN

A R A B I A

Sea (Reed
Sea)

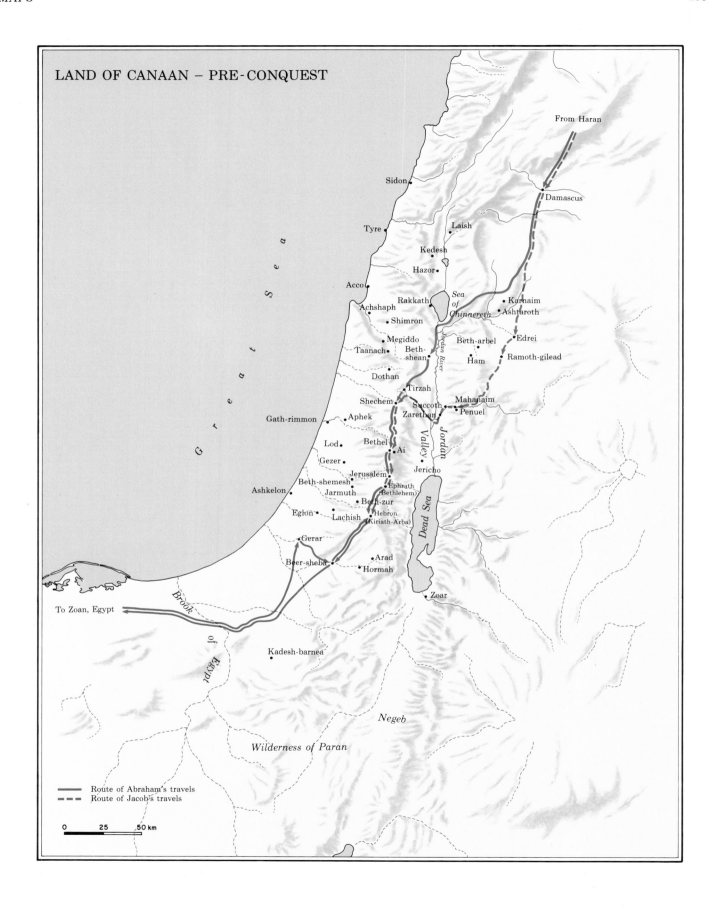

LAND OF CANAAN – PRE-CONQUEST

From Haran

Sidon

Damascus

Tyre

Laish
Kedesh
Hazor

Acco
Achshaph
Rakkath
Shimron
Karnaim
Ashtaroth
Sea of Chinnereth

Megiddo
Beth-arbel
Edrei
Taanach
Beth-shean
Ham
Ramoth-gilead

Dothan
Tirzah
Shechem
Succoth
Mahanaim
Zarethan
Penuel

Gath-rimmon
Aphek

Lod
Bethel
Ai

Gezer
Jerusalem
Jericho

Beth-shemesh
Ephrath (Bethlehem)
Ashkelon
Jarmuth
Beth-zur

Eglon
Lachish
Hebron (Kiriath-Arba)

Gerar

Arad
Beer-sheba
Hormah

Zoar

To Zoan, Egypt

Kadesh-barnea

Great Sea

Jordan River

Jordan Valley

Dead Sea

Brook of Egypt

Negeb

Wilderness of Paran

——— Route of Abraham's travels
- - - - Route of Jacob's travels

0   25   50 km

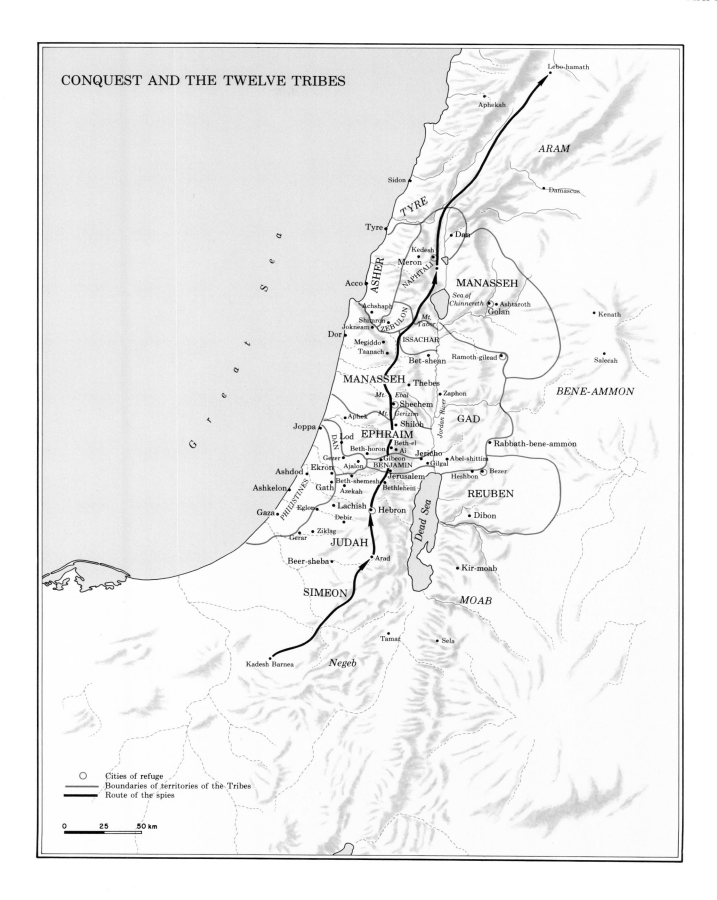

CONQUEST AND THE TWELVE TRIBES

Lebo-hamath

Aphekah

ARAM

Sidon

Damascus

TYRE

Tyre

Dan

Kedesh

Meron

NAPHTALI

MANASSEH

Acco

Sea of Chinnereth

Ashtaroth

Golan

Kenath

ASHER

Achshaph

Shimron

ZEBULON

Mt. Tabor

Jokneam

ISSACHAR

Dor

Megiddo

Taanach

Bet-shean

Ramoth-gilead

Salecah

Gr e a t   S e a

MANASSEH

Thebes

Mt. Ebal

Shechem

Zaphon

BENE-AMMON

Mt. Gerizim

Aphek

Shiloh

GAD

Joppa

Lod

EPHRAIM

Beth-el

Jordan River

DAN

Beth-horon

Ai

Jericho

Rabbath-bene-ammon

Gezer

Gibeon

Gilgal

Abel-shittim

Ekron

Ajalon

BENJAMIN

Ashdod

Beth-shemesh

Jerusalem

Heshbon

Bezer

Ashkelon

Gath

Azekah

Bethlehem

PHILISTINES

Eglon

Lachish

REUBEN

Gaza

Debir

Hebron

Dead Sea

Dibon

Gerar

Ziklag

JUDAH

Beer-sheba

Arad

Kir-moab

SIMEON

MOAB

Tamar

Sela

Kadesh Barnea

Negeb

○ Cities of refuge
── Boundaries of territories of the Tribes
── Route of the spies

0   25   50 km

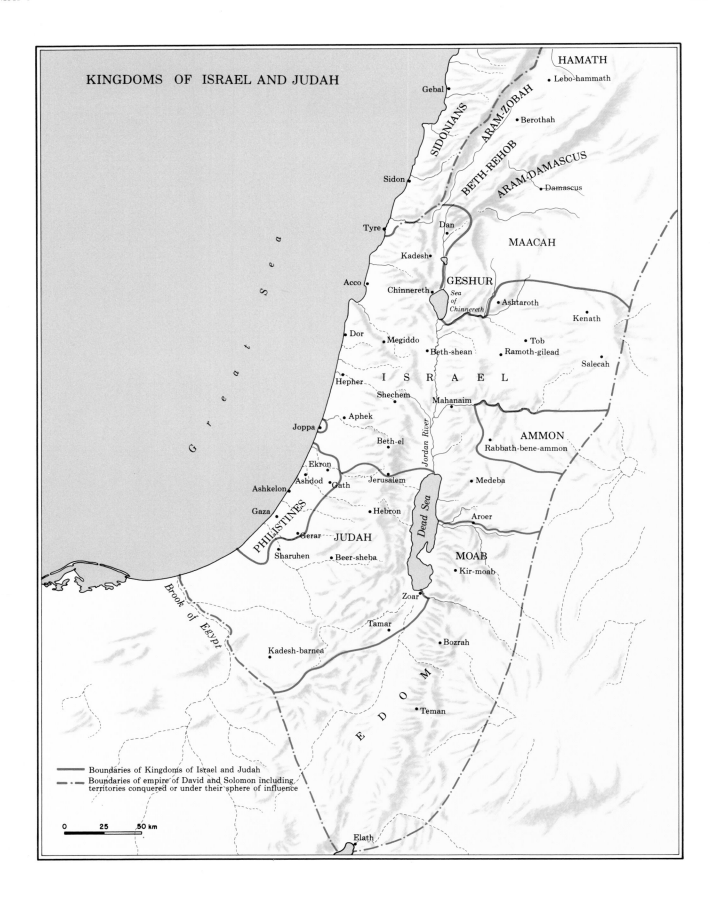

KINGDOMS OF ISRAEL AND JUDAH

HAMATH

Lebo-hammath

Gebal

SIDONIANS

ARAM-ZOBAH

Berothah

BETH-REHOB

ARAM-DAMASCUS

Sidon

Damascus

Tyre

Dan

MAACAH

Kadesh

GESHUR

Acco

Chinnereth

Sea of Chinnereth

Ashtaroth

Kenath

Dor

Megiddo

Tob

Ramoth-gilead

Beth-shean

Salecah

Hepher

I S R A E L

Shechem

Mahanaim

Great Sea

Aphek

AMMON

Joppa

Beth-el

Rabbath-bene-ammon

Jordan River

Ekron

Jerusalem

Ashdod

Medeba

Ashkelon

Gath

Gaza

Hebron

Dead Sea

Aroer

PHILISTINES

JUDAH

Gerar

MOAB

Sharuhen

Beer-sheba

Kir-moab

Zoar

Tamar

Brook of Egypt

Bozrah

Kadesh-barnea

E D O M

Teman

—— Boundaries of Kingdoms of Israel and Judah
—·—· Boundaries of empire of David and Solomon including
territories conquered or under their sphere of influence

0   25   50 km

Elath

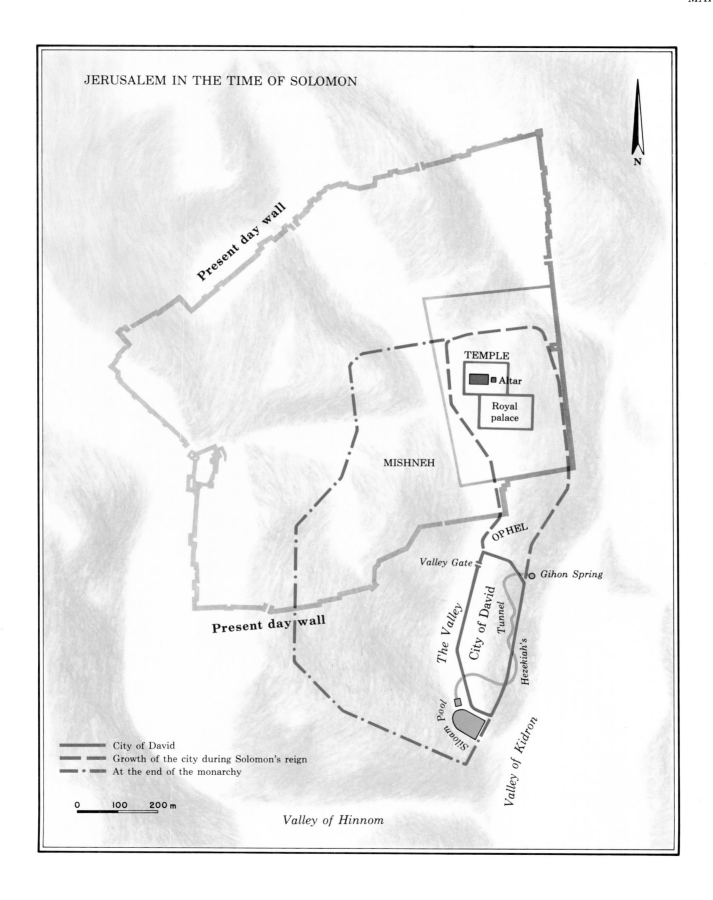

JERUSALEM IN THE TIME OF SOLOMON

N

Present day wall

TEMPLE

■ Altar

Royal
palace

MISHNEH

OPHEL

Valley Gate

Gihon Spring

The Valley

City of David

Tunnel

Hezekiah's

Present day wall

Siloam Pool

Valley of Kidron

City of David
Growth of the city during Solomon's reign
At the end of the monarchy

0   100   200 m

Valley of Hinnom

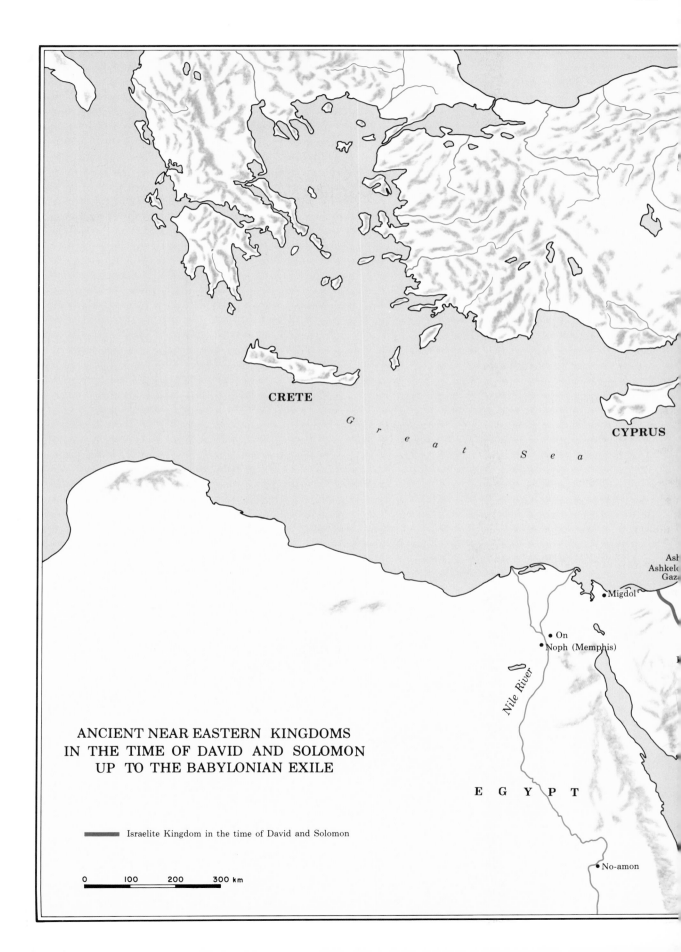

CRETE

CYPRUS

G r e a t   S e a

Ash
Ashkelo
Gaz

• Migdol

• On
• Noph (Memphis)

Nile River

ANCIENT NEAR EASTERN KINGDOMS
IN THE TIME OF DAVID AND SOLOMON
UP TO THE BABYLONIAN EXILE

E G Y P T

▬▬▬ Israelite Kingdom in the time of David and Solomon

0   100   200   300 km

• No-amon

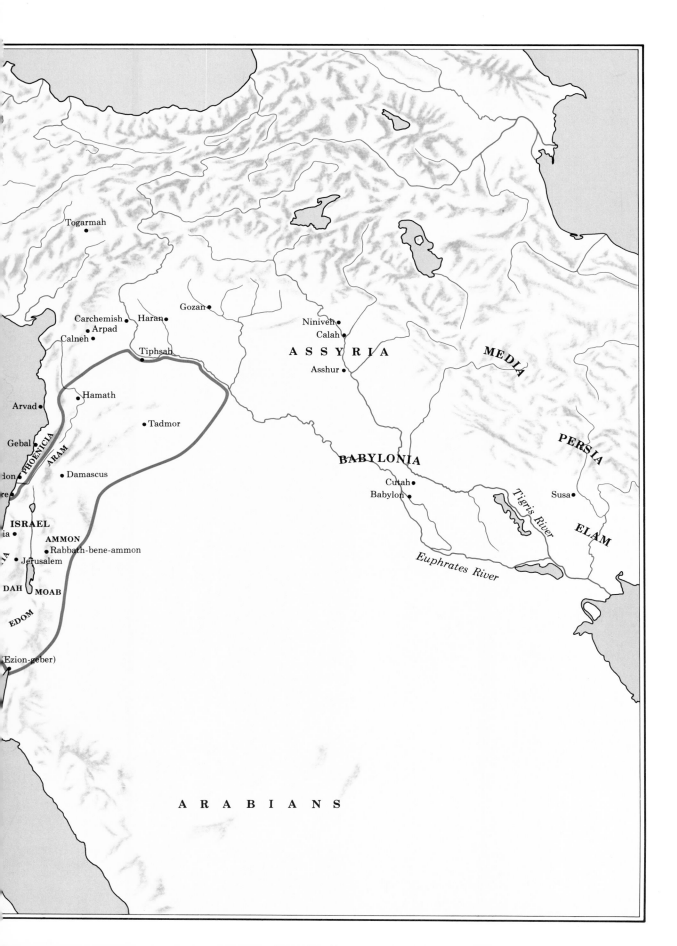

Togarmah

Gozan

Carchemish • Haran •
Arpad •
Calneh •
Tiphsah •

Niniveh •
Calah •

A S S Y R I A

M E D I A

Asshur •

Arvad •
Hamath •

Tadmor •

P E R S I A

Gebal •

PHOENICIA
ARAM

B A B Y L O N I A

Cutah •
Babylon •

Tigris River

Susa •

E L A M

•don
•re

Damascus •

ISRAEL

•ia

AMMON
• Rabbath-bene-ammon

Euphrates River

• Jerusalem

DAH   MOAB

EDOM

(Ezion-geber)

A R A B I A N S

The numbers refer to pages in which the entries in this Index are mentioned in the Bible text or in the captions of the illustrations.

ACKNOWLEDGEMENTS

GENESIS
1. Tree of Life – Photo Zev Radovan
2. Snake – Photo Azaria Alon
3. Creation – Sarajevo National Museum. Photo Moshe Caine
4. Noah – Sarajevo National Museum. Photo Moshe Caine
5. Gilgamesh Epic – British Museum, London
6. Lion Hunt stele – Baghdad Museum
7. The Standard of Ur – British Museum, London
8. Mesopotamian warrior – Musée du Louvre, Paris. Photo Erich Lessing
9. Nubian; from the temple of Ramses III. Photo Erich Lessing
10. Philistine; Private collection. Photo Erich Lessing
11. Egyptian scribe; from a wall painting. Photo David Harris
12. Elamite – Musée du Louvre. Photo Erich Lessing
13. Cretan – Heraklion Museum, Crete. Photo Erich Lessing
14. Greek warrior – Delphi Museum. Photo Erich Lessing
15. Libyan; from the tomb of Ramses III. Photo Erich Lessing
16. King of Accad stele – Musée du Louvre, Paris. Photo Erich Lessing
17. Bull's head from Ur – Photo Unesco
18. Ishtar Gate – Vorderasiatisches Museum, Berlin
19. Ziggurat – Sir Leonard Woolley
20. Shechem – Photo A. van der Heyden
21. Shechem – Photo David Harris
22. Mamre – Photo David Harris
23. Sodom – Photo Palphot
24. Dead Sea, salt mounds – Photo Zev Radovan
25. Dead Sea – Photo Moshe Caine
26. Tell Beer-Sheba – Photo Zev Radovan
27. Abraham's Well – Photo A. van der Heyden
28. Ivory figurine, Beer-Sheba – Israel Department of Antiquities exh. Israel Museum, Jerusalem. Photo IM/ Zev Radovan
29. The Dome of the Rock – Photo David Harris
30. Sacrifice of Isaac; mosaic – Photo A. Hai
31. Cave of Machpela (interior) – Photo Palphot
32. Hebron – Photo Werner Braun
33. Rachel's tomb (interior) – Photo David Harris
34. Rachel's tomb (exterior) – Collection Dr. N. Gidal. Photo Eric Matson
35. Joseph in the pit – Illuminated MS. Bibliothèque Nationale, Paris
36. Figurine of a mourner – Department of Antiquities and Museums, Jerusalem. Photo Zev Radovan
37. Hieroglyphic writing – Turino Museum
38. Temple at Karnak – Photo A. van der Heyden
39. Egyptian scribe – Photo Hirmer Verlag, Munich
40. West Semitic tribe; from an Egyptian wall painting. Photo David Harris
41. Embalming; drawing from an Egyptian wall painting. Photo J.P.H.
EXODUS
42. Ramses II– Photo David Harris
43. Field work; Egyptian wall painting– Photo Erich Lessing
44. The Nile – Photo David Harris
45. Moses taken from the Nile – Dura-Europos wall painting. Photo David Harris
46. Burning bush – Photo David Harris
47. On the way to Sinai – Photo A. van der Heyden
48. Serabit-el Khadem – Photo A. van der Heyden
49. Bricklaying in Egypt – Photo Erich Lessing
50. Seder from Darmstadt Haggadah – Darmstadt Museum. Photo Moshe Caine
51. Pharaoh in his chariot – Photo Hirmer–Verlag, Munich
52. The Red Sea – Photo David Darom
53. Bird snaring; Egyptian wall painting – British Museum, London
54. Manna – Photo David Darom
55. Quail – Photo David Darom
56. Wilderness of Zin – Photo Azaria Alon
57. Sinai – Photo A. van der Heyden

58. Jethro's tomb – Photo Zev Radovan
59. The Ten Commandments – The Jerusalem Publishing House, Ltd.
60. Tablets of the Law on stone – Photo Moshe Caine
61. Doors of the Ark of the Law – Israel Museum, Jerusalem. Photo IM/ David Harris
62. Jebel Musa – Photo David Harris
63. Jebel Musa – Photo David Harris
64. Ark of the Law curtain – Hechal Shlomo Synagogue Museum. Photo David Harris
65. Ritual objects of the Temple, on panel from Ark of the Law – Israel Museum, Jerusalem.
66. High Priest's vestments – Illuminated MS., Israel Museum, Jerusalem.
67. Torah Scroll breastplate – Israel Museum, Jerusalem. Photo IM/ David Harris
68. Moses on Mount Sinai – *Sarajevo Haggadah* – Zemaljski Musej, Sarajevo. Photo Moshe Caine
69. Aaron lighting the candlestick – Illuminated MS., British Library, London, Add. 1139. Fol. 114

LEVITICUS
70. Horned altar – Department of Antiquities, Jerusalem. Photo David Harris
71. Consecration of the tabernacle – Wall painting, Dura-Europos. Photo Moshe Çaine
72. Leprosy – Illustrated MS. The Jewish National & University Library, Jerusalem
73. Hyssop – Photo David Darom
74. Woman bathing, figurine – Israel Department of Antiquities and Museums, Jerusalem. Photo Dalia Amotz
75. Ivory wine goblet – Hechal Shlomo Synagogue Museum. Photo David Harris
76. Page from *Darmstadt Haggadah* – Photo Moshe Caine
77. Winnowing; from Egyptian wall painting – Photo A. van der Heyden
78. Kindergarten children celebrating *Shavuot* – Photo David Harris
79. Farmers offering produce – Israel Museum, Jerusalem.
80. *Succoth* service – Photo David Harris
81. Slaves – Ashmolean Museum, Oxford
82. Slaves – Drawing from Egyptian wall painting

NUMBERS
83. Torah crown – Israel Museum, Jerusalem. Photo IM/ David Harris
84. The Ten Tribes; Illuminated MS. British Museum, London
85. Weights and scale pans – Department of Antiquities and Museums, Jerusalem. IM /David Harris
86. Silver ingots – Israel Department of Antiquities and Museums, exh. Israel Museum, Jerusalem. Photo David Harris
87. Weighing precious metals – British Museum, London
88. Phylacteries – The Shrine of the Book, Israel Museum, Jerusalem.
89. Desert of Zin – Photo David Harris
90. Model of Kadesh Barnea excavations – Israel Department of Antiquities and Museums. Photo David Harris
91. Kadesh Barnea, oasis – Photo David Harris
92. Figurine from Kadesh Barnea – Israel Department of Antiquities.
93. Arad – Photo A. van der Heyden
94. Snake – Nature Preservation Society. Photo Yossi Eshbol
95. Moab – Photo David Harris

DEUTERONOMY
96. Mount Horeb – Photo David Harris
97. Court of Law; Illuminated Biblioteca Apostolica Vaticana, Rome
98. *Mezuzah* – Israel Museum, Jerusalem.
99. The Nash Papyrus – Israel Department of Antiquities and Museums, Jerusalem.
100–106. "Seven species" – Photos Azaria Alon
107. Stele "Baal of Lightning" – Musée du Louvre, Paris. Cliché Musées Nationaux
108. The Gezer Calendar – Exh. Israel Museum, Jerusalem. Photo IM/ Zev Radovan
109. Bird's nest – Nature Preservation Society. Photo Yossi Eshbol
110. *Halitza shoe* – Israel Museum, Jerusalem. Photo IM/ David Harris
111. Mount Ebal – Photo David Harris
112. Moab mountains – Photo A. van der Heyden
113. Pentateuch Scroll – Photo David Harris

JOSHUA
114. Signpost to Jericho – Photo A. van der Heyden
115. Jordan River – Photo A. van der Heyden

116. The Ark carved on stone – Photo A. van der Heyden
117. View in the Dead Sea region – Photo A. van der Heyden
118. Weapons – Israel Department of Antiquities and Museums. Photo David Harris
119. Pottery in the shape of a head – Department of Antiquities and Museums, Jerusalem. Photo David Harris
120. Plastered skull – Prof. Kathleen Kenyon
121. Site of ancient Jericho – Photo A. van der Heyden
122. Excavations at Jericho – Photo A. van der Heyden
123. "The Joshua Roll" – Illuminated MS. Biblioteca Apostolica Vaticana, Rome
124. Ai – Photo Zev Radovan
125. Valley of Affliction – Photo A. van der Heyden
126. Incense stand – Israel Department of Antiquities. Photo Zev Radovan
127. Canaanite – Oriental Institute, University of Chicago
128. Execration texts – Ha'aretz Museum, Tel Aviv. Photo David Harris
129. Canaanites; Egyptian wall painting. Photo David Harris
130. Valley of Ajalon – Photo David Harris
131. Canaanite victory celebration – Department of Antiquities and Museums, Jerusalem. Photo Zev Radovan
132. Fertility goddess – Israel Department of Antiquities and Museums, exh. Israel Museum. Photo Dalia Amotz
133. Meron – Photo David Harris
134. Hazor – Photo A. van der Heyden
135–136. Stelae from Hazor – Israel Department of Antiquities, exh. Israel Museum, Jerusalem.
137–138. Shiloh – Photos David Harris
139–140. Tomb of Joseph – Photos Zev Radovan

JUDGES

141. Clay horse's head – Israel Department of Antiquities, exh. Israel Museum, Jerusalem.
142. Achzib – Photo Palphot
143. Acco – Photo David Harris
144–145. Goddesses – Israel Department of Antiquities. Photos Zev Radovan
146. Mold for casting figurines – Israel Department of Antiquities, exh. Israel Museum, Jerusalem. Photo Zev Radovan
147. Egyptian daggers – Photo J.P.H.
148. Mount Tabor – Photo David Harris
149. Amorite charioteer – Photo Hirmer Verlag, Munich
150. Kishon River; woodcut – Collection National Maritime Museum, Haifa, Inv. 1618
151. Spring of Harod – Photo David Harris
152. Philistine – Oriental Institute, University of Chicago
153. Eshtaol and Zorah region – Photo David Harris
154. Philistine pottery – Israel Department of Antiquities, exh. Israel Museum, Jerusalem. Photo David Harris
155. Plain of Lebonah – Photo David Harris

RUTH

156. Ruth and Boaz, from the *Admont Bible* – Nationalbibliothek, Vienna
157. Women gleaning – Photo Garo

I SAMUEL

158. Site of biblical Shiloh – Photo A. van der Heyden
159. Remains at Shiloh – Photo A. van der Heyden
160. Aphek – Photo Zev Radovan
161. The Ark on wheels – Photo Erich Lessing
162. Figurine from Ashdod – Israel Department of Antiquities, exh. Israel Museum, Jerusalem. Photo IM/ David Harris
163. The Philistine returning the Ark of the Covenant, wall painting from Dura-Europos. Photo Moshe Caine
164. Beth Shemesh – Photo A. van der Heyden
165. Kiriat-Jearim – Photo David Harris
166. Mizpeh – Photo David Harris
167. Gibeah – Photo David Harris
168. Michmash – Photo David Harris
169–170. Fields near Bethlehem – Photos A. van der Heyden

171. Horn from Megiddo — Department of Antiquities and Museums, Jerusalem. Photo David Harris
172. Samuel anointing David — Wall painting from Dura-Europos. Photo David Harris
173. David playing the harp — Photo Museum for Music and Ethnology, Haifa
174. Valley of Elah — Photo David Harris
175. Mycenean soldier — Archaeological Receipts Fund, Ministry of Science, Greece.
176. Slinger — British Museum, London
177. Nebi Samuel — Photo David Harris
178. Nebi Samuel (interior) — Photo David Harris
179. Gilboa mountains — Photo David Harris
180. Beth Shean — Photo David Harris
181. Philistine coffin — Israel Department of Antiquities. Photo David Harris
II SAMUEL
182. Egyptian archer — Metropolitan Museum of Art, New York
183. Excavations at City of David — Institute of Archaeology, Hebrew University, Jerusalem
184. Fertility goddess — Institute of Archaeology, Hebrew University, Jerusalem
185. Niche for Torah Scrolls — wall painting from Dura-Europos. Photo Moshe Caine
186. Impression of Ammonite seals — Israel Museum, Jerusalem.
187. Ammonite figures. Photo J.P.H.
188. David and Bathsheba; from the *St. Louis Psalter* — Bibliothèque Nationale, Paris
189. Women mourning; from an Egyptian wall painting — Photo A. van der Heyden
190. The death of Absalom; from the *San Isidoro Bible* — Catedra de San Isidoro, Léon, Spain
191. Absalom's Tomb — Photo David Harris
192. Huleh Valley — Photo A. van der Heyden
193. King David's Wells — Photo A. van der Heyden
I KINGS
194. Gihon Spring — Photo David Harris
195. David's Tomb — Photo Palphot
196. Gibeon — Zev Radovan
197. King Solomon's stables — Photo David Harris
198. Tyrian coin — Department of Antiquities and Museums, Jerusalem.
199. Sidon — Photo Zev Radovan
200. Model of the First Temple — Israel Museum, Jerusalem.
201. Hazor — Photo David Harris
202. Megiddo — Photo David Harris
203. Gezer — Photo A. van der Heyden
204. Consignment of gold from Ophir — Israel Department of Antiquities, exh. Israel Museum, Jerusalem.
   Photo Zev Radovan
205. Pharaoh's Island — Photo David Harris
206. Canaanite merchant ship — National Maritime Museum, Haifa
207. Seal from Megiddo (Jeroboam) — Photo IM/ Zev Radovan
208. Baboon — Israel Department of Antiquities. Photo /IM Zev Radovan
209. View of Samaria — Photo David Harris
210. Elijah's Cave — Photo A. van der Heyden
211. Phoenician seal — Department of Antiquities and Museums, Jerusalem.
   IM/ Photo David Harris
212. Cave on Mount Carmel — Photo David Harris
213. Desert broom — Photo David Darom
214. Plain of Jezreel — Photo David Harris
215. Vineyard — Photo David Harris
216–218. Samaria ivories — Israel Department of Antiquities, exh. Israel Museum, Jerusalem. Photos Zev
   Radovan
219. Jordan Valley — Photo A. van der Heyden
II KINGS
220. Elisha's Spring — Photo A. van der Heyden
221. Sartaba — Photo David Harris
222. Stele of Mesha — Musée du Louvre, Paris. Cliché Musées Nationaux
223–225. Models of furniture — Department of Antiquities and Museums, Jerusalem.
226. Bitter cucumber — Photo David Darom
227. Naaman in the Jordan — British Museum, London
228. Jordan River — Photo A. van der Heyden

229. Dothan — Photo David Harris
230. Woman at the window — British Museum, London
231. Gilead — Photo A. van der Heyden
232. Detail from "Black Obelisk" — British Museum, London
233. Hazael — Musée du Louvre, Paris. Cliché Musées Nationaux
234. Bay of Elath — Photo David Harris
235. Tiglath-pileser — Musée du Louvre, Paris.
236. Captives on Assyrian relief — Photo David Harris
237. Ostracon from Lachish — Israel Department of Antiquities and Museums.
238. Perfume container — Israel Museum, Jerusalem
239. Seal from Mizpeh — Israel Department of Antiquities. Photo Zev Radovan
240. Siege of Lachish — British Museum, London
I CHRONICLES
241. Incense burner — Israel Department of Antiquities and Museums. Photo Zev Radovan
242. Dancing youth — Photo Scala Firenze
243. Philistine stand — Department of Antiquities and Museums, Jerusalem. Photo Zev Radovan
244. Gath — Photo David Harris
245. Jar handle — Photo David Harris
II CHRONICLES
246. Beth-Horon the Upper — Photo David Harris
247. Beth-Horon the Lower — Photo Zev Radovan
248. Ahiram sarcophagus — Photo Zev Radovan
249. Ahiram's tomb — Photo Zev Radovan
250. Zechariah's Tomb — Photo David Harris
251. Uzziah inscription — Israel Museum, Jerusalem. Photo IM/ Zev Radovan
252. Siloam — Photo David Harris
253. Siloam tunnel — Photo A. van der Heyden
254. Hezekiah inscription — Photo David Harris
EZRA
255. Cyrus Cylinder — British Museum, London
256–257. Persian coin — Private Collection
258. Ostracon from Arad — Israel Department of Antiquities, exh. Israel Museum, Jerusalem
259. Ezra; from the *Northumbrian Bible* — Biblioteca Medicea Laurenziani, Firenze
NEHEMIAH
260. The Dung Gate — Photo A. van der Heyden
261. En Rogel — Photo David Harris
262. Myrtle — Photo David Darom
263. *Succoth* on roofs — Photo A. van der Heyden
ESTHER
264. Scroll of Esther — Hechal Shlomo Synagogue. Photo David Harris
265. Susa, aerial view — Photo Maurice Chuzeville, Vanves
266. King Darius — Oriental Institute, University of Chicago
267–268. Esther — wall paintings from Dura-Europos Photos Moshe Caine
269. Mosaic, month of Adar — Photo Zev Radovan
JOB
270. Weaver — Musée du Louvre, Paris. Photo Erich Lessing
271. Banias waterfall — Photo A. van der Heyden
272. Mallow — Photo David Darom
273. Chiromantic signs — Bayerische Staatsbibliothek, Munich
274. Brass mirror — The Shrine of the Book, Israel Museum, Jerusalem. Photo David Harris
275. Ivory lions — Israel Department of Antiquities, exh. Israel Museum, Jerusalem. Photo Zev Radovan
276. "The Universe" — Kunsthistorisches Museum, Vienna. Photo Erich Lessing
277. Camels in the Negev — Photo Azaria Alon
PSALMS
278. Egyptian bas-relief — Photo Erich Lessing
279. *Shiviti* — Israel Museum, Jerusalem
280. Assyrian war chariot — Musée du Louvre, Paris. Photo Erich Lessing
281. Ivory stag — Badisches Landesmuseum Karlsruhe. Photo Erich Lessing
282. Hebrew papyrus — Israel Department of Antiquities, exh. Israel Museum, Jerusalem. Photo Erich Lessing

283. Painting on soles of sandal — Museo Egizio, Turin. Photo Erich Lessing
284. Tributaries — Musée du Louvre, Paris. Cliché Musées nationaux
285. On the way to Shiloh — Photo Erich Lessing
286. Inscription found on Temple Mount — Israel Department of Antiquities, exh. Israel Museum, Jerusalem. Photo Zev Radovan
287. Trumpeter — Hittite Museum, Ankara. Photo Erich Lessing
288. Fertility goddess — Musée du Louvre, Paris. Photo Erich Lessing
289. Captives on Babylonian relief — Musée du Louvre, Paris. Cliché Musées Nationaux
290. Catching birds, Egyptian wall painting — Photo Erich Lessing
291. Willow tree — Photo David Harris
292. Incense stand — Israel Department of Antiquities and Museums. Photo IM/Zev Radovan
293. Tambourine player — Israel Department of Antiquities, exh. Israel Museum, Jerusalem. Photo Zev Radovan
294. Flute player — Musée du Louvre, Paris. Photo Erich Lessing
PROVERBS
295. The Judgement of Solomon, illuminated MS, British Museum Miscellany. Add 11639/518R.
296. Captain and mate, from an Egyptian relief — Photo Erich Lessing
297. Goddess with scales — Photo Erich Lessing
298. Fragment from Qumran Scroll — the Shrine of the Book, Israel Museum, Jerusalem.
299. Agricultural scenes, from an Egyptian wall painting — Photo Erich Lessing
300. Goldsmith, from an Egyptian wall painting — Photo Erich Lessing
301. Egyptian official — Musée du Louvre, Paris. Photo Erich Lessing
302. Soldiers eating; Babylonian relief — Photo Erich Lessing
303. Farmer plowing with ox and ass — Photo Azaria Alon
304. Preparing perfume — Musée du Louvre, Paris. Photo Erich Lessing
305. Dignitaries drinking — Archaeological Museum, Istanbul. Photo Erich Lessing
306. Woman kneading dough — Department of Antiquities and Museums, Jerusalem. Photo Zev Radovan
ECCLESIASTES
307. Solomon's Pools — Photo A. van der Heyden
308. Ointment jar — Egyptian Museum, Cairo. Photo Erich Lessing
309. Safed cemetery — Photo A. van der Heyden
310. Birds in flight, from an Egyptian wall painting — Photo Erich Lessing
311. Almond tree — Photo David Darom
THE SONG OF SOLOMON
312. Fountain of the Kids — Photo David Harris
313. Young girl — Photo David Harris
314. Narcissus — Photo David Darom
315. Wild tulips — Photo Azaria Alon
316. Sea daffodils — Photo David Darom
317. Anemones — Photo Azaria Alon
318. Flock of sheep near pond — Photo Azaria Alon
319. Dan spring — Photo A. van der Heyden
320. Myrrh — Photo David Darom
321. Mandrake — Photo David Darom
322. Gazelle — Photo Azaria Alon
ISAIAH
323. Table with offerings — Staatliche Sammlung Aegyptscher Kunst, Munich. Photo Erich Lessing
324. Winged genii — Musée du Louvre, Paris. Photo Erich Lessing
325. Scribe, from an Egyptian wall painting — Photo Erich Lessing
326. Copper saw — Israel Museum, Jerusalem. Photo Zev Radovan
327. Tomb of Shebna — Photo David Harris
328. Blind harpist; from an Egyptian wall painting — Photo Erich Lessing
329. Carpenters and goldsmiths, from an Egyptian wall painting — Photo Erich Lessing
330. Garden, from an Egyptian wall painting — Photo Erich Lessing
JEREMIAH
331. Anata — Photo David Harris
332. Valley of Hinnom — Photo David Harris
333. Lachish — Photo David Harris
334. Leopard — Photo Azaria Alon
335. Qumran Scrolls container — The Shrine of the Book, Israel Museum, Jerusalem

336. Seal "Berachiah" – Israel Museum, Jerusalem
337. Weapons, from Egyptian wall painting – Photo Erich Lessing
LAMENTATIONS
338. Cruel treatment of enemies – Musée du Louvre, Paris. Photo Erich Lessing
339. The Western Wall – Photo David Harris
340. Hemlock – Photo David Darom
341. Wormwood – Photo David Darom
342. Stairs to Temple Mount – Photo Erich Lessing
EZEKIEL
343. Scorpion – Photo Azaria Alon
344. Ritual vase – Aleppo Museum, Photo Erich Lessing
345. Incense burner – Israel Department of Antiquities, exh. Israel Museum, Jerusalem. Photo Erich
    Lessing
346. Cherub on seal – Hecht Museum, University of Haifa. Photo Erich Lessing
347. Captives – Musée du Louvre, Paris. Cliché Musées Nationaux
348. Model of a cow's liver – Israel Department of Antiquities, exh. Israel Museum, Jerusalem. Photo
    courtesy Prof. Yigael Yadin
349. Assyrian ship, from a relief – Photo Erich Lessing
350. Canaanite jewelry – Israel Department of Antiquities, exh. Israel Museum, Jerusalem. Photo Na-
    chum Slapak
351. Watchtower – Musée du Louvre, Paris. Photo Erich Lessing
352. Vision of Dry Bones, from wall painting Dura-Europos synagogue. Photo Moshe Caine
DANIEL
353. Fragment of Epic of Gilgamesh – Israel Department of Antiquities, exh. Israel Museum, Jerusalem.
    Photo Zev Radovan
354. Mede dignitary – Staatliche Museen, E. Berlin. Photo Erich Lessing
355. Winged lion – Musée du Louvre, Paris. Photo Erich Lessing
356. Alexander the Great, fresco – Photo Alinari, Firenze
357. New Paphos, Cyprus – Photo Erich Lessing
HOSEA
358. Shrine, from Megiddo – Department of Antiquities and Museums, Jerusalem. Photo Erich Lessing
359. Terracotta farmer plowing – National Museum of Archaeology, Beirut. Photo Erich Lessing
JOEL
360. Locusts – Photo David Darom
361. Soldiers in rank – Damascus Museum. Photo Erich Lessing
362. Tomb of Jehoshaphat – Photo A. van der Heyden
363. Valley of Jehoshaphat – Photo A. van der Heyden
364. Man with sickle – Hecht Museum, University of Haifa. Photo Erich Lessing
365. Valley of Shittim – Photo David Darom
AMOS
366. Tekoa – Photo David Harris
367. Gilead – Photo David Harris
368. Wagon driven by oxen – Dagon Museum, Haifa. Photo Erich Lessing
369. Incense stand – Israel Department of Antiquities – Photo Erich Lessing
370. Sycamore fruit – Photo David Harris
371. Grain measuring cups – Dagon Museum, Haifa. Photo Erich Lessing
OBADIAH
372. Edom – Photo David Harris
JONAH
373. Ship in storm – Musée du Louvre, Paris. Photo Erich Lessing
374. Jaffa – Photo David Harris
375. Castor-oil plant – Photo David Harris
MICAH
376. Bethlehem – Photo A. van der Heyden
377. Warriors embracing – Aleppo Museum. Photo Erich Lessing
NAHUM
378. Thorns – Photo David Darom
379. Military expedition – British Museum, London
HABAKKUK
380. Canaanite figurine – Arch. Collections R.E.H. Haifa, Photo Zev Radovan

381. Worship of the Sun, from an Egyptian wall painting. Photo Erich Lessing
382. Ibex – Photo Azaria Alon
ZEPHANIAH
383. Siege of Ekron – Drawing of detail from Assyrian relief
384. Ammonite figurine – Department of Antiquities and Museums, Jerusalem. Photo Zev Radovan
HAGGAI
385. Transport of cedar wood, from an Assyrian relief – Photo Erich Lessing
386. Capital of column – Department of Antiquities and Museums, Jerusalem. Photo Erich Lessing
ZECHARIAH
387. Candlestick of Zechariah's vision – Illum. MS. Biblioteca Nacional de Lisboa
388. Man praying – Israel Department of Antiquities. Photo Erich Lessing
MALACHI
389. Valley of Megiddo – Photo A. van der Heyden
390. Model of granary – Dagon Museum, Haifa. Photo Erich Lessing
391. Elijah. Miniature from "The Washington Haggadah" – Library of Congress, Washington

Endpaper: Genealogy – The Jerusalem Publishing House
Title page: Photo Erich Lessing
Jacket:Detail of Isaiah Scroll – The Shrine of the Book, Israel Museum, Jerusalem. Photo Nir Bareket.

Maps: Yuval and Shlomit Greenbaum

The publishers have attempted to observe the legal requirements with respect to copyright. However, in view of the large number of illustrations included in this volume, the Publishers wish to apologize in advance for any involuntary omissions or errors and invite persons or bodies concerned to write to the Publishers.

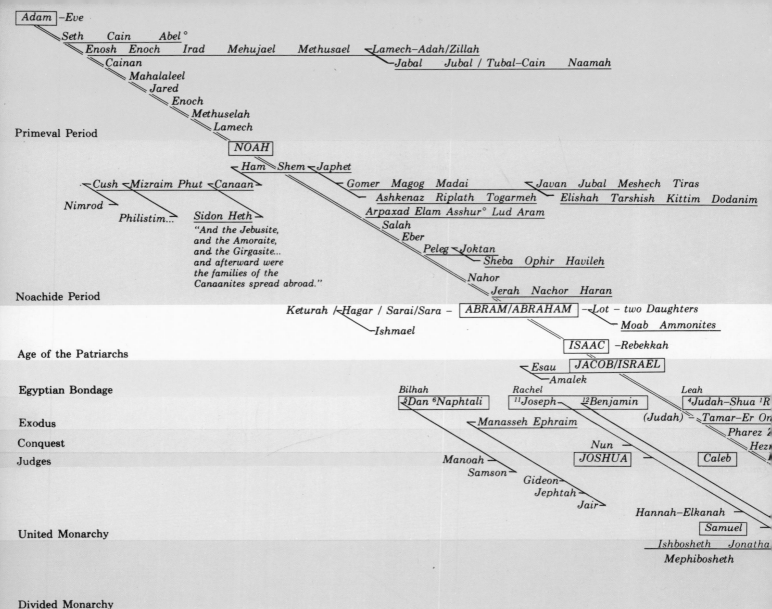

Primeval Period

Noachide Period

Age of the Patriarchs

Egyptian Bondage

Exodus

Conquest

Judges

United Monarchy

Divided Monarchy

Exile of Northern Kingdom of Israel 721 B.C.

Exile of Kingdom of Judah 586 B.C.

Return from Exile – Period of Restoration